0278579

Long Loan ✓

This book is due for return on or before the last date shown below

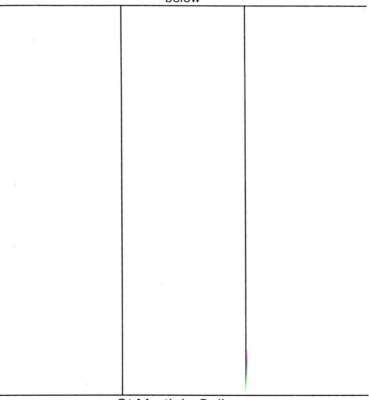

St Martin's College

EXPLORING THE ROLE OF THE INTERNET IN GLOBAL EDUCATION

EXPLORING THE ROLE OF THE INTERNET IN GLOBAL EDUCATION

John P. Anchan
and
Shiva S. Halli

Mellen Studies in Education
Volume 78

The Edwin Mellen Press
Lewiston•Queenston•Lampeter

Library of Congress Cataloging-in-Publication Data

Anchan, John P.
    Exploring the role of the Internet in global education / John P. Anchan and Shiva S. Halli.
      p. cm. -- (Mellen studies in education ; v. 78)
    Includes bibliographical references.
    ISBN-0-7734-6870-6
    1. Internet in education. 2. Multicultural education--Computer network resources. 3.
International education--Computer network resources. I. Halli, Shivalingappa S., 1952- II.
Title. III. Series.

    LB1044.87 .A52 2003
    370.116'0285'678--dc21

                                2002043210

This is volume 78 in the continuing series
Mellen Studies in Education
Volume 78 ISBN 0-7734-6870-6
MSE Series ISBN 0-88946-935-0

A CIP catalog record for this book is available from the British Library.

The Edwin Mellen Press   The Edwin Mellen Press
Box 450   Box 67
Lewiston, New York   Queenston, Ontario
USA 14092-0450   CANADA L0S 1L0

The Edwin Mellen Press, Ltd.
Lampeter, Ceredigion, Wales
UNITED KINGDOM SA48 8LT

Printed in the United States of America

**Dedicated to our best friends and partners –
our families:**

Zynu, Sneha and Krupa
Rohini and Priyanka

Table of Contents

Item 2. Focus Group One (Elements Covered)
Item 3. Focus Group One Work Sheet
Item 4. Handout (Orientation)
Item 5. Observation Sheet
Item 6. Researcher Observation Sheet (Abstract)
Item 7. Conversation Sheet
Item 8. Focus Group Two (Elements Covered)
Item 9. Focus Group Two Work Sheet
Item 10. List of Web Sites Selected for Content Analysis
Item 11. Category Descriptors
Item 12 The Internet Acronyms and Symbols.

Preface

Whether Internet is a blessing or a curse in the 21st century, it is certain that its influence on people's lives can only increase in time. Findings from the 2000 General Social Survey conducted by Statistics Canada show that 82 per cent of parents reported their school-age children used the Internet, compared to only 59 per cent among parents themselves. The same survey also found 85 per cent of young Canadians (15-24) used the Internet; on average, young Canadians spent over 9 hours on Internet in the week before the survey. The Internet has become an inseparable part of the young generation, whose culture, worldview and social relation are likely to be increasingly modified by their growing intimacy with the Internet.

It is inconceivable that the Internet and its radical changes to contemporary life should escape the scrutiny of social scientists. Yet social scientists are themselves only beginning to realize how rapidly the information age has transformed society and how profoundly the digitalized technology has altered the way people communicate and the speed information travels in time and space. Professors Anchan and Halli are the exceptional intellectual pioneers who have the foresight to explore the role of Internet in global education and the courage to map the boundaries of global education in the digitalized age. Irrespective of whether one agrees with their analyses and conclusions, the intellectual world owns much to Professors Anchan and Halli for their wayward spirit and daring commitment in providing a framework by which the relationship between the Internet and global education can be explored. Even critics would have to agree that without such pioneering works, more complete and elaborate understandings of the information age would have to be even further delayed.

Professors Anchan and Halli are well aware of the promises and dangers of the cyberspace in global education, as they outline in the introduction. The potentials of how the Internet can connect people in the global village and empower them with knowledge are well known by now. Less apparent is its capability to produce a homogeneous global culture and a market-based standard of efficiency that in the long run, may also stifle creativity and diversity. At the very least, the book has challenged social scientists and educators to explore the influence of Internet on contemporary life, with the view to harness its threats to the young generation and to harvest its potentials for the advancement of global education.

Peter S. Li
Professor of Sociology
University of Saskatchewan

Foreword

This study explores the possibility of the Internet contributing to the goals and objectives of global education. It attempts to explore the content and the processes that exist in relation to the users and the technology at the connectivity level besides inquiring into the man and machine experiences at the personal level. The emphasis is on the overall *cultural context* relating to elements of global education. The discourse focuses on the intercultural relations pertaining to local and global issues. The browsing itself was confined to sites that were relevant to *human rights, antiracism education* and *cross-cultural issues*.

The methodology involved content analysis of selected global education sites on the Internet over a period of 18 months, individual conversation interviews and focus group interviews with 6 undergraduate students from the Faculty of Education at the University of Alberta.

The findings of the study show that there is a need for becoming more aware of global issues. Like all other tools, the use of the Internet requires critical analysis of the process of using technology and the nature of information available on the Internet. The development of critical pedagogy and empowerment was dependent upon the global educator rather than the medium.

The experience with the machine and technology evoked questions about issues relating to culture. It was realized that culture was neither fixed nor finite but was mutable and influenced by power and struggles. It also became obvious that in Cultural Studies, theory was actually "contextual intervention" that entailed mapping connections and articulations. The Internet experience also elicited questions pertaining to the evolution of multiple identities even as one shared the common concerns with like-minded people. In order to enhance the role of the Internet in contributing to the goals of global education, it became obvious that further appropriation of the communication network system for classroom teaching was imperative. Most importantly, there was an agreement to the crucial need for critical and judicious filtering of information available on the Internet.

As Canadian scholars, we have used many Canadian sources and examples but as it will be made obvious, many pioneers in the area of Global Education hail from the United Kingdom and the United States of America. As one increasingly studies the concept of Global Education, it is evident that many of our concerns and remedies reflect a familiar dimension of globality.

The Internet could be used as a powerful tool for classroom teaching, sharing of teacher resources, establishing better connectivity with fellow global educators around the world, join activists in support of their negotiation for social justice, and accessing enormous amount of information from authentic sources. Conversely, it allows the proliferation of hate, crime, pornography, stereotypes, subjective opinions, inaccurate and unfiltered information passed on as legitimate knowledge. In spite of the limitations, the Internet can enhance the global educator's attempt to facilitate the development of a global identity. This book is the culmination of years of work and reflects the research findings that attempt to explicate the underpinnings of a global village. We hope that the issues raised in the following chapters would challenge readers to ask critical questions about the world we live in and our own roles as responsible stewards of this planet.

John P. Anchan
August 24, 2002

Acknowledgements

We would like to express our deepest gratitude to all the participants who were willing to give up their time amidst a busy academic schedule – without their valuable input and participation, this work would never come to fruition.

Secondly, we would like to thank Linda Wood, Instructor, Dept. of Sociology, University of Manitoba, for her assistance in the formatting of the manuscript.

Thirdly, we express our gratitude to Dr. Annabelle Mays, Dean of Education, University of Winnipeg, for her ongoing support for academic pursuits; Earl Choldin, Alberta Teachers Association, for his participation in this project; and all three universities – University of Alberta, Edmonton; University of Winnipeg, Manitoba; and University of Manitoba, for offering us the best environment to pursue this initiative. We thank *Edwin Mellen Press* for presenting our work to the community.

Our special appreciation goes out to Jim Carroll and Rick Broadhead for allowing us to use some of their selected material as a backdrop for narrating the history of the Internet.

To our families, we owe a special indebtedness, for allowing us to spend more time at work than with them – thereby, forfeiting their right to enjoy quality family time.

Finally, we are indebted to all our students, who have given us the opportunity to enjoy the "*art of pedagogy*".

Chapter 1: Introduction

1.1. The Global Neighbourhood: "Your Backyard; My Front Lawn!"

September 11, 2001 changed the world's perception of reality in terms of how a terrible event in one part of the world could closely affect rest of us. What had occurred in one part of the world had deeply influenced rest of the world community. While the actual shameless terrorist act shocked the world, the powerful after-effects of this dastardly act were quite evident long after the events of terror. Financial markets became volatile, stock exchanges shivered in uncertainty, law enforcement reconsidered intelligence, and state security became crucial. Politicians clamoured for revenge and defence budgets were drastically increased in billions of dollars. The erstwhile war against communism was followed by the cold war, and now, a new enemy had evolved, resulting in a "war on terrorism." In fact, it became evident that the criminal elements around the world had successfully employed the Internet to coordinate the evil schema and had reaped the benefits of technology in general, and information technology, in particular. Following "Black September", unemployment soared, cyberspace laws were revised, censorship and privacy laws were revisited, freedom of speech was questioned, and immigration laws were tightened. As the United States embarked on finding the enemy from within, unrest in the Middle East flared up and as many countries began to initiate racial profiling and stereotyping of vulnerable groups, the lawmakers and politicians grappled with the difficult task of protecting citizens' rights even as they targeted identifying potential terrorists. On one hand, distrust, and vulnerability freely flourished along with anti-American and anti-Jewish sentiments, creating a landscape of crucial divide – not only in the Middle East and North America but also around the world. Critics complain about the "imperial colonists" controlling the agenda, multinational corporations influencing the economy of countries, international financial bodies regulating the future of nations, and powerful trade partners ignoring the indigenous rights. On the other hand, industrialized nations claim the moral responsibility to address some of the crucial world issues surrounding environment, development, migration, health, poverty, human rights, security, education, political stability, and trade. It is indeed undeniable that the interventionist foreign policies of world powers have consistently created tensions among the members of the developing world[1]. In any case, the events of September 11, 2001 have reinforced the reality about how, by choice or by chance, we have become citizens of an intricately interconnected global community. Despite geopolitical borders, we cohabit a shared space where finite resources demand of us a very responsible stewardship. As members of a global village living on a closely-knit planet and bound to each other by technologies, we no longer can afford to ignore each other or become parochial in our quest for a peaceful humanity.

1.2.   Information Technology in a Shrinking World

In February 1997, 1,200 members of the World Economic Forum comprised of political and business elite converged in Davos, Switzerland to talk and experience networking technology. With laptops, cell phones, multipoint video-conferencing and a host of other technological wizardry, the Forum focused on the impact and implications of the information revolution (Ramo, 1997). The Internet has demanded the attention of almost everyone. The changes along with the implications of the network system cannot be over-emphasized. As one writer recalls: "'I'll put a girdle 'round about the earth in 40 minutes,' declared Puck in

---

[1] The politics of playing "global cop" is beyond the scope of this book.

2

A Midsummer Night's Dream. Four hundred years after the play was first produced, the globe is being girdled more thoroughly than Shakespeare ever dreamed" (Maroney, 1997).

Michael Miller, the Editor-in-Chief of *PC Magazine* describes the fast pace and changes that have occurred in the past 10 years and notes: "So here we stand, between the worries of George Orwell's 1984 and the wonders of Arthur C. Clarke's 2001. We are witnessing the development of the most exciting, fastest-changing technology in the history of the world. Over the next 15 years, we will choose how we use the technology. In turn, those choices will determine the kind of world we leave to our children" (1997, p. 4). This revolution in technology that has touched all of us including the determined Luddites, is exactly the reason for my interest in exploring the advent of what some call the *third wave*. Computers in specific, and the Internet in general, have dramatically influenced our lives. As one might argue, the degree of efficacy of the tool remains in the hands of the user. Yet, the Internet is not merely another tool in human history. As Neil Postman (1993), forebodes the advent of what he calls "technopoly," rightly argues that the Internet is not just another tool.[2]

Amidst the growth and influence of technology, the global nature of our lives has also become more explicit in the ever-decreasing spaces, the increasing speed of communication, the interdependency in terms of trade and commerce, education, politics, environment, and the evolution of a global citizen. As De Kerkhove (1995) describes this, "With communications travelling at the speed of thought, strictly local economies make no more sense than strictly local ecologies.

---

[2] This issue will be addressed later.

3

At every second, we are bound to one another by global events as surely as the weather" (p. 75).

In this critical juncture of history, the rapid development of information technologies has brought with it the promise of a powerful tool to educate people about world and global events. But what is the nature of this tool? While the promise and hype about the Internet beckons teachers with alluring promises, the cautious global educator will have to refrain from expecting the tool to supplant judicious and critical thinking during the process of formal education.

The focus of this book will be to understand the process of human-computer interaction and the role of the Internet/computer systems in offering elements of critical global education. In doing so, discussions will surround issues of technology and its implications in our lives as educators.

The terms *Internet, Cyberspace* and the *Information Superhighway* had not yet become passé when the seeds were sown to work on this topic. Nevertheless, the rapid growth of technology, the hype, and the proliferating literature along with the new *cybergurus* and *digiratis* has ushered in a new wave of literature and specialties.

In this age of information and electronic communication, the term *global village* has become more relevant to countries that have otherwise insisted on remaining independent "nation states." With *modernization* has come the impact of economic development and industrialization resulting in "the growth of science and technology, the modern state, the capitalist world market, urbanisation and other infrastructural elements" (Featherstone, 1991, p. 6). At the international level, the race has been to win global markets that offer lucrative promises to

4

huge profits. With the world's two most populated countries, China and India, evolving into the most promising consumer societies, governments are vying to become partners with many of the developing countries. In this rush for establishing partnerships, issues concerning basic human rights have remained sidetracked.

In light of these global changes, the emergence of global education to deal with international issues has established a critical dialectic relationship between the grassroots movements (action from below involving peoples movements, NGOs, activists, etc.) and the forces of globalization from above (transnational corporations, the IMF, WTO, global consumerism, etc.).

It is being suggested that the arrival of the electronic age—the *information superhighway,* also known as the *Internet,* is opening up the "window to the world." Countries including China, Russia, and even some parts of the Middle East that hitherto have remained closed to the influence of democratic movements have become open to the rest of the world as the citizens of these countries use the electronic digital network to establish communication with other countries. The much-heralded computer "network of networks" is being claimed as the greatest development in the twentieth century. The "electronic age" has reduced distance and time; the conventional use of telecommunications and broadcast has been further expanded upon by the computer revolution. Multimedia[3] and videoconferencing are now increasingly being used for distance learning. The electronic medium has enhanced all three types or modes of education—formal, non-formal and informal.[4] Global education encompasses all these types or

---

[3] *Multimedia* involves the Internet, CD ROMS, and interactive information services.
[4] *Formal* refers to educational activity conducted within the framework of an established system, i.e., educational institution and oftentimes synonymous to schooling; *non-formal* refers to any

modes of education in that it deals with the various aspects of understanding and dealing with issues relevant to the local and the global. In using technology to increase speed and ease of communication, the Internet has spawned innumerable projects, both at the government department levels and at the school/college level.

The challenge is to further explore the process of human-computer interaction and the role of the Internet/computer systems in offering elements of critical global education. In doing so, we explore *how* and *whether* the Internet allows global educators develop and implement critical global education. An attempt to explicate the nature or "quality" of the role of such processes and the kinds of paradigms of global education present in these processes will be made.

As a background to the topic of discussion, a brief conceptual framework will be provided before entering a fuller discussion. The definition, development, and meaning of and challenges to global education will be followed by the exposition on issues and problems of culture that will include specific aspects focused in this book — conflict, human rights, racism/anti-racism, and Values Education. No discussion on the Information Superhighway will be complete without venturing into the world of Cyberculture that relates to the computer and the Internet. The final observations and analyses in this 5-year research enterprise were based on *three* main components of research methods, namely, (a) Individual research that entailed literature review, online research, content analysis and reflection journal (b) Participant experiences involving one-on-one conversations, individual written narratives and brief reflection notes, and (c) Group experiences that were shared in a number of focus group sessions. As in

organized, systematic, educational activity, carried on outside the framework of the formal system; *Informal* refers to the "life-long process by which every person accumulates knowledge, skills, attitudes and insights from daily experiences and exposure to the environment" (Coombs, 1985, pp. 21-26).

case of purposeful research, the evolving nature of any inquiry presupposes the reality of transitory character of such an endeavour. Hence, even as the content material on the web remains in constant flux, our understanding of substantive issues including identity, race, and culture continue to alter. The following chapters will explore this aspect of information technology. The final part of this discussion will focus on the relationship between global education as a concept and the Internet as a medium.

Reflection Questions

1. The 9/11 (September 11, 2001) incidents touched the whole world. As a teacher, how would you explain the cause and effect of this tragic event to your grade 3 students?
2. How can we make critical conclusions in terms of technology vs. other needs? Should we focus on basic human needs or on using technology for the attainment of human dignity?

Chapter 2: Global Education

2.1. Understanding Global Education

Major political and economic changes have occurred as the world saw the end of the cold war in 1989. With an increasing sense of assuming collective responsibility for world peace, the nations of the world have begun to look at various ways to improve and sustain the way we treat other nations and peoples in specific and the planet in general. In a collective response envisioning a "new world," the 1994 report *by The Commission on Global Governance* put forward by an independent group of 28 world leaders and international organizations including the United Nations, the concepts of "global governance," and "global neighbourhood" have become the underpinnings of a *global village*. This report considers the "new dangers, new problems, and new challenges" faced by the world as we move towards the 21st century and calls for nation states to work together using collective power to create a better world suggesting a need for a new vision of pacifist society with a different social, economic, political and civic order ensuring abiding international law and global security. The Commission Report draws world attention to issues such as demilitarization, "sustainable development, the promotion of democracy, equity and human rights, and humanitarian action." Despite wars in Rwanda, Somalia, Northern Ireland, West Bank, Bosnia, and Sri Lanka, to name a few, world leaders have continued to press for a peaceful settlement of ethnic, racial, religious and political strife around the world.

Changes in the nation state borders such as the re-drawing of the map of Bosnia creates worry between the US and UN officials. Political resistance with the legislative election in Hong Kong raises spectres of resistance among Chinese leaders. In India, resistance to foreign influence such as the fight for *swadeshi* (self-reliant & indigenous) lifestyle causes demonstrations against the influx of North American fast-food chains from transnational companies such as Kentucky Fried Chicken, Coca Cola, Pepsi, the Texas power company Enron Development Corporation and Dupont raise questions on cultural sovereignty. International repercussions including the rapid spread of AIDS moving from sub-Saharan Africa to Asia threatens the rest of the world as the World Health Organization struggles to find ways to control it. Monetary reactions to political change such as the close call in the Quebec referendum sends the Tokyo Stock Exchange into frenzy. With another development in the phase of women's rights evolving, the UN Fourth World Conference on Women in China attracts hundreds and thousands of supporters from around the world. International trade talks between the North and South become tense due to issues of human rights; President Jiang Zemin, the architect behind the Tiananmen Massacre refuses to meet President Clinton at the site honouring human rights activists even as the U.S. and China renew trade relations. Concurrently, Harry Wu and other activists continue to expose the human rights violation in China. The assassination of Israel's Prime Minister and Nobel Laureate Itzhak Rabin, results in jubilation among extreme right-wing groups and raises a new concern for peace in the Middle East. Nigeria's execution of human rights activist Ken Saro-Wiwa and eight fellow crusaders fighting for the rights of Nigeria's Ogoni people results in the suspension of Nigeria from the Commonwealth even as Shell and Chevron's continue extraction of oil in Nigeria. Ovide Mercredi, the Native Chief in Canada defies the separatist agenda of Quebec that ignores the rights of the indigenous people. All one has to do is to pick up the *Guardian Weekly; TIME, The Globe & Mail, Newsweek, MaCleans* and a local paper *The Edmonton Journal*[5] to realize

---

[5] The events mentioned in this paragraph have been taken from the sources mentioned in just one week ending November 4, 1995.

the interconnectedness and interdependency within the global village. What occurs in one part of the world affects the rest of us and one can no longer ignore turmoil, disruptions and conflicts happening in even the remotest parts of the world.

The United Nations has celebrated its 50th anniversary even as many questions are raised regarding the 70% of its $1 9—billion budget spent on salaries of 34,000 employees. With its failure in Somalia and Bosnia, some question its role as peacekeeper when there is no peace to keep. While advocates have argued the need to depend on an institution that seems to be the only recourse towards a stable "world of nations," critics question the intentions of developed countries controlling and directing the policies and decisions of the United Nations and its innumerable corollary departments (Gunter, 1995; Atta, 1995; Arnold, 1994; Journal News Service, 1995a)[6]. One thing was unanimous among world leaders at the largest-ever gathering of world leaders in the United States in October 1995: "The prospect of a world without the United Nations was too horrible to contemplate" (Knox, 1992, p. 10). As countries look to the United Nations for dealing with international concerns, individual countries have begun to realize the collective responsibility towards planet earth.

According to Cetron and Davis (1991), 50 trends will shape the world including population, food, energy, environment, science and technology, labour, world economy, education and industry. The economies of the developing nations will grow only by 4.3% while the world economy will grow at a rate of 4.5%, increasing the gap between rich and the poor countries even further (p. 27). Some analysts predict the world population growth creating a crisis of great proportions

---

[6] See Atta,D.V. "The United Nations is Out of Control" for a scathing description of the failure & mismanagement of the U.N.

11

(Linden, 1993; Berreby, 1990; Simmons, 1992; Charles, 1992; Skinner, 1988). Environmental problems— the greenhouse effect, water, land and air pollution, and deforestation are all issues of concern to those who seek a more stable future for the planet (Silverberg, 1991; Brown et al, 1992; Muul, 1989). The relationship between the role of third world debt and trade on poverty and hunger is being explored and demands for structural adjustment are seen among development experts and activists around the world. Many countries are voicing the recognition of changing global values and the need for a clearer implementation of human rights as nations embark on trade relations and economic partnerships. Women, children and the marginalized groups have been largely ignored in the formula for development and change (Denniston, 1995; Young & Sachs, 1995; Weber, 1995). The modern *centres of production* have been replaced by *centres of consumption*, i.e., business and financial services, shopping malls, entertainment centres and theme parks (Usher & Edwards, 1994, p. 8).

In his speech at the 10th World Council for Gifted and Talented Children Conference in Toronto, actor and humanitarian Peter Ustinov suggested that in order to become a "more `global citizen,'" one needed to "become Canadian," alluding to the Canada's multicultural society. According to Ustinov, one needs to be aware of differences and problems of people elsewhere. Once we become conscious of problems in other parts of the world, we can then have the strength of character to have tolerance (Wright, 1993).

In this milieu of international interdependence, technology's part in linking people is obvious. It is increasingly apparent that computers have begun to play a vital role in understanding diversity, conflict, change, communication, and interdependence within the `global village' and technology has redefined the concept of space and time. Given its emergent role in knowledge production and

12

distribution, and in shaping consciousness, it is important to look at the information superhighway as a "source" of global education. Does and can the Internet promote global consciousness? And if so, in what paradigms does this occur? What are the implications for global citizenship?

2.2. The Development of Global Education

In contrast to most other well-known educational movements, global education has been very recent and is about forty years old (Kniep, 1985, p. 2). In 1974, UNESCO reiterated its policy of participation in a global community and recommended "guiding principles of educational policy," and by 1978, "a number of U.S. organizations had endorsed global education." (Darling, 1989, p. 5). The National Association of School Boards, the Parent Teachers Association, and the National Education Association joined the momentum to bring global awareness among children in schools. Understanding the world's problems, issues, and peoples also became a major component of global education. The earliest recorded call for global education was the 1969 Becker/Anderson report (Kniep, 1985, p. 9). In the United States, according to Wronski (1988), "The Michigan Department of Education was the first state in the United States to issue a state-wide approval and endorsement of the concept of global education in its *Guidelines for Global Education* published in 1978" (p. 147). The United States has embarked on a number of recent initiatives with federal support and other national organizations at the local, regional, and statewide levels (Crum, 1982).

In Canada, the idea of global interdependence was emphasized by the National Advisory Committee on development education in Canada and

13

thereafter, the Federal Government's role in financing programs and projects became the initial stages to global education in schools. In 1987, then Minister for External Relations and International Development Monique Landry tabled the Government's Strategy for Canadian Official Development Assistance in the publication entitled *Sharing Our Future*. Subsequent to the release of this document, the Canadian International Development Agency (CIDA), in alliance with the teachers' associations in various provinces, began to establish global education projects across Canada (CIDA, 1987, p. 81; Toh, 1992a).

As North America continued its global studies under "global education," other parts of the world had similar elements under the label "world studies" (Hicks, 1990). In fact, the World Studies Project, set up in 1980, had clear resemblance to what the North American global educators had begun to articulate. The objectives of the Project stated that it would deal with "contemporary global issues such as world inequality, human rights, peace and conflict, social change" as a basis for developing in students an "understanding [of] other cultures" from a global perspective (Hicks, 1990, p. 62). Eventually, the Project underwent changes to become the Centre for Global Education at the Education Department of the University of York in the United Kingdom. Educators in the Netherlands had formally treated elements of global education under "development education" in their educational planning policies from 1986 to 1991 (Blankert, 1992).

In Europe, global education surfaced under a variety of labels. Three examples of "interdisciplinary" studies at the secondary level in Europe schools are the "Scottish `modern studies,' the Federal Republic of Germany's `Gemeinschaftskunde,' and the Swedish `civics programme'" (O'Conner, 1982, p. 226). According to O'Conner, while the Scottish approach emphasized "social, economic, and ecological issues of concern to individuals and groups at local,

14

national, and international levels," the German emphasis was "on political education" dealing with contemporary issues and problems. The Swedish programme dealt with a very broad range of concerns such as "world issues, including population, energy, international trade, and on area issues" (p. 226). In Australia, the Australian Geography Teachers Association (AGTA) began active involvement in promoting global literacy, complemented by activities by other networks such as futures education, environmental education and development education, which was then followed by peace education (Toh, 1992b). Published details provide a record of the commitment to develop global perspectives among different nations, and especially among educators around the world, including France, Switzerland, Belgium, Russia, and Costa Rica. Elements of global education were dealt with in varying degrees and approaches in the European curriculums that included "International Peace and Conciliation," "World Decolonization," "Peoples of the World," and "Racial Problems" (Bacchus, 1992). As the UNESCO continued its attempt to encourage elements of global education under its "world studies" label through the Associated Schools Project around the world, Australia had begun using the term preferred in North America. Nevertheless, as Toh (1992b) notes, there was a strong tendency to understanding global education within a "liberal paradigm" (as it was in North America), in that it promoted paternalistic, technocratic assumptions rather than a "critical paradigm" that questioned the superficial understanding of concepts like *intercultural relations, development* and *interdependence* (pp. 2-3).

In September of 1991, Russia held the first international conference on the future of education where the focus was on the development of global education in Russian schools. Educators at the Conference conceded the importance of global education in Russia and other republics because, "it teaches about the interdependence of world cultures, it increases social and cultural awareness and

15

communication with other cultures, and it transforms and integrates a culture/nation into the world community and from a closed society to an open society" (Tucker, 1991).

In the development of global education in its various forms across countries, peace education and other specific movements (human rights education, environmental education, multicultural education, disarmament education, etc.) remained complementary in their development as putative areas of global education.

2.3. Meaning of *Global Education*

Educators have understood the term "global education" in different ways. It may include common elements that address issues and concerns that are cross-cultural and international with an emphasis on interconnectedness of systems involving cultural, political, economic or ecological in nature. Global concerns such as disarmament, environment (acid rain, global warming, ozone layer depletion, desert encroachment, deforestation, water and air pollution); social justice (human rights—aboriginal rights, racism, gender inequality, prejudice and discrimination, basic human needs, poverty and famine); cross-cultural awareness; and international relations (trade, development, foreign policy, aid) are some examples of areas that would concern global education. This understanding does not preclude recognition of other paradigms of understandings as to what the term "global education" means to different educators in this area of discourse.

Due to the rapidly changing concept and interpretation of global education, the defining of *global education* has not only become a matter of contentious debate but a challenge to many academics (Kobus, 1983, pp. 21-22). In November 1988, delegates from 25 countries, representing all five UNESCO world regions, met at the UNESCO Conference held at the Georg Eckert Institute for International Textbook Research in Braunsweig, West Germany to discuss global issues. The Conference recommended goals and objectives labelled under two main categories, namely, (1) Attitudes (self-respect, respect for others, ecological concerns, open-mindedness, vision, commitment to peace and justice), and (2) Skills (critical thinking, cooperation, empathy, assertiveness, conflict resolution, and political literacy) (Fien, 1989, p. 4).

There have been a number of attempts to define the concept of global education. Hanvey (1976) defines global education as "learning about those issues that cut across national boundaries and about the interconnectedness of systems, ecological, cultural, economic, political, and technological (p. 45). According to Ramler (1991), "Global education involves perspective taking, seeing things through the eyes, minds, and hearts of others; and it means the realization that while individuals and groups may view life differently, they also have common needs and wants" (p. 44). Tye and Kniep (1991) define global education as something that, "involves learning about those problems and issues which cut across national boundaries and about the interconnectedness of systems—cultural, ecological, economic, political, and technological" (p. 47). While the notions of "interconnectedness" and "interdependency" are problematic within a critical paradigm, most definitions do contain elements such as *interconnectedness, empathy, cooperation, interdependence, cultural diversity, global vision* and *understanding* (CIDA, 1987; Kniep, 1985; Kobus, 1983, Pradervand, 1987). The vision has been that of a global community which implies change from an egocentric approach to an altruistic, humanitarian, and considerate mode of living. It infers that we respect our fellow humans and value, treasure, and protect our

17

environment—not only for our own sake but for future generations (Hall, 1992; Anderson, 1982; Goodland, 1979).

According to Pike and Selby (1988), "to understand any global issue, it has to be viewed within a four-dimensional framework." Firstly, the "spatial dimension" with emphasis on the notion of `interdependence' implies that a global issue would have "an impact across many, if not all, parts of the world." Secondly, the "temporal dimension" suggests that a global issue will have to be "seen as a process with a past, present and future" (p. 22). Thirdly, the "issues dimension" requires the recognition of the systemic nature of global issues which will have to be dealt from within a "systemic/holistic paradigm"[7] rather than a "mechanistic paradigm." Fourthly, the "human potential dimension" that should enable students to be exposed to aspects of other cultures in order to understand the world without the "narrow categories of their own way of looking at the world" (pp. 24-29).

Gilliom (1981, 1990), suggests that "Global education seeks to develop the knowledge, skills, and attitudes needed to live effectively in a world possessing limited natural resources and characterized by ethnic diversity, cultural pluralism, and increasing interdependence" and considers the process as "education designed to cultivate a world view and to develop knowledge, skills, and attitudes needed to live effectively in a culturally diverse world characterized by increasing economic and social interdependency" (p. 169). Thus, understanding the world's problems, issues, and peoples has become a major component of global education. As much as students, both at the school level and

---

[7] The systematic paradigm "views phenomena and events as dynamically interconnected" whereas the mechanistic paradigm "divides knowledge into subjects or disciplines and into separate modes of perceiving and interpreting reality.

at the post-secondary level, will have to understand the notion of `interdependence' of countries and the relationship of nations in a global community, it is imperative for students of global education to go beyond the "superficialities and trivialities" (Toh, 1992b) to problematize the situation in order to understand and negotiate the meanings and outcomes of a discourse. Otherwise, the exercise will tend to become a "token" of intellectualizing issues and concerns without actually addressing the root causes of such problems (Hall, 1992). Emphasizing the interconnectedness, Mackwood (1991) argues for a critical perspective of global relations, especially when analyzing economic influences in relation to the environment, between developed and developing nations.

To be truly global, Kniep (1986) proposes "four elements of study" that should be included in a basic global education curriculum, namely, the (a) study of human values (b) study of global systems (c) study of global problems and issues, and (d) study of the history of contacts and interdependence among peoples, cultures and nations (p. 437). Lamy (1983a) takes a more critical approach by linking relationships between state and private negotiations that impinge on cultural commonalities and differences and suggests that a global perspectives curriculum must attempt "to build an understanding and appreciation of public and private actions which recognize...the linkages between state and non-state actors...the value and importance of cultural commonalities and differences and the necessity for foreign and domestic policies which minimize conflict behaviour and reinforce cooperation and accommodation" (p. 18). Bacchus (1989) defines global education as a process in which "our youngsters can be brought to see how the political, social and economic problems of the world extend beyond national and regional borders to include all members of the planet" (p. 21) while Selby (1993a,b), proposes four dimensions of global education, namely, temporal ("futures" perspective), spatial (geographical interconnectedness of events), issues (environment, human rights, peace and development), and inner dimension (connections between personal and planetary well-being) (pp. 3-6). Including global education under humane curricula, he attempts to link global education with environmental education and human rights education. Urch (1992) includes global education under three dimensions, namely, study of world cultures, major global issues and the planet as an interdependent system and suggests that global education should consider perspective consciousness, state-of-the-planet awareness, cross-cultural awareness, systematic awareness, and strategies for participation. Cornbleth (1979), suggests that four characteristics of global perspectives program should be that it is holistic, humanistic, conceptually based and issue oriented.

Some propose promoting critical thinking, intercultural literacy and peace in our schools through global and multicultural education curriculum (D'Andrea & Daniels, 1996; Cummins & Sayers, 1996). One of the trends has been internationalizing the curriculum by incorporating global elements in the areas of art, biology, business, chemistry, communication, computer, political science, psychology, religion and sociology (Sypris, 1993). According to Hanvey (1983), while historically global education has concentrated on altruistic concerns such as the world environment, peace, and international understanding, it is imperative that we now focus on helping solve problems of individuals, groups, and nations through appropriate analysis of global changes.

One aspect of this debate is obvious—The term "global education" is complex and multi-faceted in that it not only has different roots but most recorded attempts have been from theorists from the North. In essence, the North American quest for an operational definition of global education has evolved as the United

Nations Charter and the UNESCO's goal in developing a "world citizen" resulted in a number of organizations in the country endorsing global education or elements of global education in their policy statements and school curriculums (Darling, 1989; Peters, 1986; Crum, 1982). Choldin has suggested that a global education program should help "students develop an understanding of the global issues they face and help students empower themselves to deal with those issues as responsible citizens. There are, therefore, knowledge, skill, and attitudinal goals [as elements in a global education program]" (Anchan, 1992).

Debates have raged over the differences and similarities between global education and peace education, development education, environmental studies, and international education (Eckhardt, 1988; Husaini, 1990; Nnandi, 1990; Bacchus, 1989). For example, Pradervand (1987) disagrees with the term "development" in that the term has been used in "so many conflicting and contradictory ways, to describe so many utterly heterogeneous and often opposed trends" and contends that the transformative paradigm has been sacrificed for a liberal paradigm ignoring the side effects of industrialization on the developing countries. Global education and peace education have been mutually non-exclusive and quite integral. Both, global education and peace education emphasize cooperation aimed at co-existence rather than competition. Both contain common and diverse issues such as, structural violence, environment, militarization, human rights, cultural solidarity, personal peace, and Freirean "conscientization." Peace education has had a long history of thought and practice and "political or secular movements of peace, first visualized as `disarmament movements' are only 160 years old" and peace education has come a long way from being understood merely as an attempt to analyze and prevent war or even simply create "an awareness of the issues of disarmament and antimilitarism" (Husaini, 1990, p. 80). Variations in the meaning of the concept of peace

21

education have been promulgated by anti-war groups, political activists, World Federalists, churches (Brethren, Friends, and Mennonites), and more recently by the activist Greenpeace movement, that has linked environmental concerns with peace and disarmament (Eckhardt, 1988, p. 180). According to Hicks (1988), education for peace "is an attempt to respond to problems of conflict and violence on scales ranging from global and national to the local and personal. It is about exploring ways of creating more just and sustainable futures" (p. 5). While the term `peace' has been explained in many ways, one could accept the simplest of meanings, namely, "peace of mind at the `personal level" (the intrapersonal level of peace) and peace at the interpersonal level that aims at "non-violence, non-hurting, or non-injury (ahimsa in the Gandhian tradition)" in order to coexist harmoniously and without conflict or misunderstanding (Eckhardt, 1988, p. 179). The `negative' definition of peace (absence of war) has recently come under increasing criticism and has given way to the `positive' definition of peace (attaining justice in terms of `realization of values', a term borrowed from Galtung) stressing the building up of justice. Positive peace education that encompasses the belief of achieving global justice (in the form of universal human rights, environmental considerations, economic equality, prevention of war, education for development, etc.) directly links in with the objectives of global education. The basic principle underpinning global education attempts to expect justice in order that the human race may live at peace with one another.

Without being constrained by terminologies and semantics, academics will have to focus on achieving humanitarian goals in order to make our world more liveable and safe. To realize this goal, political awareness must follow political participation. A "holistic understanding" that does not divorce bits of otherwise related information must attempt to link issues that tend to cause conflicts (Toh & Floresca-Cawagas, 1987, p. 29). The need to address the cause of such conflicts rather than the symptoms of the problem is crucial. By dissecting the source of conflict or violence, the individual would be able to analyze the problem more critically. It is thus our responsibility to facilitate such an environment within classrooms. To ignore is to acquiesce and to knowingly disregard resolutions to problems that should not have existed in the first place implies the shirking of our personal responsibility as human beings. From the personal level to the interpersonal level, to understand global peace, one must be willing to go beyond narrow geographically defined nation states, beyond national boundaries towards a global village that subsumes all nations to form one single unit of human residence.

Since the spectrum of globality includes a broad number of issues, such as disarmament, environment, political awareness, social justice, and literacy development, global education is all embracing. From providing basic human needs to respecting cultural differences; from amelioration of the suffering to establishing global justice; and from matters of international trade policies to developmental education, global education is a challenging concept of such diverse and massive concerns. This explains the variations in its application by professionals hailing from different fields of expertise. Global education is a concept, rather than an approach and involves developing a global perspective. In fact, while it emphasizes interdependence, one might question whether the term "global education" is used to express a narrow economistic explanation that tends to ignore the underlying meanings and relationships of superficial liberal understanding. The liberal technocratic paradigm tends to be "friendly and also paternalistic" in contrast to the "transformative paradigm" which emphasizes critical analysis and explores "structural complexities" of problems and issues (Toh, 1992). The transformative paradigm "empowers learners not only to critically understand the world's realities in a holistic framework, but also to move learners and teachers to act towards a more peaceful, just and liberating world" (Toh, 1993, p. 11).

Peace, as we understand, appears to be an elusive concept relegated to the political rhetoric among nations around the world. With the attenuation of East-West tension, the North-South conflict has emerged to become the subject of more recent debate on the world scene. While the industrialized world and, increasingly some of the developing world arms exporters, have continued to sell arms to the developing world, the North has cornered itself into a schizophrenic frenzy of confusion about whether "to sell or not to sell?" One is reminded of the UNESCO Preamble: "Since wars begin in the minds of men [and women], it is in the minds of men that defences of peace must be constructed." (Harris, 1986, p. 5). What can we, as educators, do? Where does one begin? Toh & Floresca-Cawagas (1987) suggest, "a more peace-oriented consciousness, encouraged through cooperative education and training in non-violent conflict resolution skills, [as] a vital starting point towards building a long-term peaceful society" (p. 1). Interpersonal peace would be corollary to intrapersonal peace developed through "critical and democratic thinking" and "peaceful dialogue" (Toh & Floresca-Cawagas, 1987, p. 30). This involves critical thinking and critical action, i.e., action and praxis (reflective thinking followed by appropriate action). It is necessary to change attitudes— attitudes that are peace oriented and that include "tendencies toward democracy, socialism, internationalism (including world federalism), and pacifism (including arms control and disarmament)" (Eckhardt, 1988, p. 181). At the interpersonal level, a peaceful dialogue would occur without imposition of the teacher's dogmatic beliefs and would involve exploration of curriculums and including value concepts relating to peace and global envisionment. Concepts such as stewardship— "fundamental value to be developed as a response to ecological crisis," citizenship— of the global village to

24

develop "global responsibility," and relationship - "positive human interdependence" will help understand and deal with human values, international development, nuclear disarmament and non-violent conflict resolution (Reardon, 1984, pp. 19-22).

Toh (1988b) suggests three essential value orientations of global peace education, namely compassion and justness; selflessness and love; and harmony and tranquility (p. 287). Within the north-south relationship, compassion and justness need to replace pity. This presents a number of issues relating to inequities, imbalances, and justice (pp. 289-290). These issues can be effectively addressed through Values Education, a variant from the objectives identified in the training package of the Department of Education, Culture and Sports (DECS) and the Center for Research and Communication (CRC) in the Philippines. Focusing on the "personal development through education," a moral component to *values education* resulted in the Moral Recovery Program (MRP) in the Philippines (Floresca-Cawagas, 1988). Emphasizing critical thinking as it looks at the sociological implications of such education being translated at both personal and societal level, Toh & Floresca-Cawagas (1990), identify six main issues of conflicts, violence and peacelessness, namely, structural violence, militarization, human rights, personal peace, cultural solidarity, and environmental care (pp. v-viii). Values education aims at sustainable development, peace, development of collective consciousness, empowerment, and evolution of a global citizen in a global village. Nevertheless, values education (affective education, character education, or moral education) has remained controversial with certain values being readily acceptable (honesty, respect, kindness, empathy) while others raising questioned (academic freedom, censorship, ethical choices, change in the way we have considered traditions and thinking) (Braun, Jr., 1992, pp. 47-56). In the framework of nurturing a sense of community in the classroom, Braun, Jr.

describes a values education model engaged in the creation of a climate of caring, strengthening of citizenship and development of conscience and civic participation.

The pedagogical process engaged in values education not only involves issues of peace but also includes a peaceful teaching-learning exchange that is holistic (multiple linkages), democratic (dialogic), and empowering (conscientization) in its nature. The uniqueness of values education is that it attempts to identify the links between individual versus structural and typical versus systemic. It explores the translation of individual values shaping or influencing common social values that in turn affect structural changes. Thus, "making people moral will not be enough to change society" (Toh & Floresca-Cawagas, 1990, p. vii).

> Whether it be the suffering of poverty, malnutrition, or infant mortality; the incidence of wars, civil conflicts, torture, disappearances, and other violations of human rights; the plight of street children; or the destructive rate of deforestation—the awakening of learners to why these dehumanizing realities about ought to be accompanied by empowerment, or a self-determined will and commitment to participate actively in the non-violent transformation of institutions, communities, and structures from the local to national to global levels. (Toh & Floresca-Cawagas, 1990, p. 5)

Toh & Floresca-Cawagas (1990) ask "Can values be effectively and meaningfully taught and learned as an abstract set of ideals?" Peace educators underscore the crucial need to help learners interpret and analyze values as expressed in concrete personal, interpersonal, social, political, cultural, and economic relationships and structures. Only then can students learn to become personally and socially responsible for local, community, national, and global situations (p. 6). The process involves progressive exploration of causes and effect in an unjust society to the attainment of peace through a specific path of action entailing 6 elements:

26

(a) Compassion (empathy) (b) Conscientization (understanding the root causes) (c) Constructiveness (War to peace, an alternative paradigm of sustainable development) (d) Conciliation (meaningful non-violent intervention), (e) Communion (collaboration across delineation), and (f) Contemplation (reflection toward a peaceful spiritual equilibrium) (p. 19). Without exception, areas such as Sri Lanka, Kashmir, Ireland, Eritrea, West Bank, Bosnia, Rwanda, Somalia, Cyprus, Egypt, Afghanistan, and East Timor, have all resorted to violent strategies to resolving differences between factions. While peace education can be vital in evoking pertinent action strategies such political turmoil, the responsibility does not lie vested in the individual. Not only does every individual transform oneself to becoming personally "peaceful in thought and action," Toh and Floresca-Cawagas (1990), recognize the need for other dimensions within the society at large engaged in this process. As they explain: "[A] peaceful world will be impossible to create by peacemakers working solely as individuals and in individualistic fashion. The tasks of educating and acting for peace require cooperation, solidarity, and linkages between individuals, groups, institutions, and communities at the local, national, regional and global levels" (pp. 11-12).

In establishing a communion, one crosses or overcomes ethnic and other cultural divisions which can be so destructive of human sisterhood and brotherhood" (p. 12). There is a need for resocializing, cultivating self-critical evaluation, developing courage to act, challenging oppressive governments, and critically questioning consumerism and accumulation of wealth.

Perhaps, the global mission contained in the preamble of the constitution of the *World Council for Curriculum and Instruction* (WCCI), as described by Matriano, may offer us some insight into why global education can and should be an integral part of our curriculum:

27

As members of the world community, educators have a responsibility to ensure that education contributes to the promotion of equity, peace and universal realization of human rights. To this end, curricular and instructional programs of all educational enterprises for children, youth or adults should aim to develop in every person self respect, social awareness and the capacity to participate at all levels of world society from local to global. (Matriano, 1988, p. 19).

The 1986 Board of Directors of the World Council for Curriculum and Instruction identified *5 universal values* that WCCI should address and develop in a global curriculum, namely, human rights and human dignity; equality and social justice; ecology and care for the environment; civic and social responsibility; love, friendship, compassion, and care for each other" (Matriano, 1988, p. 22). Learning from each other; developing co-operative projects; engaging in holistic education that recognizes differences; establishing linkages and networks; promoting exchange; and sharing of resources are some of the recommendations by the World Council for Curriculum and Instruction for a humanized global curriculum building (Matriano, 1988, p. 23). According to Matriano & Reardon (1976), the development of a global curriculum would have certain "core values" including: (1) peace to overcome the problem of violence (2) economic equity and just distribution of resources to overcome poverty and inequities (3) social justice to overcome all types of discrimination (4) ecological balance to overcome environmental destruction, and (5) political participation to overcome oppression and lack of political power.

Awareness of the social conditions should lead towards action that leads to change. But unless the question of economic disparity is addressed, amelioration of the suffering cannot be achieved. With inequalities in existence, addressing problems of social justice becomes difficult. Global educators will have to recognize this and attempt to explore and explicate the inequalities that exist

28

within and between nations. To be able to become an efficient global educator, one has to transcend beyond local issues and be able to relate to issues and events that occur around the world. This entails a personal interest and the willingness to not only familiarize oneself with the historical changes that have led to present crises but also to critically analyze contemporary international policies and changes. At heart, a global or peace educator should be willing to understand and act in an interdisciplinary mode including perspectives from a range of fields such as politics, science, history, philosophy, sociology, and economics.

2.4. Challenges faced by Global Education

There has been varying degrees of opposition to global and peace education (Toh, 1988). In fact, some global educators have acknowledged the lack of clarity but have provided insights into possibilities for global education as an area of promise (Selby, 1993a). Nevertheless, until the mid-80s, few questions were raised about global education's rationale, goals and objectives, content, and method of instruction (Schukar, 1993). While Nnandi (1990) recognizes that "there are institutional obstacles to both global education and peace education" he states that "there is very little overt opposition to `global education'" whereas "'peace education' has met with open, organized hostility in some countries" (p. 77). Cox and Scruton have objected to peace education, claiming that it is "contentious and politically charged discussion" and that it is ` likely to inculcate guilt towards [an individual's] own inheritance and to encourage him to place blame for conflict in the camp to which he belongs" (White, 1988, p. 40). In reality, global education has met with some vocal "right-wing" attacks in the United States and has been subject to opposition by some "fringe" groups in Alberta. Some critics see global education as a form of political indoctrination where, for instance, peace studies "blame wars, conflicts, social injustices, racism and militarism on capitalism" (Toh, 1988).

Even among the critics, the understanding and interpretation of the objectives of global education tend to differ. One of the allegations of global education is that it reflects the Marxist agenda and contains values that are "pro-Soviet, anti-capitalist and anti-American," and yet, "Marxists have played a minimal role in global education (Lamy, 1989, pp. 41-42). They also question the supposed conflict between global versus "national" (read "nation state") interests. Besides, global education has had some degree of opposition due to the perception that it is "subversive," "with hidden agendas," "radical movement," and "leftist motivated crusade" and teachers have criticized the lack of a common definition of global education— that it is very vague, too broad, extremely elusive and hence, difficult to comprehend, making its implementation more difficult (Anchan, 1992, p. 120). As the Cunningham/ Tancredo paper suggests, "every issue raised by any program of global education...[is] a political issue— of the most controversial sort" (Wronski, 1988, p. 147). Wronski suggests that the current attacks on global education may "discourage teachers from introducing controversial issues into the curriculum" and may "diminish critical thinking skills in students" (pp. 148-149).

According to Metzger, "understanding the barriers to teaching global education is to increase the opportunity for overcoming the barriers [and] educators in general must rationally consider and solve the criticisms that face global education" (p. 15). More often, "cultural relativism" is confused for "moral relativism" (Wronski, 1988, p. 150) and clarifying criticisms of this nature will avoid confusion and eliminate misunderstanding about global education. In order to be effective global educators, we need to question our beliefs, values, and philosophies in understanding issues of relevance. We must clarify our understanding of goals and objectives of global education by identifying the principles and practice of global education. In order to have a global vision that is holistic, transformative, and truly global, we must explore opportunities and strategies that allow us to work toward achieving a liberating curriculum (Toh, 1993; Selby, 1993). In globalizing the curriculum *global community education*— a term Matriano (1987), prefers over the usage *global education*— one may infuse 6 elements into the existing curriculum. These include, (1) the "earthship" (study of the planet earth) as the habitat of the members of global community (2) intercultural studies and communication explicating the interdependence and interrelationships in the global community (3) issues and problems that relate to conflicts and tensions arising from discrimination, inequities and imbalances (4) disarmament education analyzing the threat of war and possible solutions (5) computer education in the development of technical and cognitive skills, and (6) peace education in relation to promoting peaceful relationship among members of the global community (pp. 70-71).

The need for global education at all levels has been expressed by a number of educators (Wood, 1991; Merryfield, 1992). Currently, global educators have argued for the infusion of global education at all grades from kindergarten (Cogan, 1981) through elementary (Thompson, 1993; Lickteig & Danielson, 1995; Evans, 1992; Cogan, 1978) to the high school level (Doane, 1993; Thorne, 1992). Some suggest the inclusion of global education within pre-service and in-service teacher education (Merryfield, 1997; Tyson et al., 1997; Haakenson, 1994; Merryfield, 1995a,b,c; Wooster, 1993; Merryfield, 1992). In the area of social studies, global education has become an integral part of citizenship education (Pellicano, 1982). Global education can also be incorporated into language curriculum as seen in the English courses at Stevenson High in Michigan (Swift,

31

1980). In all these, it is quite imperative that the there needs to be a fair degree of commitment on the part of the leadership including the Dean, the faculty members, and perhaps the local teachers' association in order to infuse global education in the curriculum (Case & Werner, 1997; Boston, 1997; Jarchow, 1997;Wilson, 1997).

There is some evidence to show that teachers are sensitive to the background of their students (race, ethnicity, religion, and gender), thereby, reflecting this in their classroom teaching (Merryfield, 1994). While this is responding to what one would call the "international classroom," there remains some doubt as to whether teachers would be so multicultural if their students were not so diverse. Some North American studies do show that in certain cases, teachers claiming to have accepted global education, fail to incorporate multicultural and global education materials into their curriculum or do not apply the knowledge to classroom activities (Farmer, 1992-93; Brown & Kysilka, 1994). In fact, a number of other factors including how teachers define global education, intensification of work, faculty commitment, and sensitivity to the issues, influence whether teachers introduce global education perspectives into their teaching (Tye & Tye, 1993; Gilliom, 1993). In essence, Lamy (1983b), argues that without a global dimension in our schools, our students will be ineffective citizens within our communities and our nation.

While Merryfield (1993), suggests a critical reflection among teachers as they attempt to infuse global education in their classrooms, Begler (1993) argues for a closer focus on the process-content relationship in teacher education programs. McLaren (1995), proposes a critical approach to analyzing overpopulation, environmental degradation, human security, and poverty—the outcome indicators of unsustainable capitalism. Werner (1996), suggests integrating global education through infusion involving *Moral issues* (the sharing of our common causes within the global village, our relationship to the other human beings on the planet), *Systems approach* (interdependency, interconnectedness on issues that are global including human rights, environment, economic exploitation), and *Reflexive inquiry* (recognizing multiple perspectives, world views, and centricity). Merryfield (1995), proposes linking multicultural education with global education arguing that global education should be a two-way approach in that it should engage in the teaching process even as it involves learning. Despite their separate histories and identities, Cortes (1983), notes that both multiethnic and global education have similar goals and content in that they include four identical areas of interest: the meaning of groups and group membership, group image formation, perspectives, and intercultural communication.

The significance of global education in the understanding of the "global village" is undeniable; yet, one tends to seek the specific issues that can be situated within such a discourse. Despite its enormity, global education can be dealt within the framework of the troika—*cause, concern and conduct*. Firstly, causes of conflicts, tensions, inequalities, and disturbances; secondly, concern toward our fellow humans in questioning some of the assumptions as to how these causes of disruptions came to be; and finally, defining our own conduct at the personal and interpersonal level and thereby seeking resolutions to issues that are manageable even at a microcosmic level. While the debate is ongoing as to what global education should include or exclude, keeping the triad framework presents us with a number of issues and concerns that can loosely be considered elements of a global education discourse.

33

Nevertheless, this is not to suggest in any way, a taxonomy of global education. What one may consider as "concerns under the global education umbrella" may include environment[8], pacifist movement or peace education[9], social justice[10], economic relations[11], development education[12], basic human living conditions[13], and cross-cultural awareness[14].

If this is so encompassing in terms of issues, global education surely appears daunting and indeterminate. Yet, complexity is not necessarily indeterminacy or a weakness and one does not have to deal with all the issues concurrently in order to be a true global educator. As explicated earlier, this discussion will entail cultural areas of global education. In the following chapter, we shall focus on the notion of culture and its positioning in relation to race and identity.

Reflection Questions

1. How would you respond to critics of global education?
2. How are teachers attracted to technology? How can Internet pedagogy further develop?
3. Can we practise global education without having to pick nations as oppressors and/or victims? Why or why not?
4. As a global education teacher, how would you implement successful and effective classroom practices?

---

[8] Concerns such as global warming, desert encroachment, water pollution, deforestation.
[9] Nuclear and conventional disarmament.
[10] Rights and freedom, anti-racism, gender inequality, child labor.
[11] Trade and international debt crises.
[12] Literacy and self-empowerment.
[13] Food, shelter and health care.
[14] Cultural pluralism and autochthony.

Chapter 3: Understanding Culture

3.1. Culture

Having raised the question of whether the computer is merely an instrument to access information, there appears to be an historical basis to believe that the human versus social functions can and will influence our way of thinking. While "culture is the representation of lived experiences" it has been analyzed as both "lived experience and as commodity" (Apple & Weis, 1983, pp. 15-16). The study of culture "as it is produced in ongoing interaction and as a terrain in which class, gender, and racial meanings and antagonisms [are] lived out" has become more acceptable and meaningful to many phenomenologists, and therefore preferred over the approach of studying culture as a commodity. While social analysis may range from classical Marxism to neo-Marxism (humanism, Critical Theory) and to post-structural analysis, the notion of culture and power within the context of understanding culture is relevant to this discussion. Many critical theory and post-modernist writings on *popular culture* have emerged recently and that work is beyond the scope of this discussion. (see Giroux, 1993; Giroux 1991; Olson, 1987; Sullivan, 1987; Repo, 1987). As the focus of this study is on the cultural consciousness, a brief look at the notion of *culture* and its derivatives is imperative.

Culture is "the human creation and use of symbols and artifacts" and is characterized by the historical nature, its relativity, and its diversity (Jary & Jary, 1991). Culture has been understood as a "collective noun for the symbolic and learned, non-biological aspects of human society, including language, custom and convention by which human behaviour can be distinguished from that of other primates...human behaviour [that] is largely culturally and not genetically determined" (Abercrombie et al., 1988). Traditional definitions have ignored the fundamentally political nature of culture (Giroux, 1985, 1983, 1981); the oppressive forces of *cultural invasion* (Freire, 1985, 1983, 1978); the social impact of cultural reproduction and the need for *cultural capital,* i.e., the ability to absorb the *dominant culture* (Bourdieu, 1977, 1973); and the role of hegemonic power (*cultural hegemony,* a Gramscian interpretation of control and power) in cultural manipulation, i.e., *cultural imperialism* (Carnoy, 1974). In fact, as early as 1950, Ogburn's theory of *cultural lag* a critique of the theory of economic determinism attempted to question the degree of determinativeness between the economic base and cultural superstructure.

The notion of a *dominant culture* raises a number of questions as to whether a single monolithic culture exists or if dominant ideology exists despite social differentiation and ethnic diversities (Abercrombie, 1988). Giroux (1983) describes two conditions active in defining the nature of culture—the "asymmetrical relations of power and the principles emerging from different classes and groups who use them to make sense of their location in a given society [and] the relations between capital and its dominant classes, on the one hand, and the cultures and experiences of the subordinate classes on the other" (p. 163). According to Giroux, this constant ongoing struggle over day-to-day experiences involves a dialectic of conflict and power giving rise to a continuous relationship between dominant and subordinate cultures with the former appropriating more out of this experience from the latter. In suffocating or suppressing the voices of the "other" subordinate cultures, a struggle for being heard is ensued through a process that envisions a notion of cultural democracy (Darder, 1991).

Many of the early sociologists dealt with culture as a monolithic theoretical concept, and some emphasize "[T]he complex relationships that exist between culture, knowledge, and power. Issues of identity and representation directly raise questions about who has the power to define whom, and when, and how" (McCarthy & Crichlow, 1993, p. xvi). It is now clearer that culture "whether in its material or symbolic form, is an attribute which people(s) are said to have..." (King, 1997, p. 1). Abu-Lughod (1997) notes that *culture* is "more than 'traits,' everyday practices, and even institutions — economic, educational, technological and political. The early anthropologists insisted it was, fundamentally, beliefs, 'world views,' and special constructions of reality" (p. 134). The leading sociologists of the classical period were "insensitive to what has come to be called globalization — particularly cultural aspects thereof" (p. 84). The "myth of cultural integration"[15] ignored the inner logic of how "cultures of particular societies are, to different degrees, the result of their interactions with other societies in the global system... By the same token, global culture itself is partly created in terms of specific interactions between and among national societies" (Robertson, 1997, pp. 84-89). We now understand that culture cannot be understood as a single existing concept or thing. King (1997) articulates this as well:

> With a potentially exponential growth in international migration, with many cultures existing far from their places of origin and indeed, not necessarily for any length of time, there is no "nationally grounded" theoretical paradigm which can adequately handle the epistemological situation. It is not just that, increasingly, many people have no roots; it's also that they have no soil. Culture is increasingly deterritorialized. (King, 1997, p. 6)

With its evolving nature, culture cannot be understood as a unitary "thing" that follows pre-determined stages of development as suggested by early theorists.

---

[15] According Margaret Archer the *myth of cultural integration* implies "all societies that are considered viable are normatively integrated, with culture performing the major function in that regard" (Robertson, R 1997, p. 85).

With the industrialized nations defining development as linear and sequential, the Modernization theory has fallen into disrepute in development and culture studies. Similarly, a theory that assumes a linear tendency among all societies evolving through parallel stages of development towards one political world, one economic world, one cultural world – towards one single world culture is in error as it ignores the multiple counter-cultures that struggle against uniformity (Wallerstein, 1997, pp. 93-94). Wallerstein argues that the "history of the world has been the very opposite of a trend towards cultural homogenization; it has rather been a trend towards cultural differentiation, or cultural elaboration, or cultural complexity" (p. 96). Nevertheless, this explanation does not account for the enforced cultural assimilation and the consequent loss of hundreds of languages in the world throughout history. Apple (1993) elucidates the transient nature of culture and race that cannot be confined to one single universally acceptable thing:

> Like race, words such as this [culture] do not (or at least should not) signify an already existing and unitary thing. Rather, they are place markers for a complex political arena in which the fundamental educational question of "What knowledge is of most worth?" is transformed—as it should be—into the even more challenging question of "Whose knowledge is of most worth? Knowledge and power become inextricably linked here. Thinking about this relationship in terms of the politics of race is crucial. (viii)

Cabral (1994), posits that culture is "simultaneously the fruit of a people's history and a determinant of history, by the positive or negative influence which it exerts on the evolution of relationships between man and his environment, among men or groups or men within a society, as well as among different societies" (Cabral, 1994, p. 54). For Cabral, culture is "an essential element of the history of a people" and it is the "fruit of history" and "denying the historical development of the dominated people, necessarily also denies their cultural development" (pp. 55, 61). According to Fanon (1994), culture is:

first the expression of a nation, the expression of its preferences, of its taboos and of its patterns. It is at every stage of the whole society that other taboos, values and patterns are formed. A national culture is the sum total of all these appraisals; it is the result of internal and external extensions exerted over society as a whole and also at every level of that society. (Fanon, 1994, p. 50)

Culture has also been understood as a hybridized state that is a resultant of relationships. Tiffin (1995) describes the dismantling of the constraints imputed upon the histories of the colonized:

Post-colonial cultures are inevitably hybridized, involving a dialectical relationship between European ontology and epistemology and the impulse to create or recreate independent local identity... It has been the project of post-colonial writing to interrogate European discourses and discursive strategies from a privileged position within (and between) two worlds; to investigate the means by which Europe imposed and maintained its codes in the colonial domination of so much of the rest of the world. (Tiffin, 1995, p. 95)

With the "hybrid, lived-in simultaneity," the "hybrid writer is already open to two worlds" and the historical placement makes hybridity subject to reclassification (Sangari, 1995, p. 144). Hybridity, as Bhabha argues, is "textual insurrection" that entails reappropriation effected through deconstructions of the post-colonial writing. This rewriting of the truth by the colonized is not a repetition of the colonialist original; it is the taking back of the right to write one's own history, to displace the non-authentic colonizer's discourse (Parry, 1995, p. 42). Smart (1996) suggests that, "Following the realization that there are different cultural universes, that we live in a multicultural world, and that all forms of life, including our own, are marked by an acute sense of "historicity, contingency, and finiteness," there is the possibility of recognizing the existence of an opportunity to be different, to be, as Foucault...suggests, other than we are" (p. 418). For Bhabha (1994), "The margin of hybridity, where cultural differences `contingently' and conflictually touch, becomes the moment of panic which reveals the borderline experience. It resists the binary opposition of racial and cultural groups, sipahis and sahibs, as homogeneous polarized political consciousnesses" (p. 207).

The sum of its parts makes culture and if the alteration of culture and race can become elusive to theoretical categories, so can identity be understood as inconstant in its nature.

3.2. Culture, Race and Identity

The traditional concept of *identity* (and all the other variables such as race, gender, and culture) as a stable signifier has been critiqued by post-modern and post-structural theorists. According to Britzman and coworkers (1991), this perception of immutability persuades the reproduction of existing relations of power and hence, forms a challenge to conventional understanding (p. 89). In response to this assumption, Hall (1992), argues that *identity* "is not necessarily a stable, permanent, united center that gives consistent meaning to our lives. It too is socially and historically constructed, and subject to political tensions and contradictions" (Apple, 1993, p. vii). Stuart Hall and Cornel West suggest *culture* and even *racial identity* are both hybrids. Both are products of "encounters between and among differently located human groups" (McCarthy& Crichlow, 1993, p. xv). Hall (1997b) explains this nuance of hybridity:

> Identities are never completed, never finished... they are always as subjectivity itself, in process... Identity is always in the process of formation. [Identity] means, or connotes, the process of identification [and] the structure of identification is always constructed through ambivalence. Always constructed through splitting. Splitting between that which one is, and that which is the other... This is the Other that one can only know from the place from which one stands. This is the self as it is inscribed in the gaze of the Other (sic). (pp. 47-48)

According to Hall, "The notion that identity has to do with people that look the same, feel the same, call themselves the same, is nonsense. As a process, as a narrative, as a discourse, it is always told from the position of the *Other*. What is more is that identity is always in part a narrative, always in part a kind of representation" (1997b, p. 49). It is a derivation from history and the present and as Foucault contends, is not invented by an individual. According to Foucault, the practices constituting one's identity "are patterns that he finds in his culture and which are proposed, suggested, and imposed on him by his culture, his society and his social group" (Spencer, 1995, p. 33). Emphasizing that these patterns are integral components to the relationship within the aggregate, Goldberg (1994) defines identity as a "bond, as the affinity and affiliation that associates those so identified, that extends to them a common sense or space of unified sameness" holding the members of the collective cohesively (p. 12). As to the concept of *cultural identity*, Hall (1990) sees it as "a matter of `becoming' as well as of `being.' It belongs to the future as much as to the past. Far from being eternally fixed in some essentialised past, they are subject to the continuous `play' of history, culture and power" (p. 225).

Identity and cultural practices, according to some like John Dobson, are indigenized and hybridized (King, 1997a, p. x). In this process of hybridization, there exists the complex evolution of multiple identities. King (1997b) describes this process as follows:

> The history of the world, rather than moving towards cultural homogenization, has demonstrated the opposite: a trend to cultural differentiation and cultural complexity. With these developments, each individual increasingly belongs to many cultures — an alternative way of saying perhaps... that people have multiple cultural identities. Increasingly, one goes through life picking up identities. In this sense, identity construction is never finished. (p. 16)

41

This is why, "as we approach the end of the twentieth century, what seemed like stable white ethnicities and heritages in an earlier era are now entering a zone of recoding and redefinition" (McCarthy & Crichlow, 1993, p. xiii). In fact, the desirability to "mutate" and "hybridize" and go through multiple identities is emphasized by Turkle, who notes that the "goal of healthy personality development is not to become a One, not to become a unitary core, it's to have a flexible ability to negotiate the many — cycle through multiple identities" (Greenberg, 1996, p. 164). The culture of simulation offers virtual communities that allow fluid identities— identity as multiplicity (Turkle 1995, pp. 177-178). Accordingly, human identity is about "images of [difference], multiplicity, heterogeneity, flexibility, and fragmentation" with the Internet offering the opportunity to construct and reconstruct "a self by cycling through many selves" (Turkle 1995, pp. 178-180, 185). This aspect of mutability, obvious in the world of cyberspace, exhibits the "eroding boundaries between the real and the virtual, the animate and the inanimate, the unitary and the multiple self, which is occurring both in advanced scientific fields of research and in the patterns of everyday life... In cyberspace, we can talk, exchange ideas, and assume personae of our own creation" (p. 9, 10). In essence, *identity* "is not a static term either, reflective of a timeless, unchanging inner self. Rather identity is a gendered, racialized and historical construct" (Pinar, 1993, p. 61).

The concept of race too, not unlike identity, evolves over time; it is historical. As Apple (1993) explicates:

> Race is not a stable category. It has changed over time. What it means, how it is used, by whom, how it is mobilized as a social discourse, its role in educational and more general social policy, all of this is contingent and historical. Of course, it is also misleading to talk of race as an "it." "It" is not a thing, a reified object that can be tracked and measured as if it were a simple biological entity. (p. vii)

Ironically and unknowingly perhaps, the mutability of the concept of *race* can and is defined by those in control to suit their own needs of rationalizing their own positions of power. On the nature of *race*, McCarthy & Crichlow (1993) agree with Apple in positing that:

> racial difference is the product of human interests, needs, desires, strategies, capacities, forms of organization, and forms of mobilization. And that these dynamic variables which articulate themselves in the form of grounded social constructs such as identity, inequality, and so forth, are subject to change, contradiction, variability, and revision within historically specific and determinate contexts. We maintain that "race" is a social historical, and variable category. (p. xv)

Pinar (1993) contends that race is "hardly an unchanging, biological concept. Race is a complex, dynamic, and changing construct" with complex interrelation with identity. McCarthy & Crichlow (1993), assert that race intersects with a number of dynamic variables that include variables such as class, gender, sexuality, and nation (p. xxiii). They suggest that:

> The challenge before us is to move beyond tendencies to treat race as a stable, measurable deposit or category. Racial difference is to be understood as a subject position that can only be defined in what Homi Bhabha (1992) calls "performative terms"—that is, in terms of the effects of political struggles over social and economic exploitation, political disenfranchisement, and cultural and ideological repression. (p. xxi)

Omi & Winant (1993) suggest that, "The concept of race is neither an ideological construct nor does it reflect on objective condition" and it is undeniable that race will continue to be a "feature of social reality across the globe... [and] race is an almost indissoluble part of our identities. Our society is so thoroughly racialized that to be without racial identity is to be in danger of having no identity. To be raceless is akin to being genderless" [sic] (pp. 4-5). In fact, one cannot understand race without considering the other variables and interconnections that need to be analyzed as relations. Ng (1993) prefers to treat race, gender, and class as relations, rather than theoretical categories recognizing its "relational and

43

dynamic character." Arguing that Marx and Engels considered "class" in terms of "relations to the means of production," Ng posits that "class" can be examined as an actual activity rather than as purely theoretical category and emphasizes the connections between these relations. It is in this light that we should analyze the role of identity, culture, and race in relation to global culture and globalization.

3.3. Culture and Globalization

In this rapid development of congregated global forces evolving what many call "globalization," educators are faced with the notion of "global culture." While the term "global culture" has been interpreted in various ways, King (1997a) describes this in terms of centripetal and centrifugal characteristics:

> In the first, cultural forms, influences, and practices from many parts of the world locating at a place or population are seen to create a new "global culture"; in the second (more commonly), cultural influences or practices, stemming from one location, are said to be found, in various forms, in many parts of the globe. (pp. ix-x)

As examples, one may identify the former kind with multiculturalism and the latter with Christianity. Nevertheless, qualifying that such nomenclature has its own limitations of typology, we may agree that globalization is a complex process arising out of global production of cultures and culturally produced views of globality (King, 1997a, p. x).

Some believe that, "Globalization will eventually vanquish retribalization" and that both tribalism and globalism will continue to pose threat to true democracy (Barber, 1992, p. 62). In this age of globalization, the meaning of the concept of global village is changing. While global relations evolve out of necessity, the lack of a balanced interconnectedness, implications of unilateral

44

agreements, indiscriminate policies, uncontrolled free market global economies, questionable international law enforcement strategies, and continued dependence of developing countries challenge the concept of a healthy globe village Some of these concerns are not addressed by the *globalization theory* which:

> [E]xamines the emergence of a global cultural system. It suggests that global culture is brought about by a variety of social and cultural developments: the existence of a world-satellite information system the emergence of global patterns of consumption and consumerism; the cultivation of cosmopolitan life-styles; the emergence of global sport such as the Olympic Games, world football competitions, and international tennis matches; the spread of world tourism; the decline of the sovereignty of the nation-state; the growth of a global military system; the recognition of a world-wide ecological crisis; the development of world-wide health problems such as AIDS; the emergence of world political systems such as the League of Nations and the United Nations; the creation of global political movements such as Marxism; extension of the concept of human rights; and the complex interchange between world religions... More importantly, globalism involves a new consciousness of the world as a single place. (Marshall, 1994)

Thus globalization is a continuous process and goes beyond international relations. It involves "homogenization" and "differentiation" along with "complex interaction between localism and globalism" (Marshall, 1994, p. 203). Nevertheless, this process we call globalization belies the existence of resistance and contradictions. As King (1997) notes, the notion of "globalization," unlike other connotations of worldly, unworldly, has a neutral affect to it, and has "its ambiguities, irrespective of its silencing of economic, political or cultural parameters" (pp. 11-12). King is joined by Hall who "adamantly rejects the notion of globalization as a non-contradictory space; it is always contested, and is always with contradictions. Indeed, 'the most profound cultural revolution has come about as a consequence of the margins coming into representation'; 'marginality has become a powerful space'" (King, 1997, p. 14).

Thus, in this milieu of globalization, the formation of "world or global culture" is complex and does not assume similar development or results. King (1997b) reminds us that while earlier "world culture" implied belonging to the culture of dominant groups, it is now "marked by an organization of diversity rather than the replication of uniformity. It is created through the increasing interconnectedness of varied local cultures, as well through the development of cultures without a clear anchorage in one territory... Global culture results from multi-dimensional cultural flows and obviously comes from a number of different cores or centers" (pp. 16-17). According to Hall (1997a), this global mass culture has different characteristics including two main features: (a) it remains centered in the West and uses an international language— (Anglo-Japanese, Anglo-French, Anglo-German, Anglo-English), but it does not speak the Queen's English any longer. (b) it homogenizes with its enormous absorptive ability. "It does not attempt to obliterate [other economic and political elites]; it operates through them" (p. 28).

Hall (1997a) identifies *two aspects of international interdependence*. The first includes the international economic, trade, and other organizations that have an increasing influence on the sovereign or nations states thus, tying in with the economies, cultures and polities of different societies. The second is the global ecological interdependence with, for example, the Chernobyl disaster affecting Wales (or El Niño influencing North American weather), and "sources and consequences are miles away" (p. 25). In cultural terms, this new kind of globalization according to Hall (1997a), is American rather than British in that the "global mass culture" is "dominated by the modern means of cultural production, dominated by the image which crosses and re-crosses linguistic frontiers [influenced by television and by film] much more rapidly and more easily, and which speaks across languages in a much more immediate way" (p. 27). Thus, the

46

nature of globalization itself has changed from the colonial influences imputed by the Empire.

Along with globalization came the formation of powerful international bodies and coalitions which have largely been non-representative of the developing and populated countries; these structures of dominance have taken control of power based on the historical attributes of economic and military might. Having assumed the responsibility of making decisions affecting the rest of the world, the G7[16], now G8 with Russia as the newest quasi-member (at the political rather than economic level), is made up of Japan, United States, France, Germany, Canada, Italy, United Kingdom and yet, the group no longer represents current economic giants. If purchasing power of countries are considered, the "world's largest economies are the United States, China, Japan, Germany and India." In fact, the largest democracy, India, is not even a part of this coalition. One of the commentaries suggests the formation of a G10 or even G12 group (Editorials, TEJ, 1997, A8). Some envision the advent of a unified body that will represent the collective consciousness for the common good of humanity. De Kerckhove, the Director of the McLuhan Program in Culture and Technology at the University of Toronto forecasts that "we are about to create a collective mind... one that will exceed the capabilities of any individual human" (Dewdney, 1995). According to De Kerckhove:

> The groundwork for the collective mind will be laid by a political globalization whose initial stages will be accomplished invisibly by the convergence of television, telephones and computers. Internet is the nascent fetus of this collective brain, and smaller components of the final global consciousness are already forming within the interconnections of cable networks, telecommunications systems and data banks, not to mention the

---

[16] Page: 47
 The G7 "was born [to address] high inflation, illiberal trade policy, free-for-all fiscal and economic policy [which] no longer exist" (Editorials, TEJ, 1997, A8).

cybernetic think tanks soon to link researchers in commutative brains that will truly be the sum of their parts. (p. xxi)

Linking biological systems with technology for the basis of analysis De Kerckhove (1995), suggests that unlike ordinary consciousness, which is represented by the "processing of virtual reality within a single mind," VR would allow "many minds to collectively process a kind of `group consciousness'" (p. 47). There appears to be a simplistic explanation of the mechanics of collective interaction explained away as a process of collective action. In understanding the process of developing a cultural consciousness—an awareness of such issues at the global level through the Internet is a relatively new phenomenon. Besides the conventional print media, the information superhighway has *sites* of multi-dimensional proportions offering knowledge, data, and "facts" to the "netsurfer." Mendes (1997), elaborates this point in terms of human virtues:

> In the new millennium and the new Century, perhaps it is citizens engaged in the Socratic dialogue of partnership that will internalise the law and justice of proportionality and seek to implement it in a myriad of consensual alliances locally and globally. With the increasing dominance of the new information technologies, public order will depend more on the rule of Virtue than the rule of law.
>
> Perhaps the new information technologies are posing a more fundamental challenge to humanity. The challenge is to force humanity to examine whether it can survive without coercive laws to prevent the forces of evil destroying local societies and indeed the global society. Perhaps this is the ultimate goal of all human rights promotion and protection. (pp. 1-4 Online)

In response to such simplistic explanation of the role of technology in assuming dominant power within the global village, Aronowitz & Giroux (1991), pose a cautionary note:

In this new world Marshall McLuhan's (1964)[17] most radical fantasy, the global village, is on the brink of realization. Politics exists, but is viewed as a massive obstacle to the creation of the electronically mediated community in which we are all digitally linked. The struggle for social power, having been rendered obsolete by the now realized dream of total individual autonomy made possible by the machine, may be conceived as an illusion. (pp. 192-193)

Aronowitz and Giroux (1991) relate postmodernism and culture by identifying three aspects of such an approach. They consider that in problematizing the cultural sphere, postmodernism has raised three issues:

> First, [postmodernism] has pointed to those changing conditions of knowledge embedded in the age of electronically mediated culture, cybernetic steering systems, and computer engineering (Lyotard, 1984) Second, it has helped to raise new questions about the terrain of culture as a field of both domination and contestation... In doing so postmodernism has helped to redefine relationship between power and culture, representation and domination, language and subjectivity. Third, postmodernism has provided a theoretical foundation for engaging the Other not only as a deterritorialized object of domination, but also as a source of struggle, collective resistance, and historical affirmation. (p. 71)

By re-articulating the nature of the *Other*, the study of culture assumes a totally different perspective from that offered by the critical theorist. The notion of empowerment gains a new meaning in that the *Other* is not empowered by the ones who can and are able to empower them; besides, the need for such empowerment is not decided or discovered by those who are morally burdened to do so. The *Other* is not in a state of *rigor mortis* or apathy in that they are not willing participants of such domination. According to Giroux (1993), "[B]y defining culture as a contested terrain, a site of struggle and transformation, cultural studies offers critical educators the opportunity for going beyond cultural analyses that romanticize everyday life or take up culture as merely the reflex of the logic of domination" (p. 165). By recognizing this complexity in our cultural

---

[17] McLuhan,M.(1964). *Understanding the Media: The Extension of Man.* New York: McGraw Hill.

49

analysis, our interpretations of human struggles may reveal the inherent limitations of our condescending assumption of the powerless *Other*. In the discourse of analyzing and dealing with human struggles, it is imperative that we not silence the voices of the people we claim to speak for. Probematizing "the position of those `transformative intellectuals' who assume a hegemony over what theory is and themselves as the locus of what can be known and done… [suffering] from a tendency to do theory *for* instead of *with* people…" (Lather, 1991, p. viii), cultural workers need to move away from our notion of knowing and "helping" in the "enlightenment," "empowerment," and "emancipation" of people from oppression (Lather, 1991, p. xvii). We need to recognize what Apple calls the "multiplicity of relations of power" that goes beyond the conventional explanations of knowledge and power, class exploitation and domination. As cultural workers claiming to represent the *Other*, "We must shift the role of critical intellectuals *from* being universalizing spokespersons to acting as cultural workers whose task is to take away the barriers that prevent people from speaking for themselves" (emphasis, original) (Apple, 1991, p. ix).

3.4. Human Rights

Even as we speak of contestation and empowerment, the struggle in the margins is most profound among not only different cultures but also various groups of marginalized peoples fighting for their rights to survive and make decisions affecting their lives. Whether it is political, religious, ethnic, or other such markers, violation of the rights of individuals and groups is an issue of great concern among human rights workers. The ongoing oppression and repression of the powerless in both democratic and non-democratic countries have rarely made the main agenda of countries of power in negotiation. Even as the *Other* embarks

50

on a resistance to domination, international bodies instituted to intensify the struggle for democracy and freedom through human rights advocacy provide some ammunition to the struggle.

In 1998, Canada will join the world in commemorating the 50th Anniversary of the *Universal Declaration of Human Rights*, which was drafted by a Canadian, John Peters Humphrey. The Declaration consists of "a preamble and 30 articles, each stating a basic human right—civil, political, economic, social and cultural—to which all people are entitled. The Universal Declaration was proclaimed by the United Nations on December 10, 1948 as the 'common standard of achievement for all peoples and all nations'" (Canadian Heritage, 1997a).

The Declaration was a direct response by the United Nations following human rights abuses during and after the war. While not legally binding, the Declaration was the antecedent to a number of international initiatives recognizing rights, freedom, peace, justice for all humans. A number of conventions followed including the *International Convention on the Elimination of All Forms of Racial Discrimination* (1965), the *International Covenant on Civil and Political Rights* and the *International Covenant on Economic, Social and Cultural Rights* (both on December 16, 1966), the *International Protocol on Civil and Political Rights, Convention on the Elimination of All Forms of Discrimination against Women* (1979), the *Convention against Torture and other Cruel, Inhuman or Degrading Treatment or Punishment* (1984), and the *International Convention on the Rights of the Child* (1989) (Canadian Heritage, 1997a). During the launch of the year's activities, the Minister of Canadian Heritage challenged everyone to join "forces in support of human rights, [since] we have the power to make the world a better place," and the Mayor of the City of

51

Edmonton released a proclamation recognizing the Human Rights Day reaffirming the words of Article 1 of the UN Declaration that, "all human beings are born free and equal in dignity and rights" (Canadian Heritage, 1997b; City of Edmonton, 1997). In 1982, Canada developed its own *Canadian Charter of Rights and Freedoms*, a part of the Canadian Constitution, incorporating the elements of human rights recognized in the UN Declaration. The Canadian Government "is the first national government in the world to manage a social marketing campaign to commemorate March 21—the *International Day for the Elimination of Racial Discrimination* (Canadian Heritage, 1997c).

Much more needs to be done in achieving the laudable goals established by the United Nations. Over fifty years have gone by since the formation of the UN but some may argue that the world has not become a better place for those deprived of their rights and dignity. The following thought reflects this condition aptly:

> The sad reality in many parts of the world where human rights continue to be violated tells us that the world has a long way to go towards achieving its goal of basic human rights for all. They also remind us that we cannot take human rights for granted. (Canadian Heritage, 1997d)

Critics have questioned Canada's role in ignoring human rights violations. In 1997, Canada imposed limited trade sanctions on Burma but resisted invoking a ban on investments by Canadian firms. Even as Foreign Affairs Minister Lloyd Axworthy cited, "persistent ongoing repression and deterioration of rights" in Burma, critics have accused Canada for not going far enough (The Canadian Press, 1997a,b). In north western China, Xinjiang's indigenous Muslims have continued to fight for the protection of their culture and their overall survival as a people (Beckley, 1997, p. 4). In May 1997, following the lead of other Western nations, Canada dropped its sponsorship of a United Nations resolution calling on

Beijing to respect international terms. Warren Allmand, president of the Montreal-based International Centre for Human Rights and Democratic Development, "attacked the Liberal government that appointed him for losing credibility when it watered down its stand on freedom in China..." suggested that Canada had turned its back on Chinese abuses by dropping the sponsorship (The Canadian Press, 1997f).

Human rights violation around the world is not confined as an occurrence to the non-industrialized countries. Even as the world has changed over time, human rights violations continue in various forms in different countries that publicly espouse democracy or tolerance. According to an Amnesty International report, "Aboriginal children in Western Australia and Queensland are about 30 times more likely to be imprisoned than others... Aboriginal communities across Australia have repeatedly complained about continuing instances of juveniles being harassed, intimidated and ill-treated by police patrols for no apparent reason, particularly on weekend nights" (Update, New Internationalist, April 1997, p. 6). The Russian military in Chechnya is said to have butchered 50,000 people and more than 1000 Russian soldiers are still missing; the intensity of the savageness and brutality during the war is shocking (Ward, 1997, p. 3). In spite of death threats, Taslima Nasrin from Bangladesh continues to defy the Islamic morality protectors noting that, "As individuals we should use our own codes of ethics as the measuring rod" (Nasrin, 1997). In Malaysia, the government decided to construct the Bakun hydroelectric dam on the island of Bornea, flooding 70,000 hectares of land displacing 9,000 tribal people (Update, New Internationalist, May 1997, p. 4).

On December 10th, 1997, the International Day for Human Rights as declared by the United Nations was commemorated in celebrations and protests around the world. The Christian community of Bangalore in India (the largest democracy in the world) held a rally in protest against minority and Dalit rights violation. The principal of a local Christian college, Father Ambrose Pinto cited examples of, "Father Christudas who was paraded naked on the streets of Dumkha and of Father Thomas who was murdered in Hazaribagh," attesting that "such incidents pointed towards the bias against the minority communities." This rally will be a coalition of Muslim women's organizations, minority and Scheduled Castes and Tribes, and Christian groups. The event would highlight a procession through the City's main thoroughfares, which would be followed by a public gathering and street plays to be enacted by students of various Christian institutions (Deccan Herald Online, December 9, 1997).

The *Canadian Human Rights Commission* has been concerned with issues pertaining to aboriginal peoples, disability, race, origin, religion, sex, age and employment equity. One of the concerns for the Commission has been the proliferation of hate groups in their various forms including telephone lines, chapters, and the Internet. In its *1994 Annual Report*, the Commission explicitly expressed its belief in the collective rights of a society over individual rights in the matters of censorship and restrictions. Based on this premise, the Commission was successful in clamping down telephonic hate messages that "repeatedly sought to denigrate vulnerable minority groups" (p. 50). In doing so, the Commission observed:

> Much is still made, however, of the argument that where hatred exists it does so in the mind of the individual and cannot be appropriately penalized by our legal system. The spectre of thought control, like that of censorship, thus makes a convenient mockery of human rights protection. But it should be made perfectly plain that we are not concerned with unholy secrets of the heart any more than we are with legitimate debate, however controversial, or indeed with political incorrectness... [T]he prohibition on hate-lines is not a large or intolerable restriction in itself. At the same time, it carries a message for all Canadians: a society that does nothing to curb the malicious promotion

of racism puts more than its minorities at risk. (Canadian Human Rights Commission, 1995, p. 50.)

The Commission's position is surmised in Section 2 of the *Canadian Human Rights Act*, which reads as follows:

> Every individual should have an equal opportunity with other individuals to make for himself or herself the life that he or she is able and wishes to have, consistent with his or her duties and obligations as a member of society, without being hindered in or prevented from doing so by discriminatory practices based on race, national or ethnic origin, colour, religion, age, sex, marital status, family status, disability or conviction for an offence for which a pardon has been granted. (Canadian Human Rights Commission, 1995, p. 9.)

At the international level, there are various human rights bodies that focus on political prisoners, conventional refugees, women, children, and victims of war. For example, *Human Rights Watch* is a non-governmental organization established in 1978 to monitor and promote the observance of internationally recognized human rights in Africa, the Americas, Asia, the Middle East and among the signatories of the Helsinki accords. One of the projects within *Human Watch* is the *Women's Rights Project*, established in 1990 to monitor violence against women and gender discrimination throughout the world. Whether it is discrimination against women in Russia or the Bosnia refugee women, the *Human Watch* has continued to use the Internet to monitor and report abuses against women. The September 3, 1995 *Human Watch Global Report on Women's Human Rights* notes:

> Despite government pledges to respect women's human rights, Human Rights Watch concludes that abuse often occurs with the active participation or deliberate indifference of governments. Overwhelming evidence of human rights violations goes unheeded by governments. For example, rape by combatants is prohibited under international humanitarian law but until recently it was dismissed as the inevitable "spoils of war." Domestic violence and the trafficking of women and girls into forced prostitution were regarded as "private" matters only, and not as crimes that the state must prosecute and punish.

In 1995, the United Nations sponsored the 4th *World Conference on Women* in Beijing, making it the largest meeting ever (17,000 participants, including 5,000 delegates from 189 countries and the European Union, 4,000 NGO representatives and over 3,200 media staff) to address the issue of women's life conditions (World Guide 1997/98, p. 34). According to this report, a survey carried out by the non-governmental *Women, Environment and Development Organization* (WEDO), showed that while most countries actively participated in the Conference, very few governments had done anything positive or significant in women's issues. The findings of WEDO echoes implications of many such summits, conferences, seminars and government initiatives that while elegantly articulated remain rarely implemented.

3.5. Race, Culture and Contestation

According to Citizenship and Immigration Canada (1994), between 1995 and 2000, Canada plans to accept about 200,000 immigrants per year. With a rating of 0.96 out of a perfect 1.0 on the *United Nations Human Development Index*, the United Nations has once again declared Canada as the "world's best nation."[18] Yet, a recent Decima study found that racism in Canada is increasing. One-in-four (25%) of Canadians believe that there is a great deal of racism in Canada, 61% say there is "some" racism, 12% say there is "not very much" racism, while 3% believe that there is "no racism at all". Younger Canadians (31%) feel that a "great deal" of racism exists in Canada, while older Canadians (17%) are least inclined to recognize racism as an issue.

---

[18] The Edmonton Journal, June 12, 1997.

According to *Statistics Canada*, visible minorities make up 10% of Canada's population and in the next 20 years, 1 in 5 Canadian will be a visible minority[19]. There will be 2 million Chinese and 1.3 million Blacks by 2016. Based on some projections, by the turn of the century, 80% of people joining Canada's workforce are expected to be women, visible minorities and aboriginal people. Nevertheless, the 1996 Angus Reid poll found that 4 out of 10 respondents felt that the country "is changing too quickly because of all the minorities we have now" and 15% still feel uncomfortable in a room of people from different cultures speaking with accents. The 1995 report from the Canadian Council of Christians and Jews (CCCJ) notes that 85% of Canadians suggest racism as a serious problem.

The *Anti-Defamation League* Annual Report on CNN Online noted that, "the cyberspace is giving old-fashioned bigotry a new lease on life...[and that] *push-button prejudice* is thriving" on the information superhighway. As hate groups have begun to use technology quite effectively to spread their beliefs, teachers and parents have an additional concern and responsibility to deal with this issue. The Internet has become another medium that demands some kind of censorship to limit the influence of illegal and hateful groups on unsuspecting children. A number of organized bodies and individual activists have taken up the responsibility of fighting hate on the Internet. The 1996 *Alberta Human Rights Update* reports a slight decrease in the filing of individual cases pertaining to discrimination based on gender and disability but an increase in racial discrimination. This does not take into account better reporting or increase in the number of cases brought to the attention of the Commission. According to a

---

[19] In fact, the term *visible minority* remains questionable in that the "visible minorities have nothing in common with each other, except their visibility to the majority" (Synnott & Howes, 1996, p.145).

recent report, "racism is a big problem in Canada's labour movement. Canadian Labour Congress president Bob White says the report `points out that racism is endemic to every institution' in Canada, including corporations, government and labour. The report recommends labour groups develop new anti-racism education programs. And it says changes are needed in corporate hiring practices" (CFRN Eyewitness News, December 3, 1997).

What is "racism"? Racism is a belief system or ideology, which serves to rationalize and justify social and economic inequality... [and is directed against] ethnic or national minorities... and economically underdeveloped nations (Berdichewsky, 1994). As Robertson (1987), explains, racism, like sexism is an ideology, and assumes that one racial or ethnic group is inferior to another and that unequal treatment is therefore justified. The characteristic feature of racist ideologies is that they try to make social and economic inequalities among racial and ethnic groups seem "natural" or "right" (p. 291). Thus, in analyzing the immigration policies within a bureaucratic structure "the concept of race can be examined as an issue of unequal relationships, created and extended by differential power that exists between the dominant and subordinate groups (Li, 1988). Alladin (1996), suggests that, "Racist ideologies as rationalizations for various forms of social, political, economic control, have contributed to the maintenance of minority groups in social positions of inferiority."

The ideology that posits the concept of race being unitary disregards race as a social entity (see Troyna & Williams, 1986, Omi & Winant, 1986). As Smith (1995) notes, "linguistic voodoo can't hide racism and anti-Semitism here [in Alberta]," and that "We perpetuate racism even as we deny our own complicity. Additionally, it is difficult to discuss racism due to subtle changes in racist ideology." Smith quotes Carl Freedman suggesting that racism is "an ideology that does not want to know its own name, at least not too overtly." In short, racism is a form of violence that expresses itself in discriminatory manifestations. As a behaviour developed from a firm ideology, it forms the precursor to institutionalized prejudice. As Hull and others (1996) note, racism can be reckoned as a "social disease". Dispelling myths of being merely a bipolar ("white against black") phenomenon, racism is multipolar in its existence; hence, despite the traditional understandings of its nature, racism does not merely remain a "white" problem.

Aull and co-workers (1996), ask the age-old question: "Why have we made no substantial progress in eliminating racism?" They provide a plausible explanation to this scourge:

> We have failed to get to the core of the problem. Many of us thought that through the long-needed legislation passed in the 60's we had solved the problem. We can, of course, cite the gains made by some Blacks in the political, judicial, military, and corporate arenas. The problem persists because we have avoided addressing it for what it really is — a social disease, virulent and infectious, woven into the moral and spiritual fabric of society, passed from parents to children, from one generation to another, for over three centuries. The civil rights laws failed to thwart the growth of the cancer of racism, because they only dealt with two of the disease's symptoms — segregation and discrimination — but not with the disease itself. (p. 2)

Writers in the field have attempted to identify the various forms of racism. Ramcharan (1989), suggests three main forms of racism, namely, (a) *Individual racism*, which prescribes the superiority of one's race in relation to another (b) *Institutional racism,* consisting of systemic or structural racism represented in the established laws, customs, and practices (c) *Cultural racism,* which comprises of the belief in the inferior nature of cultural artefacts including implements, customs and traditions, handicrafts, history, art, economics, language, and music (p.119).

As Feigenbaum (1996) and Berdichewsky (1994) have observed, the nature of racism itself has evolved over time and the "new" racism has differentiated itself from the "old" racism by its behavioural expressions, in that, it has become multidimensional, more complex and increasingly difficult to identify and deal with. We now have moved from the "old" racism that is overt, fewer, vociferous, blatant, angry, intentional and bipolar to the "new" racism that is covert, less noisy, subtle, polite, unintentional and multipolar. One aspect of systemic racism is the existence of cultural racism that prescribes "the inferiority of the implements, handicrafts, agriculture, economics, art, music, language, traditions and story of non-Anglo-European peoples, and the belief that these people have no distinctive culture apart from that of mainstream White Anglo-Europeans. For example, one of the deliberate policies during colonial time, was to re-write the history of the colonized peoples and replace it with a European history. In Europe, racist scholars obliterated the influence of African and Asian civilizations" (Alladin, 1996, p. 34).

Racism has expressed itself at various levels and in multiple ways. A recent media report described a school in Nova Scotia being shut down due to racial tension. On October 2, 1997, Cole Harbour School experienced a series of violent skirmishes where teachers, parents and students were involved in physical violence (The Canadian Press, 1997). While teachers feared for their lives and refused to return to classes, parents and the school board along with the community at large wrote letters, demonstrated and appealed to law enforcement departments to intervene in the racially motivated tension. They also demanded antiracism courses, more visible minority teachers, and the $399,000 price tag for implementing some of the changes. The province had to step in and offer the cash since the board did not have the necessary resources. In similar racial incidents at day cares in Toronto, derogatory name-calling, making fun of physical features, and refusing to sit next to a child of different racial background were reported (Gadd, 1996). This news report also noted that the daycare workers had expressed difficulty in dealing with racial and cultural diversity.

Critics of formal race-relations education point to the conscious segregation among ethnic communities that deny integration or acceptance of other cultures including the dominant culture. According to this view, the issue of race tensions goes beyond mere understanding of each other's cultures; it is more a societal issue that permeates beyond schools and workplaces (Spink, 1996). A number of writings in the area of anti-racism education have provided some insights into dealing with racism at various levels and constitute some of the many available literature that help workers in the area of race-relations to deal with discrimination and prejudice.[20]

Aull et al. (1996), argue for the vital role that education can play in dealing with racism suggesting that, "Since racism is based on the myth of white superiority and non-white inferiority (for example), schools can make a conscious effort to expose (this myth)." They propose considering three major aspects of oneness as a basic criterion for a human family, namely, The biological relatedness of human beings ("We are at least as close as 50th cousins"); the common spiritual capacities of all human beings; and the common destiny of all human beings.

The planet earth is a tiny and fragile life support system for the 5 billion people who live on it. (The population will be 10 billion by the middle of the

---

[20] See: Estable & Meyer (1996) *Working Towards Racism-Free Child Care. An Assessment Tool* and *Awareness, Assessment, and Action... A Tool for Educators Working Towards Anti-Racism in the School System*; Alladin & Rymer (1996) *Anti-Racist Education: Policy, Implementation and Curriculum*; Hewes et al (1995) *Many Ways to Grow: Responding to Cultural Diversity in Early Childhood Settings*; Slapin & Seale (1992) *Through Indian Eyes*; Saskatchewan Education (1984) *Beyond Bias: Informational Guidelines for Reducing Negative Bias in Instructional Materials*; and Sefa Dei (1996) *Anti-Racism Education: Theory and Practice*.

21st century.) It is the only home that the human race has. The preservation of this home and the survival of the human family depend on our coming together. This "coming together," the achievement of unity, is a social process that stems from the recognition, understanding, and internalization of the reality of oneness. The resulting unity does not mean uniformity, but implies a celebration of diversity, because once the reality of oneness is understood, diversity becomes an asset rather than an obstacle. (p. 3)

At the official level, anti-racism education has been incorporated into the official multiculturalism policy in Canada. Currently, Canada and Australia remain the only two countries to have established a formal government initiated multiculturalism policy entrenched in their federal mandate. Unfortunately, multiculturalism has masked, if not ignored, the conflict and tensions arising strictly out of racism; it does not raise confronting race issues but seeks to achieve harmony. Needless to say, the evolution of the multiculturalism policy in Canada has increasingly evoked controversial debates as to its efficacy. Defenders of the policy have refuted the premise that the policy is unwanted, discriminatory, divisive, and an unnecessary expense for the taxpayers. Advocate of multiculturalism, Kymlicka (1997), argues that both Neil Bisoondath's *Selling Illusions: The Cult of Multiculturalism in Canada* (Penguin 1994) and Richard Gwyn's *Nationalism Without Walls: The Unbearable Lightness of Being Canadian* (McClelland and Steward, 1995) are wrong in making similar claims about "the results of the [multiculturalism] policy. In particular, both argue that multiculturalism has promoted a form of ethnic separatism amongst immigrants." Focusing on participation rates, naturalized citizenship, language acquisition, dependency on state support, and degree of integration, Kymlicka refutes the myth of the multicultural policy having facilitated "ghettoization," "resentments" and "antagonisms." Also supporting this argument, Stasiulus (1997) provides an insight into immigrant participation in the Canadian political process, both as voters and elected officials.

Reacting to critics of the federal initiative of multiculturalism that resulted in "song, dance, ethnic food," the Canadian Heritage has begun strategies specifically focusing on the issue of culture, conflict, and racism. Meyers (1993) notes that multiculturalism in the classroom has increasingly focused on the three F's of multiculturalism, namely, food, festivals and famous people of an ethnic group. According to Garman (1997), this "'tourist-style curriculum' does not create a mutual respect, understanding or tolerance between the various ethnic groups that make Canada a unique country" (p. 24). Thus, multicultural education within the Canadian Federal government's formal multicultural policy has begun to focus on more immediate issues identified under three categories— Identity, Civic Participation, and Social Justice (Canadian Heritage, 1997e). A number of recent publications within the realm of education reflect this move toward conflict resolution and Canadian identity formation (focusing on cohesiveness and oneness).[21] Hall (1997b) suggests that the liberal approach to multiculturalism can actually cause damage to the cause of equality:

> "the exotic" is the exotica of difference. Nobody would talk about racism but they were perfectly prepared to have "International Evenings," when we would all come and cook our native dishes, sing our own native songs and appear in our own native costume. (pp. 55-56)

> What this denies is the fact that many have been de-racinated for hundreds of years and the need to satiate the exotica, one had to conjure up a song, food, or costume. It does not realize that we are all made up of *multiple social identities*. That we are all complexly constructed through different categories, of different antagonisms, and these may have the effect of locating us socially in multiple positions of marginality and subordination, but which do not yet operate on us in exactly the same way. (p. 57)

---

[21] See: Kottler (1997) *What's Really said in the Teacher's Lounge: Provocative Ideas about Cultures and Classrooms,* Miron (1997); *Resisting Discrimination: Affirmative Strategies for Principals and Teachers;* Kilbride (1997) *Include Me Too: Human Diversity in Early Childhood;* Sawyer & Green (1993) *The NESA Activities Handbook for Native and Multicultural Classrooms;* and Ellis & Llewellyn (1997) *Dealing With Differences: Taking Action on Class, Race, Gender, and Disability.*

According to Apple (1993), tokenism in the current multicultural approaches can manifest itself in two ways. The "dominant approach" consists of either "mentioning" which is simply including a few "representative" women and men of color to the curriculum along with a brief discussion of their contributions, and "never seeing the world through their eyes" or "becoming the total relativist." In response to these two extremes, Apple suggests that "the movement toward Afrocentrism has developed specifically based on politics of identity. Only by centering the African experience(s) as the core of the curriculum can, say, African American students sustain themselves and their culture and history" (p. viii). But McCarthy & Crichlow (1993) argue that "Afrocentrism also contains within its discourse a language that masks issues of contradiction and discontinuity within the diaspora, between the diaspora and Africa, between different economically and socially situated African Americans and other minority groups, and between differently situated men and women" (p. xv). McCarthy (1993) suggests that we rethink the current discourse of multiculturalism by incorporating "critical and emancipatory terms," emphasizing the "relationality and social production of knowledge and representation" (p. xxvi). According to Mohanty (1994), "While multiculturalism itself is not necessarily problematic, its definition in terms of an apolitical, ahistorical cultural pluralism needs to be challenged." The "prejudice-reduction" workshops to "manage diversity" and improve "race relations" assumes that "'prejudice' (rather than domination, exploitation, or structural inequality) is the core problem and that we have to "'reduce' it" (p. 156).

Kobus (1992), while linking multicultural and global education in relation to equity and social justice, argues that both are not mutually exclusive of each other in a well-designed program and suggests that global education is concerned with *global equity* whereas multicultural education emphasizes *national equity.*

The notion of culture studied within this discourse must be understood as a concept being interpreted in terms of the medium being employed, i.e., the Internet. As to the nature of culture represented in the medium, some critics have argued that there exists a *Kulturkampf*—a culture war—in progress that is evident in popular culture and the multimedia (Kilpatrick, 1992, p. 183). The antagonists and the protagonists of technology make up the *reversionaries* (the Luddites) and the *technophiles*— the former who wish that the post-industrial world would return to the pre-industrial world while the latter predicting the future where science and technology mastering the forces of nature and the planet as a whole (Roszak, 1986, p. 146). Without subscribing to either of these extreme views, we will approach the subject under the assumption that appropriate use of technology by humans within reason and limitation for improving their own lives and that of others need not be detrimental to humankind.

Within this framework, is an attempt to find whether the electronic medium of communication provides a critical and effective means of achieving the goals of global education. In doing so, focus on specific issues is situated within the context of culture. The cultural issues should be dealt in relation to a number of global issues including global culture, "global citizen," indigenous cultures, international conflicts, multiculturalism, racism and gender issues. Can the Internet provide means and possibilities to allow `critical' global education across the cyberspace?

Reflection Questions

1. Does cultural relativity discriminate the rights of one culture over another?

2. If race and identity are mutable concepts, how can we use practical descriptors to identify, classify, and assist immigrants and refugees during the process of settlement?
3. Argue for and against globalization.
4. Can international human rights laws infringe upon the national culture of country not subscribing to the views and values of the North?
5. Why have we made little progress in eliminating race and gender discrimination?

Chapter 4: Understanding Cyberculture

4.1. Miracle Machine- The Computer

If global education is so crucial in enhancing our understanding of other humans on the planet, it is imperative that our educational institutions provide the venue for such discourses. In this era of rapid technological changes, the computers have begun to acquire enormous influence in the way we learn, think and act. Not only do these machines provide network or communication links between humans within a given town but establish connections between countries, continents, and even across space to satellites and space stations. Far from the industrial world, the post-industrial and post-modern world is truly shrinking in time and space. Some of the changes are phenomenal and the role of one of the most recent and powerful media—the Internet and its position in relation to this change is quite obvious. Technology in general, i.e., the Internet or the communication pathway and the use of instruments of technology, and the computer in specific, have become extremely significant factors as students access the *sites of information* on the *Information Superhighway*. Some consider that the latest advances in technology will allow children and youth to begin thinking about various issues of concern in the "global village."

According to Connor (1996), one of the challenges to contemporary sociology of culture is:

> the rapid development of information technology and the cyberculture which accompanies and impels it. The development of global networks of information and communication bids fair to accomplish the abolition of the structures of space and place which have hitherto been the indispensable correlatives of cultural life, substituting for them the virtual, manipulated, or fabricated spaces of computer communications... Cyberculture also poses distinct challenges to the definitions and experiences of the body which have hitherto been crucial in the articulation of culture and society. (p. 364)

The role and influence of computers in the 20th century have provoked considerable debate. While for some like Papert and Zuboff, the computer is a tool which implies a neutral "social and political content," others like Weizenbaum, Hubert, Dreyfus, and Sullivan question these assumptions (Aronowitz & Giroux, 1993, p. 12). Critics from a humanistic assumption "propose that the human agency is irreplaceable and that computers can do no more or no less than those who create, program, and operate them... and while recognizing the usefulness of computers as productive tools, disagree that these machines can solve most of the problems faced by educators in the teaching and learning process" (Aronowitz & Giroux, 1993, pp. 178-179). Postman (1993) admonishes:

> What we need to consider about the computer has nothing to do with its efficiency as a teaching tool. We need to know in what ways it is altering our conception of learning, and how, in conjunction with television, it undermines the old idea of school... New technologies alter the structure of our interests: the things we think *about*. They alter the character of our symbols: the things we think *with*. And they alter the nature of community: the arena in which thoughts develop. (pp. 19, 20)

Some of the greatest criticisms of computer technology has emerged from writers in technology and literature including established computer scientists in the Silicon Valley (Roszak, 1986; Stoll, 1995; Hislop, 1995). Joseph Weizenbaum at the Massachusetts Institute of Technology once described the computer as "a solution in search of problems" (Roszak, 1986, p. 51) and Clifford Stoll, a computer security expert, an astronomer and a veteran in the communications network juggernaut echoes similar sentiments in his latest work *Silicon Snake Oil* that "computers themselves don't bother [him], it's the culture in which they're enshrined... [and that] electronic communication is an instantaneous and illusory contact that creates a sense of intimacy without the emotional investment that leads to close friendships"(1995, pp. 3, 24). Stoll's warning that "the medium in which we communicate changes how we organize our thoughts. We program computers, but the computers also program us" cannot be taken lightly by anyone including educators (p. 46). De Groot (1995c) refutes Clifford Stoll's assumption that "technology is bunk." This is only true if one's "view of technology is one of unbridled progress, an ever-onward march of humanity to a material Paradise." Various writers have attempted to describe the *third wave* with their own criticisms and observations. Oswald Spengler has written about "Machine Technics," Walter Ong, "electronic cultures," Marshall McLuhan, "the Age of Electronic Communication," and Neil Postman, "technopolies" (Postman, 1993, p. 22). Postman, defining *technopoly*, compares it to an "information immune system [that] is inoperable" and "a form of cultural AIDS... an acronym for Anti-Information Deficiency Syndrome" adding that, "the uncontrolled growth of technology destroys the vital sources of our humanity. It creates a culture without a moral foundation. It undermines certain mental processes and social relations that make human life worth living. Technology, in sum, is both friend and enemy" (pp. 63, xii).

Despite the criticisms, the pervasive nature of computers in our life is undeniable. According to Turkle (1984), as we move towards the next century, computers will increasingly affect how we think and will influence how children develop and "construct such concepts as animate and inanimate, conscious and not conscious." At the same time, "technology catalyzes changes not only in what we do but in how we think... It changes people's awareness of themselves, of one another, of their relationship with the world. The new machine [the computer] that stands behind the flashing digital signal, unlike the clock, the telescope, or the train, is a machine that "thinks." It challenges our notions not only of time and distance, but also of mind (p. 13). In fact, the computer as Seymour Papert's

"Technology of a thousand uses—the Proteus of machines" has given a new meaning to the notion of anthropomorphism— the machine as "human." No tool in history has ever shared words that have been exclusively confined to the human— virus, infection, virulent, contagious, sterilize, vaccine, inoculation, system interference, busy, down, memory hungry... This machine has influenced our thinking that Postman (1993) candidly mused: "To a man with a hammer, everything looks like a nail... To a man with a pencil, everything looks like a list. To a man with a camera, everything looks like an image. To a man with a computer, everything looks like data" (p. 14).

Critics in history have been even more suspicious of the computer's role in harmless efficacy. Turkle (1984), reflecting this sentiment, elaborates:

> The computer is Janus-like—it has two faces. Marx spoke of a distinction between tools and machines. Tools are extensions of their users; machines impose their own rhythm, their rules, on the people who work with them, to the point where it is no longer clear who or what is being used. We work to the rhythms of machines — physical machines or the bureaucratic machinery of corporate structures, the "system." We work at rhythms that we do not experience as our own." (p. 170)

Marx's view is one of the many paradigms of how humans have related themselves and responded to technology. Postman (1993) notes that "Marx [even] understood well that, apart from their economic implications, technologies create the ways in which people perceive reality..." (p. 21). According to educators like Aronowitz & Giroux (1993):

> [A]lthough we can design a computer that helps us address logical, analytic problems (surely an important part of education), the computer will not be able to anticipate or respond to problems that lie outside its logical ordering, say, to the emotional, cultural, and social context within which the learner lives everyday life. While the computer may be designed to replicate the epistemological foundations of technological thinking that is rule— rather than context—, driven, it cannot be taken as a model for normative thought. It is an interesting machine, beautifully designed for some, not all, purposes. (p. 185)

70

In essence, Aronowitz and Giroux argue that "Computers have mediated work, leisure, and virtually all communications— and in this sense have become a form of culture." Shenk (1997) forebodes us that, "Once we realize that information technology truly cannot replace human experience, that as it increases the available information it also helps devalue the meaning of each piece of information, we will be on the road to reasserting our dominance over technology" (p. 199).

Rowan (1995a) describes how the computer culture can be quite confusing in terms of its design, language and interaction:

> [T]he ordinary computer screen many of us stare at every day is loaded with hidden and perhaps unconscious meaning, some of it powerful and well thought out, some of it powerful and poorly thought out and some of it confusing... In semiotics, meaning is always a social convention. You may consider a trash can to be a natural symbol for a place to discard things, for example, but many cultures don't discard anything, and other cultures don't throw it in cans, to be carried out of sight [sic].

De Kerkhove, who chairs the McLuhan Program in Culture and Technology, argues that television talks to the body rather than the mind and notes that, "With television and computers we have moved information processing from within our brains to screens in front of, rather than behind, our eyes... We have yet to come to terms with our relationship to our screens" (De Kerkhove, 1995, p. 5). Arguing for the superiority of computers over the passivity of televisions, De Kerkhove feels that, while the "television leaves us little if any time to reflect on what we are watching... TV must zap the zapper before he or she zaps the channel" (pp. 10-11). In contrast, the computer allows not only interactivity and decision-making but also control over what and how we watch. He suggests that, "computers allow us to "talk back" to our screens... and [in effect] have created a new kind of intermediate cognition, a bridge of continuous interaction, a *corpus callosum* between the outside world and our inner selves" (De Kerkhove, 1995, p. 19).

Others argue that the Internet and especially the computer is "too personal" in that it excludes sharing the experience as a group and thus, will never beat the TV which allows socializing of family members watching shows (Rowan, 1995a). Nevertheless, Putnam (1997) notes that:

> The net effect of the electronic revolution has been to make our communities, or what we experience as our communities, much wider geographically and much thinner sociologically. Every day I can easily communicate with people in Germany and Japan, but I don't know the person across the street, and the fact that I don't know the person across the street would astonish my father more than the fact that I am talking to people across the globe every day. Place-based social capital is being replaced by function-based social capital. That is what the electronic revolution does. (p. 34)

Thus, networked communities are function-based social capital and Putnam suggests that, "Much of our social capital has vanished as a result of technological and economic and social change" (p. 35).[22]

Despite the sociological implications, a number of countries have joined the technology race. Canada has always attempted to remain in the forefront of technological developments. By the end of 1992, Canada had the world's third highest number of computers per capita surpassed only by the United States and Australia. Canada had an average of 162 computers per 1,000 people in the country (Coulter, 1995). According to a report from the International Organization for Economic Cooperation and Development (OECD), with an average monthly cost of US $ 20.59 and US $ 24.13 respectively, Canada and

---

[22] According to Putnam, *social capital* refers to "the features in our community life that make us more productive- a high level of engagement, trust and reciprocity" (p. 28).

Australia offered the cheapest Web surfing among all the Internet accessible countries in the world (Evans, et al. 1997, p. 10). As more and more people begin to use the computer in their daily lives, these machines will begin to play an important role in defining how we live. While some may view this as an infringement on human lives, many tend to disagree. As the influence of computers and the implications of machines in the quality of human life are yet in their incipient stages, currently, the fulfillment reported by users is quite positive. As University of Maryland sociologist John Robinson reported. "The average home-computer user spends about 10 hours a week at the keyboard, and 70 per cent feel their lives are more satisfying as a result' (Journal News Services, 1995b).

In all these, the role of the multimedia and especially the computer has become an issue for educators. Aronowitz & Giroux (1991), in criticizing "technological utopianism" argue that "we are currently witnessing the rise of a distinctly anticritical discourse that is seemingly postpolitical and, simultaneously, worshipful of the infinite possibilities for learning and teaching inherent in *new computer technologies,*" adding that the current shift from the role of computer as an instructional tool to "the emergence of a fully elaborated cultural theory that wishes to subsume pedagogy—indeed, the entire educational enterprise, under a new will to totalization" is an uncritical approach by the futurists [Emphasis added] (p. 190). As this criticism is being levelled at both the old conservative politics (modernism) and the emerging consumer culture, the analysis questions postmodern social movements.

4.2. The Information Superhighway – The Internet

In 1983, TIME magazine bestowed its annual "Man of the Year" honor to the computer, gracing its cover with the picture of a computer. Normally ascribed to humans, this position highlighted the development of technology along with its impact upon our lives. This change and its effect have continued since the honorific title ascribed by the magazine. During these changes, the industrialized countries in the North have decidedly thrust themselves into the technological revolution as they formulate and implement policies and decisions. The growth of computers themselves has been exponential. According to TIME magazine in 1994, more than 90 countries around the world had already connected to the Internet, a global network that reaches an estimated 25 million computer users (p. 44). By some 1995 estimates, there were 40 million users in over 90 countries and this number of Net users doubled every 10 months (De Kerckhove, 1995, p. 54). As of 1997, an estimated 57 million users access the Internet with a predicted 700 million users by the end of the century (Ramo, 1997, p. 44).

From political leaders and rock music stars to sports celebrities, the cyberspace has become the venue or mode for communication (Ramstad, 1994b). The `global village' is now connected through a network of "information superhighway," shrinking "distances and differences between technological changes within the context of development." (Weiler, 1989, pp. 20, 12). The digital global network is now used for electronic methods of virtual banking as revolution in the banking industry is said to be imminent (Wanless, 1996a; Wanless, 1996b). Jim Carroll, co-author of the *Canadian Internet Handbook* and the *Canadian Internet Advantage* suggests that in 10 or 20 years, entire industries will go on the Internet and we "will increasingly become electronic consumers."

Educational institutions have been convinced of the need to be a part of this revolution. According to an earlier report, "As of June 1995, the total number of Canadian schools with a SchoolNet connection has risen to 5,500, or about one third of all Canadian schools. Students and teachers have accessed SchoolNet over 4.4 million times since its inception in the fall of 1993" (SchoolNet, 1995). Government budgets in Canada have begun to reflect the new *third wave* movement by acknowledging the need to include development of technology in the area of defence, science, research, education, and business (De Groot, 1994).

The "electronic age" has reduced distance and time; the conventional use of telecommunications and broadcast has been further expanded upon by the computer revolution. Multimedia and videoconferencing are now increasingly being used for distance learning. The electronic medium enhances all three types or modes of education—formal, non-formal and informal. In using technology to increase speed and ease of communication, the Internet has spawned innumerable projects, both at the government department levels and at the school/college level.

The terms *Information Superhighway, Internet, Intranet, Cyberspace, Information Management,* and *Information technology* have become the buzz word of the 90s. Bookstores, convenience stores, libraries, schools and educational institutions have separate sections, departments, facilities, staff and budgets for the new wave of the computer era. The hype has resulted in a frenzy of activities where cities have developed into technology-based industrial estates, people have gained international fame, billionaires have been created, and the media has responded with fervour as individual entrepreneurs and technology companies dealing with the new wave appear on the scene everyday.

Educators have begun talking computers in the classrooms, administrators of *smartcards*, teachers of computerized classrooms and technology training, doctors of computer-controlled Medicare systems, while politicians envision revolutionizing their countries with the new technology to change their defence system, industrial and commercial planning, political system, classrooms, and the workplace. Libraries have installed electronic services for patrons who now can check on-line, request, extend deadlines, research and do a host of other things over the wire. Schools have begun to favour personnel attrition or lay-off in order to buy more computers; libraries have become passé for many schools as funding is diverted to buy more technology and fewer books; students have become fascinated by the high speed access to billions of bits of information at their fingertips; and principals have changed the complete layout of schools for the arrival of computers. While only schools among the rich (within the North and in the developing countries) can afford the technology, the detractors argue that an elitist preclusive segment of population around the world will grow out of this development.

The workplace has changed dramatically. For the first time since the industrial revolution, the information technology is drastically affecting all of us as we move into the next millennium. The industries and business sectors have embraced this technology with sweeping changes as banks have begun to lay-off employees and install more instabank machines, self-service banking, Internet banking, and telephone banking.

The Canadian government has not been left far behind. The Citizenship and Immigration Canada (CIC) has instituted automated computer systems to accept applications, disseminate information, appraise applicants of their status and provide "counselling." Employment centres have installed computer systems to allow job seekers use large computerized databases to post their resumes on-line, find jobs, seek information, and tips and advice on finding jobs. Many employer/employee sites on the Internet have sections for the job seekers and employers to find their match on-line. Talking of matches, singles can find mates, researchers can find information, hobbyists can get advice, professionals can find memberships, politicians can canvass, activists can disseminate information and garner support, and dissidents in repressive countries can contact the outside world.

While teachers are attracted to the medium, Internet pedagogy still needs further development; it has to go beyond using technology to musing about technology and its effects on our lives as educators. It is not to preclude the use of technological discoveries for our own advancement even as we refuse to beatify beyond reason the machine with its radix in silicon derivation.

Reflection Questions

1. How has information technology influenced the process of globalization? What are the positive and negative aspects of the growth of the Internet in an unequal world?
2. Has the computer disenfranchised the working class?

Chapter 5: Global Education and the Internet

5.1. Global Network for Global Consciousness?

The theoretical analysis considers the relationship between global education and the Internet in a conceptual way by explicating the connections between the understandings of global education and the efficacy of the electronic medium.

In the past, advocacy, activism, and education for awareness have changed the way global education and especially, peace education have resulted in a clearer understanding of the interdependence within the international community. The move toward achieving solidarity is one of the important aspects of various programs and with the possibility of using the "Internet for solidarity," a powerful medium has become available for advocates of justice and peace (Toh, 1995, pp. 6, 7). As hate and racist literature begin to appear more frequently on the Internet, the need to challenge these has also become vital. The world beyond the formal educational institutions has begun to grow more interconnected through the Information Superhighway and a number of possibilities for peaceful enculturation of values and beliefs exist (Toh, 1995, p. 6). The role of technology in communication within the area of international development was more evident in the recent Earth Summit. Even as we plan to incorporate technology, it is important to involve developing local communities in this "revolution." They need to become active participants in attempting to achieve sustainable development (Bissio, 1995, p. 70-71). The informal, interactive, non-hierarchical, decentralized, effective and low-cost electronic medium (electronic mail) has opened up some possibilities for "dynamic dialogue' between individuals, NGOs and other international organizations, both at the local and the international level

(Bissio, p. 71). It is said that such a system would allow bottom-up approach to provide possibilities for grass-roots movements rather than a top-down bureaucracy controlling and restricting the flow of information among politicians and the elite.

It was Marshall McLuhan who "predicted in the mid-1960s that the several electrical media would transform the planet into a global village where `instant information creates involvement in depth'" (Roszak, 1986, p. 161). This notion of a desirable and powerful medium that will enhance the emancipation of the suffering has been critically questioned. With the advantage of retrospect and history behind them, a number of writers have raised alarm over the "great wonders" of the information superhighway and the expected revolution toward freedom and betterment of human lives (Besser, 1995; Neill, 1995; Roszak, 1986; Stoll, 1995). In fact, some have argued that Internet exerts overwhelming control and manipulation on the naive and unsuspecting individual (Gandy Jr.,1995, 35-47) while other have insisted that the "electronic frontier" is another way for male domination to reinforce traditional identities (Miller, 1995, 49-57). Others have raised the issue of accessibility and affordability in that the technology has served only the rich and the powerful and that too in the industrialized countries. John Naisbitt, writing in his book *Megatrends* (1982), notes that, "The new power is not money in the hands of the few, but information in the hands of the many." According to Roszak (1986), to give the reader the illusion of power by gaining access to data is "data mongering," and the notion of abundant data "available to every man and woman in their home...destined to be a liberating force" is now highly debatable (p. 161). No discussion on technology can be complete without a more critical analysis of the relationship between and beyond technology and human lives. I shall return for a more detailed deliberation on these significant issues in a later chapter.

As the debate on the value of the Internet in our lives rages on, one cannot deny the influence of the medium on our daily lives. Albeit, it is rational to acknowledge the concerns on both sides of the issue, and it is of great importance that global educators begin to consider using the medium towards achieving the goals of global education.

5.2. The Research Enterprise

Global education has evolved in that, its goals and objectives have been further clarified, and ongoing discussions among educators have elicited questions as to its role in the development of a "global citizen." One of the important aspects of global education has been an emphasis on posing challenging questions that open up spaces for critical thinking. The recent spurt in the growth of the *information superhighway* along with its increasing presence in homes, schools and other educational institutions has opened up the debate of whether such technology enhances learning in a productive way. In understanding the process of human-computer interaction and what elements of a critical global education component are available, the role of the Internet/computer systems in offering elements of critical global education should be explored.

The emphasis should be on the overall *cultural context* relating to elements of global education. Cultural, in that the discourse should limit itself to the cultural area including aspects of traditions, values, customs, cultural identities, cultural solidarities and intercultural relations pertaining to local and global issues. Specific concerns should include indigenous first nations, gender equality, multiculturalism, and antiracist education (racism, prejudice & discrimination). We should ask the following questions:

81

- What is the link or relationship between global education and the Internet?
- What is the relationship between global education as a field (with its purposes and goals) and the Internet as an electronic medium (for communication and education)? How do these two theoretically and conceptually connect?
- What role does the Internet play in the development of critical pedagogy and empowerment through global education?
- Can the Internet be an appropriate and effective medium for addressing strategies for emancipation and liberation?
- Can there be a change in the notions of global identity of Internet users as they access the Internet?

Qualitative research principles and procedures including the focus on interpretative approach arising from situational interpretative principles guide this study. A number of techniques are adopted in a qualitative research endeavor and these may range from traditional ethnographic techniques (participant observation and interviewing) to newer approaches (conversations and computer-based options) (Miller, 1997; Taylor, 1998; Morgan, 1997). *Technique* entails various procedures such as collection and interpretation of data. Qualitative research is an empirical enterprise that involves close scrutiny of social contexts (Miller, 1997). Qualitative research has been recognized for its "eclecticism of theories and methods, its adaptability and widespread application in diverse contexts, and in some cases its syncretism with quantitative research" (Montero-Sieburth & Anderson, 1998). While quantitative research has all the prerequisites for a successful analysis of human experiences within social contexts, a number of limitations with interviewing, validation, contextualizing texts, analysis of discourse, and appropriation of meanings remain important concerns among researchers (Miller & Dingwall, 1997; Montero-Sieburth & Anderson, 1998; Stewart, 1998; Erickson, 1998; Bogdan, 1998; Seidman, 1998). In essence, while recognizing these concerns, this study has attempted to minimize the limitations and maximize the promises of qualitative research enterprise by consciously addressing the respective concerns in each of the adopted methods.

This study entailed three main methodological approaches, namely, (a) *Individual Research* – Literature Review, Online Research, Content Analysis and Reflection Journal; (b) *Participant Experiences* – One-on-One Conversations, Individual Narratives, and Reflection Journals; and (c) *Group Experiences* - Focus Groups and Sharing of Experiences. The following methods of data collection were used:

(a) *Content analysis of the Internet through Web browsing*: As a part of the content analysis, various Internet sites were explored and *analyzed* to find representative samples of sources that would become relevant to this study i.e., dealing within the cultural sphere. This exercise entails critical analysis (positive and negative aspects) of such sites and looks at Web site discussions — spaces of contestation on the Internet where debates ensue between differing groups or individuals (e.g. racists and anti-racists).

(b) *Experiences of the volunteer participants*: The conversations and the focus groups provided the opportunities to gain an understanding of the participants' experiences. Each participant maintained brief observations on the Web sites that he or she visited. These experiences were enriched through information garnered during the personal conversations and focus groups. The

83

participants also completed commentary worksheets during the focus group sessions providing additional insights into their experiences.

(c) *Researcher's experiences recorded in the Reflection Journal*: The reflection Journal constituted the personal diary in which an ongoing process of analysis, comment, reflection and ideas for possible strategies occurred. These entries allowed recording of thoughts on the process and content of the study along with the researcher's own feelings and observations about the overall experience.

5.2.1. Content Analysis

The approaches to these activities involved different sources of data that constituted the basis for what Yin (1984) calls a "case study database." The content analysis of the Web sites was done through *unobtrusive research* with the Web pages (sites) in this case, being the units of analysis. According to Babbie (1989), "Social artifacts, or the products of social beings or their behaviour," may be considered as units of analysis. One class or groups of artifacts can include, "social objects such as books, poems, paintings, automobiles, buildings, songs, pottery, jokes, and scientific discoveries. Each of these objects implies a population of all such objects" (p. 84).

After grouping all sites that could be identified as *global education*, selection of clusters by sampling was followed. This was followed by sampling within it for sites specific to issues of culture. The actual coding or classification of sites was based on a pre-defined conceptual framework. Thus, in accordance with the operational definition of *global education*, the list of sites are coded for nominal categories, *Yes/No* while the coding for *Critical Value* is based on *ordinal ranking*, that ranges on a scale of 1 to 5. The details of the coding decision are described in the next sub-section. In contrast to manifest coding (where the actual list of words, terms or other such indicators are noted), latent coding (where the underlying meaning or the context) is employed in this study.

The Web sites were then subjected to content analysis. As Babbie (1989) suggests, "Content analysis methods may be applied to any form of communication...[and] is particularly well suited to the study of communications and to answering the classic question of communications research: `Who says what, to whom, why, how, and with what effect?'" (pp. 293-194). Sampling during content analysis may occur at a number of levels including, "words, phrases, sentences, paragraphs, sections, chapters, books, writers, or the contexts relevant to the works. Other forms of communication may also be sampled at any of the conceptual levels appropriate to them" (p. 297). With its advantages of affordability (time and money), content analysis is more forgiving, permits longitudinal studies, and is unobtrusive but its application remains limited to examination of recorded communications (Babbie, 1989, pp. 308, 309).

While most of the analysis in the content analysis is based on formal and systematic browsing with the Internet, data provided by the participants became a complementary source of information. In doing so, comparisons are made as to the relevance of the Internet content *actually* extracted by the researcher in relation to those that were extracted by the research participants. The content analysis of various World Wide Web sites included Home Pages from private individuals, public institutions, government and non-government organizations and departments at the local, national and international levels. The sites were selected on an incidental basis and by considering the titles/summary descriptions of the home pages or categories offered by the search engines. Primarily, selections reflect the area of this research study, i.e., the cultural sphere.

The electronic addresses and abstracts for all explored sites have been made available in the appendix of the dissertation. Due to the time-consuming nature of Internet surfing, record of accurate number of hours in total time spent on the Internet is difficult to assess. Nevertheless, as a formal research project, blocks of time were recorded if they exceeded one hour per session.

Beginning in January 1996 and ending in August 1997, the Web browsing lasted for a period of 18 months or 78 weeks. There were two phases:

- Phase I (January 1996 to October 1996) was of 10 months in duration and entailed web browsing for site abstracts and ratings.
- Phase II (October 1996 to August, 1997) was of just over 11 months in duration and involved 8 months of continued browsing for new sites along with detailed re-visiting for content analysis of selected sites.

Phase I: With[23] an average of 16 hours *actual browsing* per week, the Netsurfing began in January 1996 and ended on August 31, 1997, adding up to over 1248 hours on the Internet. These hours do not include digression, blind spots (Error 404!), downloading, automatic disconnection and reconnection, stand-alone machine lock-ups, software and hardware conflicts, and mainframe system delays. During this period, over 1300 sites were browsed and 450 sites have been recorded and catalogued. Web sites were selected through a variety of methods that involved: (a) using search engines (b) obtaining Web addresses from

---

[23] Cut off date was August 31, 1997. Total web sites in Access database: 450. Total web sites in Content Analysis: 90.

magazines, computer journals, newsletters, newspapers and books (c) selecting links from one site on to another (d) online journals, magazines and technology Web sites (e) accessing addresses from television shows on technology, and (f) following up Web addresses provided by the participants in this project.

The selection of sites was decided either on the basis of the title or reviews on the site. The method of selection confirms why there is an unusually high number of selected sites relevant to race and antiracism. The percentage of any given category of sites does not represent the numbers or percentage of the type or category available on the Internet. Based on this information, 450 sites were explored under the assumption that they were relevant to the topic. Of these, 231 sites were classified as global education or global education relevant sites. A *Yes* or *No* entry indicates this in the database for each record within the field entry for *global education*.

Each entry was recorded on a Researcher Observation Sheet and an abstract registered unless the site was inaccessible or defunct. Each site was rated, when relevant and possible, for 3 aspects: (a) Information Value (b) Critical Thinking Value, and (c) Site Emphasis. In some cases, the actual Web Site was saved and this was entered on the Observation Sheet as an item under *File Saved As*. The *Category Descriptors* were identified in order to make classification of various sites more manageable. While it is difficult to create clear demarcation to differentiate between categories, the need to establish a general guideline necessitated the rather arbitrary descriptors. (Appendix). Eventually, it became clear that ratings would have to be de-emphasized due to the nature of some sites (e.g. resource or technical sites could not be rated for critical components). The *Site Emphasis* field was discarded 14 months into the project for similar reasons and was replaced by *Global Education* field requiring Yes/No entry.

Periodically, each recorded entry from the Observation Sheet mentioned above was keyed into a database (Access 97 for MS Windows 95). Forms and tables were created reflecting the available information. During the earlier stages of the project, previous versions of the software MS Office were used and each of the downloaded HTML sites was formatted, line by line, to make the document compatible with the word-processor format. 6 months into the project, *Web Buddy*, a browser plug-in application software was used to do this formatting; this saved enormous amount of time. Each site selected for content analysis was placed on a single sheet with the actual Web page extracts on the top and a brief commentary on the bottom of the page (Appendix).

The basis for the earlier categorization of each site in terms of *Information/Action*, *Critical Value*, and *Information Value* was revised for a number of reasons [Appendix]. The scale was adopted on the following premise:

> Information/Action (I/A) seems simplistic at the basic level. Is the site aiming at dissemination of information or encouraging participatory activism (protest letters, challenges, debates, travelling to places of action, demonstrations, etc.)? Some sites had the ultimate goal of instigating activism while some others were not so obvious. The latter situation was difficult to confirm (Reflection Journal).

The scale of 1 to 5 (5 highest) was adopted to give an overall indication of whether the intent of each site was to stimulate action or critical thinking. In most cases, this is done by assumptions based on the title, topic, hosting organization or individual, presentation, and the overall content of the site. This again, is in relation to the investigation conducted by the researcher conducting the inquiry – education and the Internet with special reference to the World Wide Web (WWW).

Critical Value referred to the degree of critical thinking the site evoked. But this classification became quite difficult; was the site itself critical or was the intent critical? If the intent of the site was dissemination of information and not critical thinking, how would I rate it on a scale of 1 to 5 (with 5 the highest)? Does a low Critical Value attributed to CNN or TIME magazine home page make it less critical? Whether this information is neutral or apolitical is another question. For example, Toh (1989) raises the issue of the media conduct in reflecting superficiality, perpetuation of myths, stereotypes, distortions, biases and assumptions, sensationalism, lack of contextual understanding, and uncritical presentation of third world countries and the peoples from the point of view of "developed" nations. Toh suggests that rather than just focusing on disasters, poverty, and hunger, the media needs to raise critical questions as to why such problems and crises arise and thereby, help demystify mainstream images and themes (pp. 71-72). Given the incomplete or non-existent coverage of news relating to the developing world, initiatives to establish alternative venues of dissemination or the "New World Information Order" attempt to redress this wrong (Schiller, 1978; New Internationalist, 1981). CNN, as much as the other media stations in the West, is not less likely to present biased information. Thus, the idea of CV as it was understood and conceived for this study, became quite dissatisfactory. This problem has been addressed during the second phase of Content Analysis. This thereby, challenges a likely question: How valid are the ratings in the database of abstracts? The *Critical Value* is rated if the site has or is assumed to develop the elements of critical thinking while sites that are not perceived to be attempting to do this do not get rated.

The *Comments* section is perhaps the most descriptive of all fields, allowing a narrative summary of the site. This aspect is more elaborately extrapolated during phase 2 of the study in *Content Analysis.*

Not Applicable was used for some sites that provide a venue for individuals to post materials. These sites could not be given an Information Value or Critical Thinking Value such as in the case of a resource link site or a link site. Similarly, many of these sites were not rated *yes* for global education, as they could serve as resource sites for any research project; nevertheless, some links that clearly devoted elements relevant to the topic were marked *yes*.

In essence, a major element of measurement or rule for classifying a Web site being global education in nature, was *that the site would have to contain information, resource materials and/or links to other resource material sites that deal with global education issues.* The issue of whether the site had critical elements was not a consideration in the identification of such sites.

With the above premise as the basis for nomenclature, the rationale for categorization and inclusion/exclusion of sites was as follows:

- News service Web sites such as the CNN Interactive, ABC World News, MSNBC News, The News Electronic Web Service, Southam Newspapers, and Time's Pathfinder have been classified as "global education sites" because they deal with the various issues in global education through news, interactive discussions and topic articles.
- Sites that specifically dealt with the homeless, women's rights (feminism), children's rights, aboriginal rights, race-related issues, and human rights were included under global education.
- Censorship on the Internet was not classified as global education but censorship within a country (Singapore, Iran, China) were categorized as global education as they dealt with the individual rights in relation to daily lives rather than technology and freedom of expression.

90

- Culture, Art, History, Interactive Educational sites, information leading to sites that are global in nature were also considered global education sites.

- Promotional Web sites, both at the corporate and government levels, were not considered as global education sites. These sites, while providing some information on the country's culture, customs and traditions, economics, government, and tourism, did not really attempt to address global education issues. If a promotional site had considerable amount of information on culture relevant to a global educator, it was deemed a global education site.

- Search engine sites specifically devoted to global education elements (e.g. Yahooligan) were considered global education sites but most search engines, despite the fact this may generate excellent global education sites, remain just application sites. They are tools to finding information rather than producing specific topics and their Web links.

- Sites that dealt with international technology issues and the Internet were not considered global education sites; these are sites dealing with education and technology in general. Culture and technology sites have been included in the list but are not categorized as global education sites.

- Books, reference and encyclopaedia sites (e.g. Canadisk Online, AskEric, Book Lovers) are not considered global education sites as they, like the search engine sites, contain information beyond global issues and are tools for reference. Britannia sites are an exception to this logic as they contain links and sites dedicated to elaborate culture and history of marginalized people.

- Sites labelled as *global education* by academic institutions offering global education courses or programs have been considered promotional in that they do not provide any relevant material for the individual browsing except information about the offerings at the institution; hence, they do not classify as global education sites. Nevertheless, sites that provide global education links and resource materials are classified as global education sites.

- Sites that have *Links* as the URL reference should be accessible through other home pages dedicated to the issue (e.g. the hate site *Independent Skinheads* can be reached by linking from the hate sites *The CLOC* or the *Canada's Freedom Site*). Some sites that have *Links* did not have the WWW address (URL) available. These were pages embedded as links without their own home pages and were sites linked to other similar sites.

- International conferences, workshops, meetings, policy descriptions (including United Nations administrative sites) were not considered global education sites as they are again, resource materials for reference and even with some focused conferences dealing with global issues, the diversity among and between such gatherings could make it complex to classify. The United Nations administrative sites dealt with operational directives, management aspects, project reports, financial considerations, and personnel movements while the United Nations research sites contained articles, proceedings, economic policies relating to poverty, human rights, environment and other such issues.

- Entertainment and interactive games, despite having an international flavour, were not considered as global education sites. An exception to this rule was the *Global Recall* game site as it directly challenged kids on issues relevant to sustainable development.

As to identifying the possible sources of relevant sites, information on the sites were gleaned from: (a) search engines (b) education and technology magazines (c) word of mouth (d) newspapers (e) journals, and (f) links from sites.

- Many search engines were used including, Alta Vista Yahoo, Excite, WebCrawler 100, NearNet, and Search Browser, to name just a few.

- Some link sites do not have a URL (Web address) and hence have no address entry. Some sites that are transitory in nature (e.g. CNN News item article) are not available once they have served their time on line; nevertheless, their URL information is included.

- Throughout the project, one of the categories in classification was whether the site emphasized dissemination of information or emphasized action or activism (Information/Action). But this became vague and irrelevant to many sites and hence, was removed in favour of a yes/no response as to whether the site was global education in nature (global education- Yes/No).

- Sites that had information considered important for discussion but went beyond the first link, were considered as separate Web pages with different URL reference (e.g. human rights in Iran, human rights in Kashmir; email classroom in California, email classroom in Colorado).

The 450 sites were grouped under 27 categories (Appendix). 14 sites were recorded as *Error 404!* and 54 sites (12%) were classified under School Resources. 49 sites (11%) were relevant to race/anti-racism only because of special interest in relation to the research topic.

The basis for categorization is as follows:

- No category has been defined as *culture,* as many areas come under this category (e.g. techno-culture, cultural studies, popular culture, indigenous culture, etc.).

- Despite *404!* being reported for some sites, these sites have a category allotted to them. This is because the sites did not have a 2nd level or had the server down or were simply inaccessible (busy). Hence, only the base home page with the minimal information was used to categorize the site.

- If an area of activism was specific to a cause, it was included under the relevant topic/area (e.g. activism relating to racism/antiracism as RAR and environmental activism as ENV rather than ACT for activism in general).

- Resource sites that are main links to other resource sites (e.g. k-12 sites) are categorized as SCHOOLGEN (School—General) rather than SCHOOLRES (School—Resources) because of the base site not providing the actual resource.

- Some sites classified as SCHOOLGEN may have resources but have not been classified as SCHOOLRES only because of the intent or the identified goal of the home page. These sites have a sole purpose of providing overall connectivity.

- The category OTHER has been used for unrelated topics or areas that were difficult to be included under the identified categories. Despite many of these sites had nothing to do with global education, they may be of interest to educators.

- The category CENSOR includes debates and issues relating to censorship. This category also contains application software used for blocking content (e.g. Surf-Watch, CyberPatrol, CyberSitter, etc.).

One aspect of Web sites was that many sites had gone out of existence, moved to another location, had undergone a name change, or remained static (unchanged) for a long time. For example, when returning to some sites of interest for content analysis, it was discovered that they had moved or become extinct over a period of one year. This problem created some wasted time and blind spots during browsing. Hence, while URL addresses are provided in the attached information at the end of this dissertation, individuals may find it difficult in some cases to reach the sites. Fortunately, some sites provide the new URL at the old URL for people who may want to click on the link to reach the new site. In essence, the following comments reflect some of the immediate issues relating to Internet surfing, downloading, sorting information, and establishing communication with the participants involved in this study.

(a) *Voluminous information on the Web*: In spite of all these, the Web Search Engines remained the most powerful sources for individuals searching for anything on the Net. For example, the search engine *Yahoo!* (powered by *Alta Vista*) produced 10160 hits on anti-racism during one single search on one day within one minute!

(b) *Downloading of files and Web sites*: Hundreds of files and Web sites were downloaded on to hard drives. These provide background information on the site or the topics at the site. Some Web sites were downloaded in their entirety using the plug-in off-line browser Web Buddy.

(c) *Email communication with web site hosts*: In many cases, email communication was established with site hosts or Web masters. The facility to access site designers, content designers, site sponsors and other related individuals or institutions made it amazingly simple for easy and guaranteed communication. In many cases, responses were prompt and rewarding.

(d) *Content Analysis of Selected sites*: Based on the available information from initial browsing, 90 sites were chosen for Content Analysis. A conscious effort was made to include representative samples from each of the identified categories.

Phase II: 90 sites relating to culture in general and human rights, cross-cultural issues, and anti-racism/racism in particular were chosen as representative samples for content analysis [Appendix]. This entailed downloading each of the sites into the plug-in program Web Buddy followed by detailed alteration of each page for accommodating the graphics. The actual content has remained intact unless otherwise mentioned. Each site has a Comment/Analysis box on the same page. Of the 27 categories in the listing, 19 categories were chosen to be directly used for content analysis and 8 categories were skipped. The skipped categories included careers and jobs, games, information technology news, newsgroups, pornography, promotional materials, religion and school technology news.

Each description sheet for the Web page has: (a) Title of the Web Page (b) URL address (*can be clicked on to launch the browser*) (c) Master Sheet number (refers to the actual entry number in the accompanying Access database) (d) Date the page was accessed (to allow the reader to ascertain the actual day the site was accessed), and (e) Duration of browsing time.

As the title suggests, the analysis remains at the content level and does not attempt textual analysis. Some sites have repetitive numbers (hence the number 90 does not refer to different sites but to actual page sites during access). This is done because of the need to explain some sites in detail.

During the content analysis, the focus was on three main themes relating to culture: (a) Cultural Identity/ Cross-cultural Issues/ Multiculturalism (b) Democracy and Human Rights, and (c) Racism/ Anti-racism. While these categories have the delimitation of becoming arbitrary typologies risking the assumption of clearly defined areas, the need to categorize information, both in the database and coding of responses necessitated some kind of nomenclature.

Thus, overlapping of all three categories is normal. Cultural identity, for example, is an issue under any of these categories and whether it is human rights, democratic struggle, cross-cultural understanding or formal multiculturalism as we understand in Canada, a person or group of people may have developed their own identity beyond simple geographical demarcations. Similarly, race, identity and representation are so closely inter-linked that attempting to understand each one by itself becomes a Herculean effort.

5.2.2. Reflection Journal: A Personal Diary

The Action Research Journal constituted the personal diary in which an ongoing process of analysis, comment, reflection and ideas for possible strategies occurred. These entries were on a sporadic basis but allowed collection of thoughts about the technology itself. The bulk of information came from content analysis of sites while a lesser but equally valuable amount of information was derived from the experiences of participants. In both cases, the following questions formed the basis for focused inquiry:

- *What* have we found or explored that is relevant to this topic?
- *Why* do we feel or react the way we do to the specific sites being discussed?
- *How* do these experiences impact our daily lives in terms of our own understandings about global/cultural issues?
- *How* might I use the Internet as a tool for pedagogical process in global education?
- *What* did I experience as I surfed the Net for relevant information?

- *How* did I access this information and how useful was it in relation to the goals in mind?
- *How* did this experience influence my own thinking about global issues?

Many of the significant observations including limitations, categorization, access, development and implications that have found their way into the main text of this dissertation come from the Action Research Journal. The evolutionary changes relating to the project become evident in the nature of changes recorded as the fieldwork proceeded. Conversation questions changed or were replaced, approaches in the process of interviewing evolved, categorization of sites changed, and the importance of certain categories and even their meanings were questioned. Questions pertaining to classroom teaching were ignored in cases where the participant was not actively teaching; focusing on development issues, unfamiliar to some participants, were discarded; and arbitrary categorization of sites as "culture" or "global education" had to be questioned and rating of sites from 1-5 eventually ignored. At the personal level, the process of obtaining and recording data from the Internet also changed; this was mostly a technicality. The outcomes of the focus group sessions speak for themselves and the individual conversations provided excellent opportunities to interact with each person on a more personal note.

While development issues were the main focus of discussions, an ongoing debate on the possibilities and limitations of technology ensued.

5.2.3. The Participants

The participants were student teachers from various specialties in the Faculty of Education, University of Alberta. This component of the project activities lasted for 9 months (February 1996 to October 1996). Subsequent to the announcements inviting student-teacher participants from the Faculty of Education, a group of 6 volunteers were selected from a pool of respondents. The selection was based on the following criteria: (a) Faculty of Education (c) gender representation (d) users or intended users of the Internet (e) representative of different specialties, i.e., students majoring in social studies, physical education, English, science from elementary and/or secondary education, and (f) registered as full time students during the Winter Session starting January 1996. Most importantly, all of the volunteers were interested in the process of dealing with the substantive issues involving global education and technology.

Based on the responses in the Preliminary Questionnaire:

- 1 participant had taken at least one global education course within the past 2 years;
- 3 of the participants had attended conferences or workshops relating to global education;
- 2 of the participants had travelled abroad on overseas projects;
- No participant had travelled abroad for personal reasons;
- 4 of the participants had some experience on the Internet (using email);
- 2 of the participants had reasonable experience on the Internet (browsing the Web);
- 1 participant had been reading print materials relevant to global education on a regular basis;
- 1 participant had been reading print materials relevant to global education on a sporadic basis; and

- 4 of the participants had some personal experience in international/intercultural events that were either on-campus or off-campus at their respective educational institutions.

Students from varied interest backgrounds (environment, feminism, peace education, development education, race, pop culture, science, arts, politics) and *all* participants using the Internet in one way or another, engaged in individual and group interactions. An aspect of the research was to consider what amount or degree of global education material relating to culture and its sub-themes has been instrumental in the facilitation of the participants' understanding of "global education" and cultural issues. Two aspects of consideration here were: (a) The *perception* of the participants as to what is available on the Internet, and (b) How do participants utilize Internet for their own understanding of issues and concerns that are global?

In the discourses with the participants, the specific research questions attempted to find what ideas, views, perspectives, knowledge, skills or values were gained by the participants relating to cultural issues as they interacted on the information superhighway.

The field research method followed for conversations involved *unstructured interviews* and the measure of outcomes looked at participants over time to see whether they used the Internet for purposes of global education. The various activities and the ongoing dialectic were recorded in the reflection journal. The unstructured interviews or *conversations* mostly contained *open-ended questions*. While "Close-ended questions are very popular because they provide a greater uniformity of responses and are more easily processed" (Babbie, p. 140), open-ended responses are more appropriate in action research in that they offer the freedom to engage in spontaneous and democratic sharing of experiences that would otherwise be impossible. In the conventional interview method, the interaction between the interviewee and the interviewed is of unequal relationship— the researcher asking specific questions and the respondent attempting to answer them. The interviewer elicits information and gathers data for generalizations. The interviewee rather than the interviewed mainly controls the direction of the interview. Usually, in the interview method, there is less emphasis on dialogue and thus the interviewee and the interviewed discuss or air their views less candidly. The conversation method on the other hand, emphasizes the need for situational interpretative approach and the root activity in the situational interpretative orientation is `communication' (relating "man" to social world) and involves clarifying motives, common meanings and authentic experiences. Situational interpretative orientation entails understanding situational knowledge (Aoki, 1985, p. 10). In the conversation method. the question and answer session turns into a dialogue of sharing ideas, sometimes even going beyond the immediate subject at hand. This not only makes the participant more at ease but opens communication channels to encourage expressions of sincere feelings and opinions rather than provide tailor-made responses to barren questions. In a conversation, both individuals share the commonality of exchanging information pertaining to a common theme in life.

Unlike the conventional interview where the labels "researcher" and "practitioner" remain distinct between the interviewer and the interviewed, the conversation encourages, "openness and indeterminacy... [and] participants do not ordinarily ask for proof of assertions," and while not eliminating these differences completely, conversation bases itself on a "cooperative investigation" mode of equal participation with common questions (Carson, 1986, pp. 30-83). According to Babbie (1989), "An unstructured interview is essentially a conversation in which the interviewer establishes a general direction for the conversation and pursues specific topics raised by the respondent. Ideally, the respondent does most of the talking" (p. 270).

In exploring what the Internet offers and how it addresses challenging issues for a global educator, the issue and the process of using the medium even as the ongoing analysis of content continued was constantly re-visited.

5.2.4. Focus Groups

The Focus groups offer a similar advantage over traditional conventional methods of interviewing. The structured directive interview dominated by the interviewer with its predetermined and close-ended questions versus non-directive "interview" with open-ended questions in a non-threatening environment provides ample opportunities to share experiences without being guided by pre-conceived ideas of the interviewer. Focus group interview is thus, shifting attention from the interviewer to the respondent and "is a particularly appropriate procedure to use when the goal is to explain how people regard an experience, idea, or event" (Krueger, 1988, pp. 19-20). In short, the advantage of a focus group interview is that it is socially oriented research procedure ("people are social creatures") and has the flexibility to explore unanticipated issues.

Orientation and the first focus group session were held on Wednesday January 24, 1996 at the Faculty of Education, University of Alberta. This session addressed: (a) Project Introduction (introduction of the group, objectives of the project, ethics and understandings, procedures and commitments) (b) Topic Introduction (global education, the Internet). Initial conversations at the

Orientation session provided opportunity to formulate additional questions for the second focus group session. Due to the dynamics of the small groups and the limited time available for discussions, there were no Sub-Groups as originally planned. The group consisted of 6 participants; 3 females and 3 males (incidental and not planned). The Orientation consisted of two main areas: (a) Project Introduction (Introduction of researcher; participants; objectives of the project; ethics and mutual obligations; procedures and commitments; preliminary questionnaire) [Appendix] and (b) Topic Introduction (Global Education & The Internet) [Appendix]. After formalities concerning Ethics and Consent Forms were completed, the researcher provided a brief outline on the definition, significance, concerns of global education. Working copies of Observation Sheets were given to each participant. The total duration in hours of both focus groups and the Orientation was about 3.5 hours (total group time for this project).

Obtaining supplementary information through focus groups was one method of data collection process. Two focus groups of [1.5] hours each in duration were conducted [Appendix]. The first focus group was held at the beginning of the project (January 1996) and was preceded by a half-hour Orientation/ Introduction session. During the first session, elements relating to the following questions were addressed:

- Why do you want to be a part of this Project?
- Are global issues important to us? Why?
- Do we have to concern ourselves with global issues? Why or why not?
- Do you think we need global education? Why or why not?
- What did you find or expect to find on the Internet that was relevant to cultural issues that are global?

- What are the different cultural issues you have seen or expect to see that would be relevant to this discussion?
- What area/areas of cultural dimension has interested you?
- What do you expect to achieve for yourself by the end of this project?
- Besides this Project, how do you plan to use the information you have accessed?

The activity also entailed dealing with four major aspects of the study:

1. The Need for Global Education and My Role in it
2. Clarifying the Concept of Global Education
3. The Internet and its Role in the Lives of Global Educators
4. A Vision of the Internet's Future in Global Education

The second focus group with the same participants as the first was held in November 1996. Proceedings of both these sessions were maintained through agendas, stick-pads, flipcharts, participant-summary sheets, and focus group summaries. During the course of the project, participants were able to communicate among themselves and with the facilitator using email. In fact, during the summer vacation, one participant continued web browsing and maintained email contact from Ontario.

5.2.5. Conversations

Informal but planned dialogues, i.e., conversations, rather than formal and structured interviews with each of the participant were conducted [once every month]. There were [3] conversations of [one hour in duration] (each session) with each of the participants over the complete duration of this project. The participants committed a total of 3 hours for this exercise. All sessions were recorded on compact cassette audiotapes.

Participants maintained an ongoing concise record or notes of their observations, comments and responses on issues related to the cultural sphere. These observations were concise reflection of their experiences rather than deep reflection and/or narration and were collected once during the project and finally, by the end of the project. Participants referred to their Observation Records during group and individual meetings. The writings reflected the participants' own process of change and around themes such as: How might I use the Internet as a tool for pedagogical process in global education? What did I experience as I browsed the Net for relevant information? How did I access this information and how useful was it in relation to the goals in mind? How did this experience influence my own thinking about global issues?

The information collected was synthesized to form narratives of individual experiences and involved continuation of the content analysis on the Internet. Emphasis was on such questions as: What is *actually* available on the Internet that is relevant to this project? How accessible is it for users? How relevant and useful is it to global education?

There were eight conversations with 4 of the 6 participants over a period of 9 months (February 1996 to October 1996). One participant withdrew during the earlier stages of the project and the second participant withdrew 2 months into the project. Both individuals cited work/study overload. The conversations were transcribed from audiocassettes. Though not the primary source of contribution for content analysis, secondary information of relevant materials accessed and reported by the participants were identified and used as supplementary material for analysis. The information provided in the participant Observation Sheet contained comments and the WWW http addresses. Participants were expected to spend around one and half to two hours per week in exploring the Internet. This time also included 5 to 10 minutes of recording observations. Additional time was spent in communicating with the researcher via electronic mail.

The interactions with participants complied with established ethical guidelines as described in the University of Alberta's *University Standards for the Protection of Human Research Participants.*

Chapter 6: The Internet

6.1. The Background

6.1.1. What is the Internet?

According to Yellin (1994), the term *information superhighway* "made the American Dialect Society's word—or expression of the year. But many people don't know what it is, or what they can get from it." Al Gore described the Internet as a "network of networks," while LaQuey and Ryer called it a "loose amalgam of thousands of computer networks reaching millions of people all over the world" (LaQuey & Ryer, 1993, pp. vi, 1). As the popular Internet gurus Carroll & Broadhead (1996) explain, "Probably some time in 1995 (or even before then) the phrase 'information highway' obtained the dubious status in Canada and elsewhere of perhaps being one of the most disliked phrases in popular culture. Certainly it is an overused phrase" (p. 13). Art Buchwald, the humor columnist, wrote: "I am also starting a campaign to stop people from using the phrase 'information highway' as a means of describing a new method of communicating with another electronic system. I am recommending a five-day jail term for anyone who uses the term" (Carroll, 1997b). As to the term 'cyberspace,' it was coined by Vancouver science-fiction writer William Gibson who used it in his 1984 novel Neuromancer. The cyberspace, "is a populous, vast, and exciting realm which knows no boundaries... While it is a place that cannot be seen directly, we know cyberspace exists from what grows there" (Ogden, 1995, p. 15).

According to Carroll & Broadhead (1996), the Internet is the world's largest (a) computer network (b) pen pal system (c) global information service (online library database) (d) technology platform (e) marketplace without boundaries, and (f) information distribution system (pp. 3-5). The Internet may be used for: (a) sending and receiving email (b) conducting discussions and debates (USENET) (c) engaging in research (d) accessing news and information (e) dissemination of information, and (f) carrying on telephone conversations (pp. 5-7).

As the Canadian Prime Minister Jean Chrétien describes, "A century ago, it was the railroad that linked Canadians together. Today, the Information highway is playing a similarly important role. It is vital to Canada's future prosperity... It's been said that in the electronic global village, the Internet is the main street" (Carroll & Broadhead, 1996, p. xii). According to Fife (1996), "The Internet is best understood as a vast, baroque, virtual symphony composed and constantly modified and expanded by cyberspace freelancers of wildly divergent abilities, styles and interests. It has no management, no uniform technical standards, no strategy or blueprint" (F2). Frank Ogden describes the Internet as:

> [A] global village of 44,000 computer networks. Its citizens come from 160 countries. At present rates of growth, by 1998, 100 million individuals will exchange electronic mail through this system, a rival to world post. Those on the Net already access three million free computer programs and files. Citizens of cyberspace are creating a new planetary society wherein time and space have new meanings, national boundaries are largely ignored, and gender and personal identities are irrelevant. (1995, p. 20)

The Internet— "a network of networks that allows very precise narrowcasting and puts control in the hands of the user" —is not as invasive as the telephone, and has 40 million users in over ninety countries, doubling every ten months (De Kerkhove, 1995, p. 54). With 3.6 million web sites around the world, it is predicted that there will be 720 million users by the end of 2005 (OCLC, 1999; Paquet, 1999). In fact, the State of the Internet Report suggests that by the end of 2005, there would be a billion users around the world (State of the Internet, 2000).

In fact, Nielsen Ratings in 2001 reported that 41% of the global audience that accessed the Internet were from the United States and Canada (Nielsen Ratings, 2001). Nevertheless, Keegan notes that in terms of world population, the "Internet revolution" has not reached 98% of the planet's population (Keegan, 2000).

The Internet allows transmission of electronic mail (email), provides entertainment, allows electronic or online shopping, facilitates discussion groups or newsgroups, delivers current and updated news, connects to and allows downloading of free software (shareware or freeware), links to vast resources centres, and enhances business delivery and promotion. For example, the 1995 *Netguide*, a resource book, lists its contents under the following categories:

> Entertainment (movies, TV, music, theater & dance, fashion); home and family (parenting, kids & teens, genealogy, home improvement, cars); mind & body (health & medicine, disabilities, death, drugs); recreation (sex, sports, games, travel, food & beverages); on the fringe (New Age & the occult, magic, humor); Computers (the Net, Cybersociety); News & Business (news, weather, investment, employment, real estate, taxes, consumer advocacy, shopping); politics & government (issues & debate, crime & punishment, abuse & support, international politics, ideologies & parties, election, the military); identity & society (religion, ethnic identity, gender issues, women and feminism); and online university (education, colleges, reference desk, libraries, art, literature, books online, astronomy). (Maloni et al., 1995)

The above *partial listing* shows how vast and diverse, the Internet can be. The Internet "seems to be both institutional and anti-institutional at the same time, massive and intimate, organized and chaotic" (LaQuey & Ryer, 1993, p. 27). Ultimately, it is the user's responsibility to decide what to search for and where to search followed by extracting appropriate material from this voluminous information.

While the many computer manuals and reference books provide the details of the technology behind the functioning of machines and network, a brief description of how the Internet works is necessary. What exactly is the Internet? According to Carroll & Broadhead (1996):

> The Internet is a massive network with all kinds of people, information, and organizations—it can be a wonderful place to explore. It is also frustrating, disorganized, anarchic network that sometimes will cause you to shake your head in anger...Yet, you will also discover on the Internet something that you have never seen before: a global sense of community; information riches of untold depth; fascinating and ongoing developments in business activities; people who share your interests; knowledge about topics that you never knew existed. (pp. 21-22)

In essence, a number of computers are inter-connected to each other to form a network which in turn, are linked to more networks to eventually hook up to the network of networks—the Internet. Irrespective of the brand, make, platform (IBM or Apple), or the computer language of individual computers around the world, a standard Internet protocol, Transmission Control Protocol/Internet Protocol (TCP/IP) developed by DARPA has become the universal conduit for communication.

The exchange of information across networks is done through someone who has direct access to the Internet. Internet Service Providers have direct access to the Internet with their high speed machines. The Internet service providers (ISPs) "are organizations that provide access to the Internet for a fee or for free. Categories of ISPs include for-profit organizations, co-operative (not-for-profit) networks, community networks (also known as FreeNets), and many bulletin board systems" (Carroll & Broadhead, 1996, p. 85).

The Internet Address follows an accepted protocol and a known nomenclature[24]. The IP address is made up of four sets of numbers separated by

---

[24] This section contains information based on writings from Carroll & Broadhead (1996). Used by permission.

110

periods (200.182.116.3) preceded by the *http* for *hypertext transmission (transfer) protocol*. The *www* stands for the World Wide Web. The IP address can also be written using Domain Name System (DMS) that consists of the name of the organization in some form or another along with an extension called *zone name*. For example, http://www.cnn.com is the domain name for the Cable New Network.

Despite the freedom to establish and maintain sites of all nature, the functioning of the Internet and its protocols do not follow a "free-for-all" situation. International and national standards are maintained by specific institutions. Some of the professional bodies influence and partly control Internet protocols and standards. These include, *Internet Society, Internet Architecture Board (IAB), Internet Engineering Task Force, Internet Network Information Centre (InterNIC)*, and *Canadian Domain Registry* (Carroll & Broadhead, 1996, pp. 111-112). While they decide the technical protocols and standards, substantive issues relating to the content on the Internet remains relatively free and unrestrained.

In essence, one can identity *four* main uses of the Internet namely, (a) correspond/communicate (b) access, (c) discuss/debate (research), and (d) disseminate.

One of the most commonly used features of the Internet is for correspondence through electronic mail or email. The email has become ubiquitous on business cards, letterheads, title masts in magazines, TV shows, Newscasts, calendars and information brochures from organizations and institutions. While individual email directs mail at one or more groups of people on the distribution list, electronic mailing lists involving subscription to a given newsgroup or USENET will result in announcements sent via email to subscribers. Thus not only does email provide two-way communication between individuals, it allows distribution of information from one individual to a group of individuals and delivery of information to an individual from many individuals or groups. In most cases, one can search any email address or the conventional address and telephone number of a person who is linked to the Internet by a number of search engines (Husted, 1997).

The Internet also consists of the World Wide Web (WWW). The Web pages can contain text, sound, pictures, images, static video and active animation videos. According to Highfield (1997), "The Word Wide Web was born in 1992, when a British scientist at the CERN atom-smasher in Geneva developed a way of finding text on the massive databases of the Internet by linked references, called hypertext. Key words in a document that referred to another document are highlighted. Clicking on the link, by using a mouse, automatically links to another document on the Internet" (F7). Thus, the *World Wide Web* "is the name of a system that interconnects various databases on the Internet by specialized links to access information automatically" (De Kerkhove, 1995, p. 54). Ogden (1995), describes the World Wide Web as:

> [A]n information highway much faster and more sophisticated than the Internet connection, will soon provide us with greater choice and a better education. The Web is interactive. You have to get involved to participate, hear, see, and learn. Higher-resolution pictures, in 16.8 million colors, with high-quality acoustics, along with animation and soon-to-be, real-time video, and almost free voice and radio transmissions will present users with unlimited information. Everyone will be able to take a trip to any destination desired, make a movie, interact face-to-face and "talk" with anyone else wired on the planet, and do it at one one-hundredth the cost of a telephone call or conventional television hookup. (Ogden, 1995, p. 27)

One writer notes that, "Everyone with a computer now has the opportunity of having the world's largest library on their desk thanks to the Web" (Highfield,

1997, F7). According to a chief scientist at Sun Microsystems, the Word Wide Web is estimated to be doubling in size every 53 days" (Carroll & Broadhead, 1996, p. 246). Michael Neubarth, editor of the Internet World Magazine, wrote in the January, 1996 issue:

> For the third year in a row, the number of registered computers on the Net more than doubled -- from 3.2 million hosts in 1994 to 6.6 million in 1995. Reliable estimates of the number of people using the Net worldwide now range between 40 million to 50 million, with projections of 200 million by year 2000. A recent CommerceNet survey found 22 million Internet users in North America alone. ... In two years, the Web has grown from 100 sites to 100,000 sites that house more than a million home pages. ... As Yahoo's Jerry Yang notes ...the Web is a land of opportunity where new ideas continue to bubble forth. (Rogers, 1995)

Another component of the Internet are the USENETS. Discussion groups or newsgroups are sites that allow similarly interested individuals and groups to congregate on the Internet to discuss and debate a wide variety of issues including business, science, research, entertainment, personal, and thousands of other topics. Newsgroups or USENET newsgroups are also known as "knowledge networking" a term used to describe "the ability to harness on-line information, either by regularly tracking information on a particular topic by receiving information on that topic or by seeking information or answers to questions by discussing a topic with others on-line" (Carroll & Broadhead, 1996, p. 25).

The Internet also has the ability to transmit documents, files and other such information through a File Transfer Protocol (FTP). Access to information on the Internet can be in the form of gaining information browsing the World Wide Web or downloading information using the FTP gophers. It can be exchanging information between USENET group members or engaging in an academic debate with colleagues who are experts in the field. Online encyclopaedias, libraries, journal publications, book abstracts, reviews and daily newspapers from around the world are just some of the few sources on the Internet that provide access to information. Whether technical or non-technical, a variety of information is available on the Internet. For example, the *Canada Yellow Pages* (http://www.canadayellowpages.com) now offers Web surfers around the world, addresses and telephone numbers of more than 3.3 million Canadian businesses at one single Web address (Evans, et al. 1997, p. 12). People can access online help using "cyberhelp" for filing income tax as they use some of the most popular tax filing programs available on the market (Bray, 1997). For some technophiles, the ease of access has become the essence of using technology. As one writer notes, "Timely access to information is becoming one of the most significant, competitive weapons in many industries driven by information. The information highway is only in the fetal stages in terms of its development in the business community" (Arab, 1996).

Canada is touted as the "first country in world" to set up the new next-generation high-speed network— *Canet2,* which will allow universities and research centres to bypass the overcrowded Internet (Southam Newspapers, 1997). The Canadian government has decided to invest millions of dollars into its program to connect classrooms. Statistics Canada reports that, "only 7.4 per cent of all homes in Canada" have the necessary equipment to get online. Topping the already announced $52 million government initiative, the federal government has added another $10 million to encourage more people to become part of the technology revolution (Beauchesne, 1997).

6.1.2. How did the Internet Evolve?

On September 10, 1994, users celebrated the 25th birthday of the Internet, a descendent of the military ARPANET (Snippets, 1994). ARPANET (Advanced Research Project Agency Network which later became the DARPA, the Defense Advanced Research Projects Agency), is known as the "Mother of the Internet" (LaQuey & Ryer, 1993, p. 2). According to Al Gore, ARPANET, the first network, "was used primarily by a few thousand computer scientists to access computers, share computer files, and send electronic mail" (LaQuey & Ryer, 1993, p. v). The early network was mostly limited to defence and academic research but as it evolved into the USENET (User's Network), became more accessible to the community in general. In 1986, the National Science Foundation Network (NSFNET) provided a link to researchers through five supercomputer centers and by March 1990, had replaced its precursor, the ARPANET (LaQuey & Ryer, 1993, p. 6).

A number of special interest groups began using the Internet to promulgate their objectives. The Environmental Law Alliance Worldwide (E-LAW) with the EcoNet/PeaceNet; medical doctors in Africa with SatelLife's HealthNet; Amnesty International with the PeaceNet (a part of the Institute for Global Communications Network); and Texas educators with the Texas Education Network (TENET) were some of the earlier users of the Internet (LaQuey & Ryer, 1993).

The mainframe computer arrived in the 1960s, followed by the minicomputer in the 1970s, the personal computer in 1980s the Local Area Network (LAN) in 1990s, and finally, the Global Area Network (GAN) or the

115

Internet as we now know it developed from all its precursors (Carroll & Broadhead, 1996, pp. 2-3).

The Word Wide Web had its own evolutionary stages within the Internet development. In March 1989, the Internet hypertext system was established at CERN, the European Laboratory for Particle Physics, which was followed by the prototype of the World Wide Web in October 1990. The Web browser software (Mosaic, Netscape, and Internet Explorer) arrived on the scene allowing users to surf the World Wide Web. Users can surf casually to discover sites serendipitously or conduct specific search for a given topic using one of the many search engines. Search engines, like the Yahoo!, Magellan, Lycos, Excite, Alta Vista, Open Text and a host of other such brilliantly designed programs, are the bright angels in a Web world of confusion to desperate seekers delving into more than 50,000, 000 pages of Web site information on the Internet. There are also specialized Web search sites for those highly specialized searches in technology, research and education (De Groot, 1997c).

Interestingly enough, one Canadian national newspaper, the Globe and Mail reported that "As the masses plug into the Internet, some of its original inhabitants are fleeing—including scientists and scholars who made it such a valuable resource in the first place" (Carroll & Broadhead, 1996, p. 12).

With the announcement of *Internet 2,* the next generation Information Superhighway has arrived. University researchers have developed the new research computer network that is faster than the Internet and with improved computer connections, "*Internet 2* introduces ways to sort and prioritize information traveling over the information superhighway." According to the development team at the University of Pittsburgh, "Internet 2 is being developed

116

because the current Internet is too congested and outdated to let researchers do such things as observe medical tests or adjust a microscope from thousands of miles away" (CNN Online, October 9, 1997). The pioneers of this technology expect to link two dozen schools to *Internet 2* by the end of 1997. According to the report, "Each participating university has committed at least $500,000 a year to upgrade its equipment. The National Science Foundation is financing much of the major intercampus wiring."[25] In February 1998, U.S. President Clinton proposed a budget to the Congress asking for $500 million or more over five years to develop the "Next Generation Internet" (CNN Online News, February 2, 1998).

In fact, some still do not consider the current Internet as the final form of developed technology, believing that the eventual and imminent merger of television, computer, and telephone technologies would result in the "true" Internet (Carroll & Broadhead, 1996, p. 3).

6.1.3. Who Owns and Controls the Internet?

According to Christopher Davis, "Lots of people, and nobody, and the National Science Foundation, kinda, sorta" (LaQuey & Ryer, 1993, p. 27). The giant phone companies who have normally shared the rights with cable companies in controlling the media now have to contend with a new and powerful enemy— the Internet Service Providers (ISP's). The technological revolution has left the traditional media corporations in a desperate attempt to regain and retain control of technology over consumers (MacDonald, 1997b). Nevertheless, the fight for

---

[25] More information on Internet 2 can be found at http://www.internet2.edu/

winning the Internet war continues among the cyber-competitors (Rowan, 1996; MacDonald, 1996).

Who then would control the content on the Information Superhighway? Carroll & Broadhead (1996) describe the scenario as follows:

> The control of the highway has been decentralized with the arrival of the Internet, which promises to revolutionize the flow of information around the world by wresting control away from the 'elite.' And it is for this reason that the Internet is a very different model from the highway first imagined by big telecommunication companies... No longer will information come just from magazines, newspapers, television, and radio sources. No longer will the means of publishing be controlled by the elites, by the mega-corporations, by government regulatory bodies. Instead, information will originate from anyone, from anywhere, on any topic imaginable. (p. 15)

As to the value of all the information available on the Internet, it remains questionable. It is possible for an individual to surf the Internet and come "across many oddities in the World Wide Web, put there for no apparent reason other than their curiosity value. The original silliness was a photograph, updated every 10 minutes, of the coffee pot in a computer laboratory in a British university" (Carroll & Broadhead, 1996, p. 19).

Government control is going to be extremely difficult. For example, the province of Quebec in Canada has begun penalizing businesses that advertise in English on the Internet. Groups advocating for the freedom of speech have begun to question the legality of the Quebec language police who enforce French only laws within the province, attempting to control the Internet. The federal government and other representatives argue that the border-less Internet is not within the jurisdiction of any government (Binder, 1997). This is just the beginning of a host of ethical, legal, philosophic and moral questions relating to the persuasive Internet (Compilation, 1997).

118

6.1.4. Who uses the Internet?

By the end of 1992, Canada had the world's third highest number of computers per capita surpassed only by the United States and Australia. Canada had an average of 162 computers per 1,000 people in the country (Coulter, 1995). With North Americans being the most active web surfers in the world, by the end of 2001, Canadians were second (after the United States), with an average of 162 computers per 1000 users (Globe and Mail, 2001). According to the US Commerce Department, as of September 2001, 143 million Americans (54%) were using the Internet (Dreazen, 2002). According to TIME magazine in 1994, more than 90 countries around the world had already connected to the Internet, a global network that reached an estimated 25 million computer users (p. 44). The five largest on-line systems in the United States- Prodigy, CompuServe, America Online, Genie and Delphi during this year had about three million paying customers and the system was being used by an estimated two million others (Ramstad, 1994b). By some 1995 estimates, there were 40 million users in over 90 countries and this number of Net users doubled every 10 months (De Kerckhove, 1995, p. 54). Other estimates suggest that there were more than 30 million users in over 200 countries and this would increase to more than 100 million users by the turn of the century (EdTel, 1995).

CommerceNet/Nielsen Media Internet Demographics Survey released in March 1997 reported that 50.6 million people in the United States and Canada were wired to the Internet. In effect, the number of users had doubled in 18 months. The survey findings also found that women users had increased from 34 per cent in 1995 to 42 per cent in1997. The report suggests that while 25 per cent of the users in 1995 had an annual average household income of $80,000, this was

119

down to 18 per cent by 1997 (Knight-Ridder Newspapers, 1997). Ramo (1997) predicts that there will be 700 million users by the end of the century (p. 44).

With computers being a vital part of the communications revolution, it is estimated that "more than 50,000 computers are sold worldwide every 10 hours" (Brehl, 1994).

Russo (1997) reported that as at March 1997, about 40 million Americans had access to the Internet. The Vice President of the United States, Al Gore notes that "the amount of traffic on the Internet has been increasing 10 percent per month" (LaQuey & Ryer, 1993, p. vi). The estimates are anywhere from 20 million users to 50 million users "depending on who you talk to" (Carroll & Broadhead, 1996, p. 3). *Canada Monitor* reports that the number of people using commercial on-line service or the Internet at work in Canada is growing drastically and "63 per cent of Canada's largest organizations are building data warehouses" (Rowan, 1995b). Software now allows online banking. In 1996, only 6 to 9 per cent of Canadian households with computers had opted for online banking while 41 per cent of Canadians have had access to the Internet (MacDonald, 1997a).

According to Patrick McKenna (1997), "A recent marketing study by The Radicati Group, Inc. shows Internet services and software is expected to gross $3 billion by the end of 1997. The consulting and marketing research firm expects continued growth and opportunities for small and large companies, as trends become more identifiable." Borrowing from the biological description of animal versus human life span analogy, Carroll & Broadhead (1996) observe that, "Six months in Internet years is like 20 human years" (p. 8).

120

There is even a group attempting to create Web sites for churches around the world. "The Houses of Worship project opened [in Pittsburgh] 16 months ago and plans to reach out to more than 330,000 North American churches by June. By 2000, project leaders expect to circle the globe connecting Christendom's estimated two million churches" (Becker, 1997).

The business world has taken to the Internet in a big way (Santoli, 1995). According to a survey by *Courtyard by Marriot*, nearly 60 per cent of business travellers carry laptop computers for online flight and accommodation reservations, travel information, weather and roadmaps, email contacts, faxing, presentation development, document creation, and even games (The Washington Post, 1996). The applications are endless and promoters of technology believe in the intervention of technology in everyone's life.

6.2. Access to the Internet

6.2.1. Connecting across Continents

A $22.5 million pilot project initiative named CANARIE (Canadian Network for the Advancement of Research, Industry and Education), linking national and regional networks to encourage technology among companies, universities, hospitals, and government research has been launched. This non-profit corporation seeks to address tele-medicine and distance education needs (Vancouver Sun, 1994). Many developing countries have begun to use technology for distance education.

Home schooling is one area within the developed world that is increasingly adopting technology for distance learning. Virtual classroom for home schooling, where students living in rural areas can access lessons through online services is gaining popularity in Alberta. One such initiative is the Edmonton Public School's *LearnNet* that links students with a number of schools, teachers and university researchers. A number of schools in the City have joined this venture to allow more access to off-site students (Thorne, 1996b). Peerless Lake, a relatively isolated place north of Edmonton has no running water or paved roads but now has a school that has gone online. With funding from Industry Canada's CAP (Community Access Project) program, the school has acquired computers and online connections resulting in its own Web site (http://www.comcept.ab.ca/peerless/). The school is collaborating online with Japan and Sweden (Gal, 1996a).

In 1995, the Canadian Parliament signed on the Internet and similarly, the United Nations intensified its use of the Internet inviting, "young people to advise world leaders on how to reduce poverty, unemployment and social conflict" (Carroll & Broadhead, 1996, p. 9). Many of the developing countries have started to incorporate technology into their day-to-day living. While such changes have mostly favored the middle class and upper middle class in many of these countries, trends have shown that accessibility and affordability may eventually become minor barriers.

6.2.2. Technology and the South

While changes in technology and the access to technology are drastically evolving, many technophiles are optimistic that despite the lack of access and affordability, technology would evolve to become a part of everyone's life. At the TeleCon '94 Conference, Greg LeVert, president of the telecommunication company MCI's Integrated Client Services commented, "So you think the world is wired? Despite talk of an information highway, half the world's population- three billion people- have never made a phone call. [Yet], nearly a billion more people will have access to a telephone by the year 2000" (Brehl, 1994). Nevertheless, as Toffler & Toffler (1991) caution, "Of the 600 million telephones in the world, 450 million of them are located in nine countries" and this lopsided distribution could be a problem. "The next century can be a promising one for all—but only if we see to it that the slow world is plugged into the fast one, closing the informational and electronic gap" (p. 58).

Predictions aside, the current form of technology in many of the developing countries needs to develop and become more applicable to the lives of the average person. While email access has improved considerably in the developing world including restrictive nation states in the Middle East, it remains far more elusive to the average person in Asia and the African continent.

Cost, access, speed, control of knowledge, and effect on the labour market are some issues that concern the developing world. The role of technology in education remains another concern, not only in the developed world but now also in the developing countries. Not unlike the transitory, mobile, unrestrained capital that moves from country to country, abandoning labour and their communities, the transnationals have begun to use technology to ignore boundaries and local

123

cultural needs. In the North, transnational corporations have begun to donate money and equipment to desperate schools in search of financial support even as they try to control and influence a captive audience through advertisements and consultations. This has raised legitimate concerns among critics that with privatization and reduced government funding businesses will assume control of our kids and education system (Chalmers, 1996).

Despite these criticisms, the Information Superhighway also offers peoples movements and NGOs the opportunity for ongoing, mobilizing, critical educational and empowerment initiatives in a most efficient and affordable way. According to KC Wildmoon, the Nobel Prize winning *International Campaign to Ban Landmines* used cyberspace to grow from a group of three people wanting to do something about anti-personnel devices, to a network of 1,000 organizations in just six years. Wildmoon notes that the coordinator for the campaign, Jody Williams, successfully used the cyberspace for their coalition building (CNN Online News, December 1, 1997). The *Association for Progressive Communications* (APC), a "global computer network for change," is a consortium of 21 international member networks that "offers links of communication to over 40,000 NGOs, activists, educators, policy-makers, and community leaders in 133 countries." The APC allows a cheaper alternative to the telephone in developing and maintaining an informational system around the world for NGOs and citizens engaged in people's movements for social justice, environmental sustainability, solidarity and related issues (The World Guide 97/98, p. 43).

The nature of the Internet is far more controversial than technology at large, in that the Information Superhighway remains without particular ownership, accountability or national identity, making it the most difficult of all technologies to regulate or control. As De Groot (1997a) observes, "The most

124

likely capital of cyberspace is 'nowhere and everywhere,' which is where cyberspace itself is. And that, while difficult to depict cn an atlas, will nevertheless be a revolution in human society... It is hard where this [setting of standards] will end up. Today, Seattle and Silicon Valley set the standards, but a few decades hence it could easily be India and China."

Spending priorities of developing countries have been subject to suspicion for a long time where, regimes have indiscriminately spent huge amounts of loans and monetary aid for armament or military defence, even at the expense of education, health and eradication of poverty. It now appears that technology and its application may be used for the very same purposes—diverting spending to maintain political regimes and satiate the elite in the developing countries, even as the poor remain untouched or unimpressed with the advent of the *third wave*.

6.2.3. Censorship and the Internet

Censorship on the Internet is a hotly debated topic. The unrestricted access and option to post whatever excites the individual and the possibilities to disseminate uncensored and unedited information is subject to criticism by many scholars. The censorship debate has become a major issue of contention within the Internet culture. Critics argue that while the youth can find pen pals, friends and groups around the world to exchange information, unsuspecting youngsters can also find violence, pornography, hate groups, and guidelines to illegal activities on the Internet.

As controversial as it may be, issues of censorship continue to spark heated debates. Along with the call for censorship accompanies the demand for freedom of speech. The Web site *Censorship, Freedom of Speech, Child Safety on the Internet*, contains anything that relates to censorship and freedom on the Internet. There are also extensive links to other sites dealing on this issue.

An important legislation relating to this issue is the Communications Decency Act (CDA). During the last three years, the issue of censorship on the Internet has become the most debated, highly volatile and emotional topic for academics, educators, ethicists, sociologists, politicians and last but not least, computer professionals. The CDA, a legislative attempt to ban the transmission of obscene or indecent material across the Internet, was signed by the US President Bill Clinton into law as Title V of the Telecommunications Act in February 1996. Many Web sites showed their disagreement by turning their Web site backgrounds black. Lawsuits by American Library Association, American Civil Liberties Union, Microsoft, and Apple resulted in federal courts blocking the act. The CDA initiative was taken to the Supreme Court, where Reno vs. ACLU was quashed—a ruling that determined how the First Amendment and traditional free speech principles apply to the Internet within the United States.

Of all the areas under censorship, child pornography has attracted the most intense debate. Blocking software industry has proliferated and many basic Internet software packages now integrate screening/filtering programs as a minimum requirement. For example, the Internet Explorer 3.0 has settings for parents to regulate what their children access. As one can see, this is only the tip of the iceberg. From arguments, home pages, and elaborate Web sites on preventing children from accessing the Internet to the various regulatory mechanisms available to enable children to browse the Internet, one search word

126

in a good search engine will bring up thousands of relevant sites. In Europe, some countries like Sweden and Germany have moved toward making Internet service providers responsible for the content they supply while the U.S. computer industry is mainly depending on voluntary controls. screening and filtering of undesirable materials. According to one expert, "It's difficult if not impossible to suppress content on the Web because there are so many ways to evade controls. Which does not mean that one should not take steps to limit behaviour, but coming up with foolproof controls is virtually impossible." (CNN Online News, November 11, 1997). As a reaction to the increasing calls for self-restraint, Netscape Communications, Microsoft Corporation and CompuServe have all assumed some responsibility by offering screening software (Mendes, 1997).

The Web site *Content Blocking* describes the formation of a Working Group to deal with Internet and issues such as censorship and children, defamatory materials, intellectual property and culturally inappropriate materials. The need for an Internet Law and Policy Forum has been highly under-rated. This is only a working group (at the time of this browsing). Censorship and the fear among ISP (Internet Service Providers) regarding unnecessary government intervention besides loss of Freedom of Speech has stimulated the establishment of a monitoring body addressing formation of regulatory mechanisms. An issue that will never be completely resolved, Content Blocking will increasingly become a subject for hot debate among politicians, technologists, social workers, educators and parents.

While Canada has not yet legislated the nature of online interaction itself, laws pertaining to hate propaganda, child pornography and obscenity have been ratified (Mendes, 1997). Even as technology has offered unprecedented freedom

127

to disseminate information, there is the suggestion that there be a balance of proportionality:

> Justice demands that proportional safeguards are put in place to make sure neither the individual interest, nor the societal interest is overwhelmed and sacrificed at the expense of the other. The individual interest in free expression is to be kept in proportion to the societal interest in protecting society, especially the vulnerable in society, against hate propaganda, pornography and obscenity. (Mendes, 1997, p. 6)

The *Simon Wiesenthal Centre* has tried in vain to stop racism and hate on the Internet but since the Internet is "not a place, or a company, or an institution, or an association," controlling the material on the Net remains largely unsuccessful. What is legal in one country may be illegal in another and since Web sites can be launched from anywhere in the world, the costs to control the Internet is far too overwhelming and enormous to be practicable (De Groot, 1995).

The Canadian Human Rights Commission has initiated a process to shut down Holocaust denier Zundel's hate site on the Web. While the commission has been successful in shutting down Canadian telephone sites that had hate messages against the Jews, removing Zundel's site based in California may be more challenging. It did, as predicted, spark "a debate over freedom of expression in cyberspace and the right of any government agency to control messages on the Internet" (Bindman, 1996). The case before the Canadian Human Rights Commission has begun to apply human rights legislation to the issue of hate groups on the Internet and the case against Zundel is said to be the first of its kind. A University of Alberta linguist, Gary Prideaux, has provided results of his analysis to prove that Zundel's site is propagating anti-Semitism (Tobin, 1997; Hooper, 1997; The Canadian Press, 1997h). Prideaux's analysis has come up with indisputable evidence that Zundel's site is anti-Semitic in nature. Yet, Matthew Friedman, an author of a book on the Internet, thinks that controlling the Internet

128

is unadvisable, impractical and impossible. According to Friedman, the Internet "exists pretty much beyond any one nation's jurisdiction... [Censorship is] like killing a cockroach with a sledgehammer. The Internet has done us a great favour by exposing people like Zundel and (the issue) of racism. Let them hang themselves with their own bizarre ideas" (Hooper, 1997). Friedman thinks that the Commission is over-reacting and that the government attempts to control the World Wide Web is like "herding cats. It is just not possible."

In June 1997, in spite of free speech advocates, Germany's parliament passed the first comprehensive national Internet law dealing with rules relating to confidentiality of personal data along with issues of pornography and hate materials on the Internet (Mock, 1997, p. 3). In spite of opposition from many proponents of freedom of speech against restrictions, it is encouraging to note that the laws in Germany make it extremely difficult for hate groups to operate from within the country.

Despite the fact that the Canadian government has considered hate propaganda as a criminal offence since 1970, the application of the law itself remains difficult due to the nature of the Internet being without specific national borders (Mock, 1997, p. 3). Nevertheless, Mock remains convinced that, "Ultimately the battle against racism and hate on the Internet will be won through increased efforts to incorporate Holocaust education, multiculturalism, anti-racism and human rights education in our schools" (Mock, 1997, p. 3). Mock suggests that we incorporate computer literacy courses with critical elements addressing the identification and recognition of issues that relate to credibility and facts available on the Internet.

Groups of individuals have sprouted around the world to promote or dissuade Internet censorship, illegal cyberspace activities, distance education, Internet polling, citizens poll-back, rights of individual privacy, and access to information. Some Internet experts are even concerned about censorship per se: "Baby boomers—that idealistic generation of the 1960s, once so full of passion and enthusiasm for issues of democracy and freedom—are calling for censorship. It is a strange state of affairs" (Carroll & Broadhead, 1996, p. 12). A segment of the digital 'evangelists' have begun to cry foul arguing that kids have their rights— "cyber rights," to access the culture they are creating on the Internet, and that the political left and right are supposedly "exploiting children to advance their own ideological agendas" (Katz, 1996).

The widespread presence of money laundering, international drug activities, illegal and questionable operations has also raised questions about controlling the Internet. As increasing number of crimes are committed on computers and over the Internet, law enforcement officers are in the process of establishing legal ground rules to identify and convict lawbreakers. For the third time following establishment of specific law enforcement team dedicated to investigating Internet crime, police seized pornographic material from an Edmonton man and charged with downloading and transmitting more than 2,000 child pornographic images (Gold, 1997). Another Edmonton man is one of the first people in Alberta to be sentenced for collecting child pornography on his computer. Sentenced for 30 months in prison, the 33-year old man had pornographic images depicting 22 children. Initially, the issues of censorship, access to his computer accounts, and privacy were in legal debate but eventually, the court agreed to accept the evidence, clearing way to other similar offences on the Internet (CFRN, January 30, 1998). In Toronto, the largest seizure of computer child pornography files in Canadian history has set the law enforcement officials concerned about tackling cybercrime and cybercriminals (Poling, 1996). With an industry that makes $1 billion in online sex sites, pornography Web sites have even crashed as a result of overwhelming demand by people hungry for online erotica. In fact, "sex is still the most searched for word on the Internet," says an online porno model, who has invested thousands of dollars in the Internet pornography business (Silver, 1997). As the pornography business grows, business corporations and employers are extremely concerned with employees browsing entertainment and mostly pornographic sites on company time (Stafford, 1997).

With the U.S. Supreme Court's decision to block the Communications Decency Act, major service providers like CompuServe and America On-Line have established their own controls over pornographic materials (Russo, 1997). In Canada, the federal communications regulations body, the Canadian Radio-television and Telecommunications Commission (CRTC), is considering regulating the Internet (Southam News, 1996). There is even a new Web site that lists convicted sex offenders that includes 500,000 photos of child molesters from Canada, Mexico and the United States (Mercer, 1992). Hundreds of Internet users and law enforcement departments have begun to identify and deal with people engaged in cultivating pornography on the Net. (Powell, 1996; The Canadian Press, 1996b). In one case, pranksters have managed to insert pornographic images on seemingly harmless computer software aimed at the public creating chaos among unsuspecting publishers (Farrell, 1997). In fact, it takes only three inputs to reach a pornographic site. Finding pornographic material on the Internet is as simple as spelling S-E-X. For one investigator, a single search for "sex" produced 662,255 hits (Gold, 1996).

Some parents argue that censorship should remain with the users. As one parent whose children get on the Internet's *Cyberkids*, an online magazine written for and by children, notes that their four-year-old daughter "pretty much knows about things that are wrong," and "she knows when she sees a picture that disturbs her. She does not talk to anyone she doesn't know. It's just an extension of the real world. The same limits have to be set" (Donnan, 1995). According to Donnan (1995), "Concerned that the difference between right and wrong may not come as easily as surfing the net to pubescent hackers, computer industry and education groups are increasingly trying to teach computer ethics to children and their parents. Even as computer experts are concerned about the way technology is appropriated by young children, some feel the critical need for teaching them how to go about it" (p. 10).

Presently, as the Net does not belong to any one individual company or country, the notion of regulatory mechanisms may be established only at the various nodes of dissemination. Net Shepherd Inc., a Calgary software developer company has released a freeware program called daxHOUND, that rates many of the Internet sites with classifications as General, Child, Pre-teen, Teen, Adult, or under a skull and crossbones allowing parents to decide what to filter [Appendix] (Duvall, 1996). *Net Nanny, SurfWatch,* and *CyberPatrol,* are some of the many screening software packages available to parents eager in blocking out undesirable Web sites (Gal, 1996b). Perhaps the issue of censorship is appropriately described by Mendes (1997):

> Throughout human history, the rights of individuals and groups have been sacrificed for what is alleged to be the common good of all. Tyrants, dictators and those who lust for power throughout history have come up with compelling reasons, in their view, to censor, to suppress, to oppress through laws and force. Human rights advocates have fought against these forces and continue to do so. The battle is again joined in the world of cyberspace. This time, perhaps for the

first time in human history, the technology of cyberspace gives the upper hand to those who advocate freedom of expression. (p. 15)

At the school level, monitoring by responsible staff remains the main option. A group of school officials in Calgary have written a "code of conduct" to help students navigate safely on the Internet. As John Hogan, superintendent of secondary education at the Calgary public school board commented: "There's a black side to the Internet. We believe while it's an incredible learning resource for students... that we have to have students and parents understand that there is this ugliness [pornography, gambling, hate groups] associated with it." According to this news item, half of the 200 public schools in Edmonton have student access to the Internet (Calgary Herald & Journal Staff, 1995).

6.3. Implications of Using the Internet

In using the Internet, one must consciously make an effort not to attribute anything supernatural or beyond the expectations of a conventional tool. The Internet can be compared to a library of resources. How does the Information Superhighway compare to the conventional library? Both systems have many similarities in that the effective use of library depends upon whether the user:

- is aware of the facility;
- decides and knows how to use the facility;
- utilizes the search resources (indexes and abstracts) using appropriate descriptors;
- does the actual search for the material and identifies the area where the material is available;
- decides to physically go to the appropriate section and pick up the material (document);

- will not get distracted by other materials, people or events in the process;
- reads, understands and uses the information available in the document;
- recognizes and discards irrelevant and inappropriate information;
- treats the content of the selected document critically, and
- understands that the library is only a tool that offers the resources.

Not very much unlike the conventional library, the Internet user must:
- be aware of the technology and what it offers;
- decide and know how to use the technology;
- utilize the search engines and browsers using appropriate descriptors;
- conduct the actual Web search for the specific material or information;
- not get distracted by other sites on the Internet;
- read, understand and identify as to the credibility, reliability, accuracy and the source of information;
- recognize and discard irrelevant and inappropriate information;
- treat the content of the selected document critically, and
- understand that the Internet is only a tool that offers the resources.

Major differences between a conventional library and the Internet is that the latter:
- does not have a person or body that regulates and/or controls the system;
- does not have any monitoring mechanism (hence, the high frequency of questionable material);
- does not have any local laws to define responsibilities to the user;
- does not have any accountability procedures in place (as to the availability of materials);

- does not follow conventional censorship commitments to the author or publishers;

- thrives on its own and evolving cyber-culture designed on very clear and strict cyber-protocols and user behaviour;

- remains very fluid and in a flux as to the variety and nature of content that is available; and

- is sometimes overwhelmed by the technology hype along with the mushrooming techno-gurus who have assumed the responsibility of defining what is "appropriate."

Some predict that only those who have learned to manage technology will benefit and become successful educators. Ogden (1995) believes that the future belongs to educators who will be knowledge navigators. These cyberspace travelers, according to Ogden, will "replace teachers who are unable to keep up with changing times... Knowledge navigators do not fear geographic boundaries. They are electronic flyers who, in the words of "Star Trek," "go where no one has gone before." They cross borders electronically and gather information... In the valley of the uninformed, the information-rich knowledge navigator will soon be king or queen" (pp. 26, 29, 30). While one might hesitate to join in the chorus with Ogden, some of his sweeping generalizations hold some truth. In the evolving nature of education and its priorities, educators need to become technologically knowledgeable even as they remain cautious about its seemingly alluring promises. We need to echo the warnings of Postman (1993) in questioning some of the commonly dispersed uncritical rabidity among the believers of technology.

> It is a mistake to suppose that any technological innovation has a one-sided effect. Every technology is both a burden and a blessing; not either-or, but this-and-that... Technophiles "gaze on technology as a lover does on his beloved, seeing it as without blemish and entertaining no apprehension for the future. They are therefore dangerous and are to be approached cautiously...

The uses made of any technology are largely determined by the structure of the technology itself—that is, that its functions follow from its form" (pp. 5, 7).

Similarly, Shenk (1997), reflecting this caution agrees that the seductive myth that information is power also assumes that technology equals progress. "Information obesity" is premised on the notion that more information is necessarily better. According to Peter Sellars, easily acquired ("non-serendipitous") information is "debased, devalued and dehumanized" (p. 27). In its production being faster than we could process it, information has emerged "not only as a currency, but also as a pollutant" even as "we face a paradox of abundance-induced amnesia" (pp. 30, 124).

6.3.1. The Internet and International Development

While the industrialized nations march forward to the tune of technology revolution, the developing world does not want to be left watching the North progress. A familiar scene from the post-colonial industrial revolution has begun to reappear. Countries that do not have clear policies and sufficient budgets for reducing poverty or establish minimum standards of education have resorted to become "technologically advanced" in order not to be left behind by the *third wave*. Some countries have turned into low cost labour duty free industrial enclaves manufacturing microchips and other parts for the electronics industry that are mostly situated in the industrialized world. The notion of labour movement along with its migration, brain drain, illegal workers, borders and deportations, standards of labour and worker's union, (investment portfolio) have become evolving concepts as business and especially the computer industry, have established off-shore or overseas satellite-based labour production.

Peenya in Bangalore, India has become the Silicon Valley of Asia, not just India, in having developed sprawling electronics industry where local Ph.D. graduates with computer and engineering degrees work in modern complexes offering their expertise in programming and designing technology. Intellectual products are then sent as electronic information via satellite to California. While the information technology workers in the developing country get a considerably higher than average salary (and are delighted to work in their own hometowns without being displaced), the contracting companies in the North own intellectual property for a minimal expense, in contrast to the same job done by workers in North America. Nevertheless, this raises issues of disenfranchised and unemployed workers here in the North, even as the boundaries and borderlines between countries become less distinct. From the multinational corporations investing in low-cost labour countries and moving from country to country on their own terms and conditions, we now move into an era of electronic transactions across international networks that will deny and defy standards of labour and national boundaries.

6.3.2. The Internet and the Possibilities

The futurists predict the good times, as technology will revolutionize our living. Some believers in the promises of the digital revolution consciously ignore and downplay other pressing concerns. In fact, Peter Leyden features editor of *Wired* magazine dismisses the pessimism flippantly, "They're worried about [a] growing underclass, poverty, a shrinking ozone layer, that the world is choking in garbage. You can throw up all kinds of negative things, but it won't change the fact that we really are at an extraordinary moment in history" (Duvall, 1997). In fact, Jim Carroll notes that, "The barrier isn't technology. It's the culture, it's the

137

mindset" (The Canadian Press, 1995). Children do not have many problems in dealing with the new technology because they are willing to go through the learning process in an unfamiliar setting. Bill Gates, chairman of Microsoft Corporation notes, "[Adults] just aren't willing to put up with a few hours of confusion and sort of get over the hump. Whereas kids, they're always confused and learning new things all the time so, what the heck, they dive in" (Ramstad, 1994b).

To expect that the Internet become a conduit for positive results is natural for some. According to Raymond Morrow, professor of sociology at the University of Alberta, "the Internet's distinguishing aspect lies in its non-profit origins. It appears to provide a rationale based on the belief that something that has an altruistic beginning will naturally continue to become another tool for emancipatory goals."

While the traditionalists in North America have launched a war on technology, their counterparts in the Europe have become less critical of the techno-revolution. Focusing on lifestyles and the influence of science, "neo-Luddites" in the United Kingdom seem to be "happy for their message to be spread on the Internet" (Berens, 1996). From the "neo-Luddites" to the technology gurus, the range between techno-believers and techno-phobes is wide and diverse. Some of the more cautious experts (Stoll) argue that the lack of touch, interpersonal relationships, the replacement of the artificial for the natural, unreal for the real, and the pseudo-experience for the authentic experience (texture, feel, etc.) are really not the genuine ingredients for true learning.

Among the techno-optimists are the advocates who remind us of the disappearance of time and space, access to voluminous information at high speed and low cost, the sudden opening of world to the physically disadvantaged and isolated individuals, and the removal of restrictions for contributors on the Internet. In fact, some futurists even attempt to chide the cautious ones, predicting a brighter future to all those who believe in the new technology. Ogden (1995) suggests that, "People already competent in network surfing and instant information retrieval have become a new social class. I call its members the 'digirati.' This new class does not suffer the same apprehension about the future as today's government bureaucrats, corporate managers, and academics" (p. 15).

Other similar predictions for computers and technology seem quite optimistic. Futurist Richard Worzel envisions: "The future is going to catch you by surprise. It's not what you are going to expect. The future will also bring portable computers that can accept memos and letters by dictation, ceramic engine blocks for cars, and genetic engineering that will reverse the aging process" (MacDonald, 1994). According to another futurist, with the intertwining of computing and communications, "the Internet will lead us in new and exciting directions" (The Canadian Press, 1996a). The integration of technological applications will facilitate this change. According to Surtees (1995), "The convergence, or melding, of the telecommunications, broadcast, computer and entertainment industries is driving the global creation of faster, more powerful electronic highways that herald on-demand delivery of movies by phone or cable and wide access to the Internet." Some futurists predict the telephone, television, ATM, Plastic Cards (identity, license, debit, credit & charge), Video Terminals, and the Internet will become seemingly integrated into one system (Blythe, 1996). Technology developers predict the seemingly smooth integration between the TV and the Internet as viewers will be able to interact and even do on-line shopping using their TV remote controllers as some communities in California already do

(Whitefield, 1996). Quite a fancy world indeed, the vision of techno-wizardry paradise may not really account for the detrimental effects on humans.

In 1995, Rifkin predicted in his book *The End of Work* that computers, robotics, telecommunications and other similar technologies would replace human labour, but a study by the Conference Board of Canada suggests otherwise. According to this report, "high technology will create more jobs than it kills" (Evenson, 1997). While Rifkin's predictions are subject to ongoing debate and could be a separate topic for discussion, the eager adoption of technology among private and government institutions is undeniable. Governments in the industrialized world have begun to get involved in policies influencing and perhaps even defining the using of technology. The Information Highway Advisory Council is a Canadian federal government initiative. The 29-member council released a 227-page report containing 300 policy recommendations for the government. Recommendations, available on the Internet at their home page [Appendix], includes accepting competition, ensuring equal access, encouraging corporate involvement and research development, addressing privacy and security laws, and promoting Canadian culture (Surtees, 1995). Churches have begun to use the Internet to reach out to their congregations and businesses have begun using the Internet in a big way (Broadway, 1996; Kelly, 1996; Fife, 1996). Interactive Computer Assisted tools have begun to find new niche as teachers and schools claim better learning through technology. T. D. Baker Junior High School in Edmonton for example, has helped design a computer prototype called TELS (Technology Enhanced Learning System) with Alberta Educational Technology and Research Foundation. The pilot project tested in 14 Alberta schools has teachers claiming a remarkable improvement in math scores among students (Stepan, 1995).

140

Some language teachers have begun to argue for more language laboratories with computer-based aids to facilitate learning. The ESL (English as a Second Language) teachers now have access to *Pronunciation Power*, a software package that comes with complete graphics, sound and animation. Produced by an Edmonton entrepreneur, the CD is said to facilitate learners acquire language skills and is available at http://www.englishlearning.com. (MacDonald, 1996). One private college in Brockville, Ontario, has "taken a quantum leap into the future" by negotiating a $500,000 lease with IBM Canada to deliver laptops to all its students who will of course, pay $1,340 extra with the unanimous consent of every parent (The Canadian Press, 1996c).

Parents and schools have begun to support the increasing growth of technology in schools (Dawson, 1997, A8). Parents have Web sites like http:///www.ccn.cs.dal.ca/ tildebonny/modem-mom/index.htm where working mothers can discuss issues relating to parents and their children (The Canadian Press, 1997g). Commercial and specialized bookstores now have their own Web sites for customers (Morash, 1997). According to one report, in 1995, more than 420,000 Canadians were getting long-distance post-secondary schooling through distance education. (The Canadian Press, 1995). The craze for increasingly miniaturized technological toys such as cell phones, laptop computers, pagers, electronic day-planners, portable faxes and printers is resulting in a new generation of "road warriors" (Chmielewski, 1997). For the first time in Web history, watch a real-time videocast of a TV program and simultaneously chat online with other users, the producers of the program and the anchor. *CNN TalkBack Live* introduced this new technology and its new Web site on August 22, the show's third anniversary (CNN Online News, August 22, 1997). Web movies are the new wave among the Internet junkies who are able to watch movie serials and freely analyze without any editorial restrictions (Rodriguez, 1997).

Politicians are increasingly using the Net to seek votes and most major political parties have established their own Web sites on the Internet (Johnsrude, 1996). Nationalism and political agenda by patriotic citizens are also being disseminated on the Internet. *Proud to be a Canadian* at http://www3.sympatico.ca/clark/canadian.htm is created by Armed Forces serviceperson David A. Clark (Diamond, 1997) and offers the ingredients to becoming a patriotic citizen.

Encouraging this rapid growth of technology, billionaires of the digital world have begun to aggressively support the development and application of technology products in research and educational institutions. Bill Gates, the co-founder of Microsoft Corporation has donated $200 million ($20 million in Canada) to establish the Gates Library Foundation (GLF) with charity dollars for libraries to upgrade their computer and communications systems (Miller, 1997c, A12). Gates, expecting criticism about his intent comments, "Obviously, I'm somebody who believes that personal computers are empowering tools. People are entitled to disagree, but I would invite them to visit some of these libraries and see the impact on kids using this technology" (Miller, 1997c).

Amidst this debate on the intervening/non-intervening status of technology in our lives, some suggest that the Internet is a technology that will be able to reach unprecedented number of audience. Despite it being a buzz word "being tossed around," information technology is "not likely to become yesterday's news" (Marck, 1997). Only time will tell the effects of technology on our lives.

6.3.3. The Internet and the Emergent Problems

If the current move in capitalist monopoly and control over the dissemination of knowledge continues, it could be an indication of the ensuing imminent ethical and legal conflicts relating to power and control in the hands of few entrepreneurs. If as Naisbitt (1982), cautions, "The new power is not money in the hands of the few, but information in the hands of the many," we could ask the question if giant companies in Silicon Valley should be playing a role in the dissemination of knowledge. One is also faced with the contentious issue of who owns, controls, and distributes knowledge and whether such information can be sold to the rich alone. Critics who have become outspoken opponents of Microsoft (the anti-Microsoft or "I hate Microsoft" school) question Gates and his move to monopolize the market. In fact, as some suggest, Microsoft has bailed out the ailing Apple from potential bankruptcy and hence, neutralized any form of formidable competition in the computer industry (Quinlan, 1997). Yet, within this corporate free-market fight to gain control over the tools of technology, there has appeared new struggles and challenges. To the consternation of the Microsoft giant, a programmer's language called Java developed by Sun Microsystems, has become the standard on the Internet (De Groot, 1997b).

Apart from individual capitalistic monopolies and business competitions, there is the debate on technology and its implications in the development of a country and its citizens. Some argue that the technology hype has really taken control over how we think, live and understand. According to William Esray, president of Sprint telecommunications company in the United States:

> Too many people are being swept away by the idea of an information superhighway when what they need to do is stop and think about what they really want... I think what we need right now is not virtual reality, but a cold splash of common reality. Too many in the telecommunications, the

143

information and the cable industry seem carried away by sugarplum fairies that are dancing in their heads. (The Canadian Press, 1994)

Esray states that, "some have the wrong idea about the highway, what it can do and what people want from it" (The Canadian Press, 1994). Reacting to the U.S. Vice-president Al Gore's remark that we should attempt to link the Library of Congress to every child in every school via the network, Esray commented, "Wouldn't it be equally innovative if we could make sure that every child could read?" (The Canadian Press, 1994). Esray notes that "Not everyone will be clamoring for more information and services. Many Americans still can't program their VCRs." Shenk (1997), reflecting Esray's concern, observed:

> Gore and other politicians are sadly missing the point. The disenfranchised citizens of our country are not in need of faster access to bottomless wells of information. They are in need of *education*. There is an important difference, and the government must recognize this distinction soon... The so-called information poor don't need Internet access; they need basic classroom materials, building infrastructure, and highly qualified teachers... Above all else, it is imperative that in the coming years we strive to keep the quality of our thinking as great as the quantity of our information. (pp. 211, 213)

Ramstad has argued that *two-tier* societies may be the outcome if people do not get a chance to learn the computer and that, while the computer revolution has transformed the way industrialized world operates, "[M]illions of people choose not to live that way. Though they may be educated and affluent, computers to them are either too impersonal or daunting. Many more people have been left behind for economic reasons— they can't afford or have no access to computers" (Ramstad, 1994b). Postman (1993), a strong critic of unbridled embracing of technology cautions that, "Technology imperiously commandeers our most important terminology. It redefines 'freedom', 'truth,' 'intelligence,' 'fact,' 'wisdom,' 'memory,' 'history'—all the words we live by. And it does not pause to tell us. And we do not pause to ask" (pp. 8-9). According to Postman, "The benefits and deficits of a new technology are not distributed equally. There are, as

144

it were, winners and losers. It is both puzzling and poignant that on many occasions the losers, out of ignorance, have actually cheered the winners, and some still do" (p. 9).

One of the major effects of computerization is the displacement of workers and the resulting poverty due to unemployment. As Thomas Hirschi, a sociologist from Cornell University ponders, "With electronics, you have ubiquitous opportunities for large-scale elimination of the need for employee labour. Now, the question becomes, 'Where are people going to go?'" (Ramstad, 1994b). Sir Bernard Lovell, founder of Britain's Jodrell Bank Observatory has raised the possibility that computers may result in stifling scientific discoveries, a situation Postman notes is only part of the problem, an issue beyond cost-efficiency, efficacy and mere "antiserendipitous" condition; it could point to de-skilling of professionals (Postman, 1993, p. 121). Expecting counter-criticism, Postman thinks that "technopolists" may label critics as "Technological pessimists" (p. 122).

The reliability of technology itself is subject to criticism. The technology of the future is considered vulnerable and still at a primordial stage. Amidst a huge publicity and media coverage at the American Association for the Advancement of Science, the CEO and founder of Microsoft, Bill Gates was in the process of demonstrating a promising future for personal computers in the 21st century when his computer crashed. To be later savored by traditionalists, Gates commented, "Well, so much for that" (Haysom, 1997b; McConnell, 1997). In October 1997, electronic mail at the world's number one ISP, America Online Inc. was knocked out due to hardware problems affecting access and email services to 6 million customers worldwide (The Associated Press, 1996; CNN Online, October 29, 1997). Edmonton's community-based not-for-profit Freenet "crashed on the eve of the city playing host to a convention on the growth of Internet access" (Journal Staff, 1996). Hackers have become notorious for bringing down major networks and business systems. One of the largest World Wide Web service providers, WebCom in Vancouver was knocked out for 40 hours affecting more than 3,000 Web sites (The Associated Press, 1996b).

Internet Service Providers like *CompuSmart, TELUS PLAnet, OA Internet*, IBM's *Advantis Canada* and a host of other providers have been affected by 'pingers' at one time or another and hackers have continued to flood the Internet with information causing overload and system crashes (Thorne, 1996a). Even the NASA Web site was invaded by computer hackers who altered vital information that became available to the public raising new questions about the vulnerability of defence and other government targets for terrorists (The Associated Press, 1997b). Some terrorists have begun to use the Internet to launch electronic attacks against government computers (The Daily Telegraph, 1997). A report from Washington presidential commission considers the vulnerability of the American nation to electronic warfare. According to The Commission on Critical Infrastructure Protection, computer attacks could jeopardize the communications systems. Cautioning the government and legal authorities, the report noted in its executive summary that, "[t]he right command sent over the Internet to a power generating station's control computer could be just as effective as a backpack full of explosives and the perpetrator would be harder to identify and apprehend" (CNN Online, October 21, 1997).

In June 1997, the Associated Press reported that, "Two of the Internet's biggest rivals, Microsoft Corp. and Netscape Communications Corp., [had] announced a stunning alliance Wednesday aimed at safeguarding consumer data in cyberspace... [In fact] most people who browse the Web don't know the sites

146

they visit can collect personal information about them, but U.S. regulators are closely eyeing such privacy intrusions" (The Associated Press, 1997c). Internet users will have to face the vulnerability and problems that arise from lack of privacy in their on-line transactions including weaknesses in e-mail encryption (Port, 1997; Andrews, 1997).

The Internet yet remains slow and extremely busy due to overuse. "Until flipping through the Web pages is as fast as changing channels on a TV, the Internet will remain highly overrated—busy signals, downloading times, connection speeds, low-quality video and audio transmissions, just to name a few. Due to the long wait on the Internet some people have derisively termed the World Wide Web as the "World Wide Wait" (Whitefield, 1996; Marin, 1997). Conversely, conventional forms of knowledge distribution remain steadfast. In fact, the introduction of online magazines has only been partly successful in competing with their traditional paper-based issues. Microsoft's "grand electronic publishing experiment" the *Slate* magazine has proven that people are not yet ready for the Internet-based magazines (Haysom, 1997a). According to Terry Retter, technology strategist, the future of personal computer appears discouraging as people find computers break down far too easily, need constant technical support, tend to lack security, and remain too difficult to use (Boei, 1997).

A host of health related disorders have also begun to manifest among habitual computer addicts. Due to improper positions maintained for long hours, Computer Vision Syndrome (CVS) has caused eye problems among the Internet surfers with symptoms of blurred vision, dry and irritated eyes, neck strain, back strain, double vision, fatigue, and headache (Gallagher, 1997) The term *Mouse Potato* has appeared in our vocabulary which being "a slang for a person who

147

spends an excessive amount of time in front of the computer" (CFRN, October 10, 1997). The American Psychological Association has recognized that not unlike other addictions such as gambling, drugs, video games and eating disorders, the Internet can also be quite addictive. At their 1997 annual meeting in Chicago, the psychologists decided to certify Internet addiction as spending more than 38 hours a week online (Armstrong, 1997). The advent of the Internet has produced a group of "Webaholics" who are "maladaptive," and suffer from "psychomotor agitation (the cybershakes)," resulting in the creation of *Netaholics Anonymous, Interneters Anonymous,* a *Webaholics Web Page,* and the *Internet Addiction Support Group.* (Belluck, 1996). According to Belluck, the new modified prayer of a Webaholic from the *Interneters Anonymous* is, "Grant me the serenity to know when to log off." In fact, a mother of seven and eight-year old kids in Florida has lost custody of her children due to neglect. Addicted to the Internet, Pam Albridge has been ordered by a judge to give up her children citing that she "ignores the needs of her children" and "has been spending most of her time in her bedroom with the computer" (CFRN News, October 22, 1997).

Shenk (1997), arguing that "Computers are neither human nor *humane*" (emphasis, original) (p. 11), describes how technology can be damaging to health:

> Theodore Cross argues that we are now inflicted with "culturally induced Attention Deficit Disorder (ADD)" indicated by acute restlessness, boredom, and distraction. Trained, nurtured, and sustained by electronic bits, bites, bytes, and flashing images, our children will grow up to be massaged, addicted and hypnotized by technology, unable and unwilling to read and analyze print material (p. 36). As technology "speeds up our world in the name of efficiency and productivity, it also constricts rational thinking" and brings us to a "new wave of indecisiveness: paralysis by analysis." (p. 94)

The computer world doomsday edition of prognostication predicts that when the clock strikes 2000, computers will go into frenzy and major catastrophe awaits ticketing, billing, government record-keeping computer systems. Computers were programmed to read only two latter digits in a year and with the turn of the century, it is said that machines will begin to read the year 2000 as 1900 (The Associated Press, 1995). "Major breakdowns and confusion are predicted when the Year 2000 approaches as computers become disoriented due to the 2-digit electronic calendars programming (e.g. 79 instead of 1979)," and machines will begin to create "unpredictable chaos and confusion among major government and corporations" (Marck, 1997). Some predict that "half of the world's businesses could be in chaos because their systems will crash...millions upon millions of credit card transactions rejected...air traffic control in turmoil... [and] massive data processing breakdown (Broder & Zuckerman, 1997). Industries are hiring lawyers to sue computer manufacturers over the Year 2000 (Y2K) problem, opening up a new slew of lawsuits in the 20th century (The Associated Press, 1997a).

Many schools have taken to the Internet in a big way. Cyber-High, based in St. Albert, Alberta, is a program linking 100 junior high students across the province. While parents of students being home schooled are delighted to have access to resources and teachers, the local Alberta Teachers' Association is concerned about the isolation and impersonal nature of the program. Coordinator Rus Hathaway, not addressing the issue of isolation, claims that the program is saving taxpayers money by reducing the "per student cost" for education in the province (Moysa & Kent, 1995). Concurrently, schools that cannot afford to buy computers are being forced to seek donations as matching dollars before governments are willing to approve grants for computers in the classrooms. Bureaucratic structures like the education departments, unaware of local needs and priorities, control *when* and *how* technology upgrades are done (Keith, 1997). The caution resounds repeatedly in a number of reports:

School board officials warn Alberta's efforts to expand computer technology in the province's schools are failing students' needs. And the College of Alberta School Superintendents says the ability of Alberta students to compete with those from other regions will be seriously hurt unless three key issues are addressed. The college says it is concerned about a lack of overall vision as to where technology fits into the curriculum. (CFRN, April 22, 1997)

Shenk (1997) reminds us that *education* comes from the Latin word *educare*, "meaning to raise and nurture, [and] is more a matter of imparting values and critical faculties than inputting raw data. Education is about enlightenment, not just access" (p. 75). Shenk considers technology as "junk food" with no nutritional value in it. Allow Steve Jobs, the co-inventor of Apple computers, explain this:

> I used to think that technology could help education. I've probably spearheaded giving away more computer equipment to schools than anybody else on the planet. But I've had to come to the inevitable conclusion that the problem is not one that technology can hope to solve... You're not going to solve the problems by putting all knowledge onto CD-ROMS... Historical precedent shows that we can turn out amazing human beings without technology. Precedent also shows that we can turn out very uninteresting human beings with technology." (Shenk, 1997, p. 74.)

Neil Postman (1993) mused that historically, "Tools did not attack (or, more precisely, were not intended to attack) the dignity and integrity of the culture into which they were introduced... Tools are not integrated into the culture; they attack culture. They bid to *become* the culture" (pp. 23, 28). Perhaps, in many ways, technology has spawned and nurtured its own kind of culture that belies commonly accepted boundaries. With its own rules and opportunities, the Internet has offered a venue for criminals and crime, raising a host of concerns and questions. The increasing abuse of the Internet by people who forge abusive e-mail messages using legitimate names of innocent subscribers is going to be a major source of risk and nuisance (Gillmor, 1997). The Internet has also provided a fertile venue for conspiracy theorists, investigators, con men and intelligence personnel (Coates, 1996).

At the business level, corporate Web sites are sources of industrial espionage where competitors lurk around in search of ideas and vital information creating a situation termed, "competitive intelligence (CI)." "Competitive intelligence is a peaceful form of espionage used by companies around the world. Information about your company will be analysed, interpreted and then used against you by competitors, suppliers and even loyal customers" (McIntosh, 1997). Amidst legitimate Web sites that are information sources for stock analysis, the cyberspace has also become a conduit for misinformation. The Bre-X disaster was preceded by unsuspecting investors relying on feedback from chat room discussions to decide as to the viability of an impending major disaster (MacLean, 1997).

Online illegal betting on sports has become a new activity that concerns the U.S. government. Mike Rogers, president of Supernet Sports, an online betting service notes that, "The Internet is akin to the wild, wild west in the 1800s... It's wide open, with limitless opportunities that are legitimate. But it is also ripe for fraud and scams" (CNN Online News, Wednesday, October 29b, 1997).

Cyberspace marketers are offering "prizes" or freebies as incentives to young kids in return for personal data about themselves and their parents. Critics argue that the exploitation of young and vulnerable kids is "deceptive advertising" that breaks privacy laws (Humphreys, 1997). Cults like Heaven's Gate (now called *cybercults*) have begun to use the Internet for attracting followers (Page, 1997). Students now can plagiarize term papers by downloading pre-written term papers available on the Internet. *The School Sucks* site and the *Evil House of Cheat* site (with 658,000 visitors as of June 23, 97), are two sites that offer "services" for students desperate in submitting readable school essay papers (Miller, 1997a). Teenagers are being incriminated for making pipe bombs using easily available instructions on the Net. A 17-year-old Edmonton city male was recently charged making and detonating home-made explosives using recipes found on the Internet (Williams, 1997).

As described earlier, pornography remains another area of concern. Culminating in an exhaustive 2-year investigation, the FBI made a dozen arrests and searched 120 homes across the United States for distribution of child pornography and sex trade (The Associated Press, 1995). With the US Supreme Court having turned down the Communications Decency Act law enforcement departments and police departments have intensified their monitoring of the Net for readily available obscene materials and other criminal activities (Canadian Press, 1997d; Bronskill, 1997).

The Internet Service Providers have begun to get concerned about the rapid proliferation of Hate propaganda on the Internet and have decided to police themselves (Southam Newspapers, 1996). The *Anti-Semitism World Report* surveyed 60 countries and found religious hatred had decreased in general and that, "The Internet remains a growth area for the publication and dissemination of anti-Semitism, and neo-Nazis and Holocaust deniers claim that it presents them with an opportunity to achieve a breakthrough in terms of influencing the wider public" (News Clippings, 1997).

While librarians rejoice the US Supreme Courts decision to not regulate the Internet, most librarians are concerned about the availability of questionable

152

material on the Net suggesting a move towards establishment of filtering systems in libraries across the nation (Dienkelspiel, 1997). Set up by the Canadian Association of Internet Providers and Golden Triangle On Line, the Internet providers have established their own policing system, *Net-Scams Alert* (http://www.golden.net/promos/scams), to stem hoaxes, scams and other crimes on the information highway (The Canadian Press, 1997). Police in Edmonton have warned parents to keep a close watch over what their children access on the Internet. According to detective Dave Johnston, "Children are vulnerable because they are children, they are not wise in the ways of the world; they're too trusting" and the department has developed a guide for parents called *Children and Computers: The Hidden Danger* (Rusnell, 1996).

6.3.4. The Internet and the Global Educator

According to Carroll & Broadhead (1996), "The Internet is bringing cultures together around the world and is probably doing more to provide a greater understanding between different peoples than any other human invention" (p. 4). As De Kerkhove (1995), muses, "With communications travelling at the speed of thought, strictly local economies make no more sense than strictly local ecologies. At every second, we are bound to one another by global events as surely as the weather" (p. 75). As Carroll & Broadhead (1996), explain:

> For some, the Internet is a sociological revolution, a system that is helping to return "power to the people" from the "media and government elites." It is a system that cuts through today's power and information structures and a system that is changing society in a dramatic ways by doing so. To others, the Internet is a global nation that transcends national borders. (p. 5)

To some, the arrival of the *electronic democracy* is the zenith in the evolution of democracy. According to the optimist gurus, "We will be able to register our displeasure directly with the Premier of the province concerning some new legislative initiative and take part in an on-line electronic poll. We will be able to visit and join new initiatives lobbying for support on some type of environmental activity. We will be electronic citizens of a network that is the ultimate form of democracy" (Carroll & Broadhead, 1996, p. 246). But does access alone provide control over democratic processes and does this form of "connection" facilitate the development of global consciousness? Some believe that technology will play the nascent role of creating a system leading to a collective consciousness. Dewdney describes how De Kerkhove understands the role of the Internet in the formation of global consciousness:

> The groundwork for the collective mind will be laid by a political globalization whose initial stages will be accomplished invisibly by the convergence of television, telephones and computers. Internet is the nascent fetus of this collective brain, and smaller components of the final global consciousness are already forming within the interconnections of cable networks, telecommunications systems and data banks, not to mention the cybernetic think tanks soon to link researchers in commutative brains that will truly be the sum of their parts. (Dewdney, 1995, XXI)

Other techno-gurus think that being able to connect has allowed us to communicate better. Frank Ogden argues that the technology has enhanced our ability to discover different cultures:

> Today we learn hour by hour about other lands and cultures. The industrial age gave us the haves and have-nots. Now is the time for the knows and know-nots. Today a wide-awake "know" can access information faster than a government, and because the individual is not a corporation or a department, that person can do more with the information in a shorter period of time... Now revolutionaries or radicals can rapidly gather, absorb, and disseminate information, and this can cause more havoc than bullets. Governments can't control the spread of information. And even if they could grab and hold on to it, they wouldn't know how to process the knowledge. (1995, p. 92)

Some cyber-gurus argue that our understanding of the political process will be influenced by technology. De Kerkhove (1995), attributes the Internet with an unprecedented characteristic of being able to offer multiple advantages:

> The space of the Internet is not neural, it has no border, it is not stable nor is it unified. It is organic. Its motion is perpetual and it behaves like a self-organizing system. Our obsolescent political notions are going to be thoroughly trashed by it... [From] the Middle Ages to the Age of Reason, and... to the Age of Mind [and] with the advent of the Internet we have the first medium that is oral and written, private and public, individual and collective at the same time. (pp. 182, 188)

Olson & Sullivan (1993) note that, "Innovations become a means of control and have different results for different classes, racial groups, gender divisions, and so on... Thus, the computer, as well as other information technologies, may possibly accentuate and amplify power inequalities within our society" (p. 425). While De Kerkhove warns that telecracy or "participatory democracy" may well play directly into the hands of the populists, he attributes the ability to control technology as a positive development that allows activists and social emancipators utilize this new tool to achieve their goals.

> As technology empowers people, consumers develop the need to exercise more control over their immediate environment. Computers [have] allowed people to talk back to their screens, to reclaim control of their mental life from television and to take an active part in the organization of their environment, both local and global. (De Kerkhove, 1995, p. 94)

There is an element of control in how technology can be manipulated and designed to suit our needs. In fact, there appears to be an appeal to ward off the harmful effects of globalization through the control and use of technologies. In his book *The Skin of Culture*, De Kerkhove, "warns that our planet is at a precarious turning point that can lead either to fragmentation or further globalization, and that only by designing our technologies, instead of letting them design us, will we be able to avert social catastrophe" (Dewdney, 1995, XIX). Yet, while such optimists do not deny the implications of technology on the lives of people around the world, the problem exists in the process of globalization rather than the technology itself.

> Computers gave us power over the screen and allowed us to personalize information-processing. It is not the world that is becoming global; we are. That's the good news. The bad news is that every technological innovation brings about an opposite counter-reaction: globalization encourages hyperlocalization, which in many parts of the world, brings social unrest, various patterns of racism and armed conflicts... To the extent that people are globalized, they will also emphasize their local identity all the more. The threat of Babel revisited lurks in the Gulf War, Somalia and the former Yugoslavia. (De Kerkhove, 1995, p. 83)

In fact, De Kerkhove argues that the analysis of globalization and the effect of technology on industrialization are said to be deficient in their approach:

> [T]he fundamental issue of globalization is that of consciousness. While social critics such as Hans Magnus Enzensberger, Jurgen Habermas, Jean Baudrillard and many others have correctly recognized consciousness as a new industrial product, their inherently political approach has narrowed their focus, away from the more comprehensive development now underway. For the first time in world history, we are accelerating towards a new level of consciousness that is both collective and private at once. (De Kerkhove, 1995, p.183)

The television provided a "kind of collective mind with no individual input" while the computer remained "private minds without collective inputs" (De Kerkhove, 1995, p. 53). Nevertheless, this has changed with the arrival of the Internet, in that the network allows collective input within the realm of collective consciousness. The power of communications can be intimidating to oppressive political leaders. When Serbian leader Milosevic clamped down on the local news media, protesters took over the Internet to communicate with the world and with other Serbians (Katz, 1996, A5).

156

Thus, the Internet is much more than just another technological tool that is used for making our lives easy. As Hugh Mehan (1989) suggests, computers differ in some ways from other technologies in that "the computer learning has less to do with the medium itself than it does with the social practices around computing" (Olson & Sullivan, 1993, p. 431). Olson & Sullivan describe this aspect quite articulately:

> Tools are used by people for particular ends (good and bad) Understanding who uses them, how, and for whose benefits—the structure of intentional action—is necessary if we are to assess how computers are likely to be actually employed... Because the computer directly affects so many of the most important areas of human activity—the organization of information, processes of production, our psychological sense of the possible, and so on—it also potentially changes relationships of social power" (1993, pp. 437-438).

Chapter 7: Culture on the Web

7.1. The Browsing and Content Analysis

With some experience in using computer hardware and software along with limited coursework in software analysis and BASIC programming, I have had a background in the use and utility of technology. Due to the previous experience in using the Internet for casual browsing and electronic mail communication, it was a pleasure to embark on a formal rendezvous using the World Wide Web. Hence, the hours and activities reported in this project constitute a partial account of all activities pertaining to the project. One aspect of this experience was the discovery that for every one hour of constructive and productive online browsing, there were perhaps three hours of unproductive and distracting exploration. Despite the advantage of familiarity with the tool, a considerable portion of the project was spent in dealing with the limitations and utter frustrations involving the much-trusted hardware, software and electronic connections, which at their best, remained unreliable and extremely disappointing[26]. Nevertheless, the option between using or not using technology was not an issue; with all its limitations, technology provides the speed, access and convenience required to complement any activity including research.

---

[26] Throughout this project, portable Toshiba laptops (T1000, T100CDS, T200CDS, T300CDS—75 to133Mhz, 40MB RAM) using Windows® 3.x and Windows 95® were used. Software applications used included Netscape 2® and Internet Explorer® 2.x, 3.x, and 4.x; MS Office Pro Suite® (MS Word, MS Access, MS PowerPoint); and Web Buddy™ (Offline Browser). The University of Alberta Dial Up Network (SLIP/PPP) was used from remote locations using US Robotics® 28.8 bps PC Card modem. Having to work off campus precluded using the campus high-speed network.

Content Analysis

During the content analysis, I have focused on three main themes relating to culture, namely: (a) Cultural Identity/ Cross-cultural Issues/ Multiculturalism (b) Democracy and Human Rights, and (c) Racism/ Anti-racism. While some examples of sites cited might not belong to just one of these three themes, many examples overlap and the classification is only for convenience. Cultural identity, for example, is an issue under any of these categories and whether it is human rights, democratic struggle, cross-cultural understanding or formal multiculturalism as we understand in Canada, a person or group of people may have developed their own identity beyond simple geographical demarcations.

7.2. Cultural Identity and Cross-cultural Communication

Our understanding of various cultures is constrained by our own cultural background and our individual histories that impose upon us the limitation affecting how we think and act. Hemminger at *Exploring Ancient World Cultures* asks the question, "Why study ancient or different cultures?" Explicating the meaning of the word *culture*, Hemminger discusses the change and limitations in various cultures, with a caution: "As you begin your study of ancient cultures, you might want to recall these questions as you forge for yourself a meaning to the term *culture*. In the process, try not to measure others against your own cultural standard, which has, in many ways, formed you and your apprehension of the world. Instead, try for a moment to see the glittering battle scene with Arjuna's eyes." The *Bhagavad Gita* character is faced with the possibility of dealing with reincarnated human relatives unlike *Schindler*, who is left with no such choice in intervening on behalf of the Jews. Hemminger then goes on to note: "The danger in looking for universals thus consists in reformulating other, possibly alien, views to fit our own. We must always guard against the assumption that other people think as we do—or that they should. Arjuna speaks within the context of one culture; Schindler acts within the confines of another." Hemminger discusses the Roman Empire, Pyramids of Egypt, Plato, Dante, Krishna and Mohammed. Even as one critically looks at diverse and ancient cultures, Hemminger reminds us that our perceptions of different cultures have an influence on our perspectives about those cultures. It is thus imperative for global educators to caution their students engaged in cross-cultural communication of the individual perspectives each one of us brings with us. Some have argued that this interaction takes place in virtual communities that have created their own cultures. Rheingold (1993), considers computer interactions and communication across the Internet as a medium that is comprised of communities resulting in new cultures. According to Rheingold, "Most people who get their news from conventional media have been unaware of the wildly varied assortment of new cultures that have evolved in the world's computer networks over the past ten years" (p.4).

The advent of the Information Superhighway has resulted in many schools resorting to cross-cultural communication across the Internet. If getting to know people and cultures through the electronic medium could enhance our understanding of diversity, one could argue for increased interactions over the Internet. Even before the arrival of technology, communication between individuals and schools (e.g. twinning) remained a popular means of exchanging information about different cultures. The Internet became a more affordable means of communication for school projects and remote schools in developed countries began to not only exchange letters through electronic mail but also gain access to voluminous information on the Internet. Besides twinning or matching for learning foreign languages (usually, Spanish, French and German), students wish to interact in order to learn about different cultures and peoples. A grade six teacher in Belgium develops themes from examples of bravery in another part of the world to enable his or her students to seek out, "everything that is happening in the world." The desire to keep in touch with the various world events and learn from them makes the Internet a powerful tool in the hands of global educators.

> **Het Molenschip** Contact Name: Geert Mortier; First Language: Dutch; eMail address: argo0073@argo.be; Classroom Grade: 6th grade; Average Student Age: 11; City/Town: Evergem (near Ghent); State/Province: Oost-Vlaanderen; Country: Belgium. Comments: 'Het Molenschip' is a boarding school for children of the occupational travellers such as barge men and fairground workers. My class has it's own name : it's called 'Omaira Sanchez' after the Columbian girl Omaira Sanchez that died in 1985 after the eruption of the volcano Nevado del Ruiz in Armero, Columbia. As my class is a Unicef-World-Class, my students took nearly a personal interest in this event and decided to call their class after the brave girl they saw dying on television.... In a whole, we are interested in everything that is happening in the world and we wish to experiment this new way of communicating with other children all over the world. Date Submitted: Tuesday, October 01, 1996 at 17:02:17 (EDT). (*Access email Classroom Exchange*)

The need to communicate with other people around the world to discuss and share cultural experiences, as in the case of students at the San Andres High school and Brisbane Elementary school can form the initial basis for students to explore cultural issues. A critical teacher may guide the students to discuss "global issues with other students around the world," as in the case at St. Catherines, one of the schools featured at *Access email Classroom Exchange*. The interaction can be rich and rewarding with the schools in the North becoming more multicultural or international. At Rockbridge Elementary School, one single classroom has a rich diversity of 45 languages with students from different ethnic groups. Yvonne Marie Andres, in her online article "Advantages to Telecomputing: Reasons to Use the Internet in your Classroom," at the *SchoolNet* site writes about how a network project evolved and developed to include students engaged in communicating with students in different cultures:

> As news of our successful writing projects spread, the educational network grew from 6 schools located in San Diego County, to include more than 85 schools from all over the United States, as well as schools in Puerto Rico and Argentina...

162

Students, some of whom had never left their own neighbourhoods, were suddenly asking for maps so that they would know where their new "computer pals" were writing from. Students learned that there are different, regional ways of expressing the same ideas. So, they took greater efforts to explain exactly what they were trying to say. Bilingual messages were exchanged and translated into both languages. Students were communicating with one another in a way that most adults were not even aware existed.

Students began to establish connections with students from other countries. In this exploration, one might be skeptical in questioning whether such communication remained at exchanging information or grew beyond that to engage in discussing critical questions. In such cross-cultural exchanges, one also needs to be wary of investigating the *Other*, the delving into the exotic unknown by and for "interesting people" as the following excerpt mentions:

> **Ridley College Middle School** Contact Name: David Mackey First Language: English eMail address: dmackey@niagara.com Classroom Grade: 7 Average Student Age: 11/12 City/Town: St. Catharines State/Province: Ontario Country: Canada. Comments: This year's class has 14 students - evenly divided between girls and boys. I have one student from Korea, one from Mexico, one from Grand Cayman. They are interesting people, and they are likely to be interested in the different lifestyles of other cultures. A class in Africa, the Middle East or India would be of real interest to them. Date Submitted: Tuesday, September 24, 1996 at 15:29:18 (EDT). *(Access email Classroom Exchange)*

Such cautions aside, electronic exchange can be rewarding as Andres describes about one incident that launched a simple online exercise into the beginning of a critical discussion between students in the United States and Russia:

> One of the Australian schools who was participating in the AT&T LDLN had their computer terminal set up at the Australian EXPO 88, in the United Nations Pavilion. All of the messages that the students were exchanging were being displayed on a large screen, so that visitors to the pavilion could read them. A message of hope was posted by some Soviet children, stating that the Russian Pavilion "wished for a world without wars. If all people unite their effort, the threat of nuclear war can be eliminated." Students from Lincoln Junior High responded with their own replies for world peace. The Soviet Ambassador was so impressed that a real time chatting session was arranged, and children from Oceanside typed back and forth for an hour, via computer and modem, exchanging information about schools in California and schools in the Soviet Union.

The notion of exploration may help learn cultural diversity by focusing on different countries. Rural schools may, despite their geographical isolation, interact with schools in chosen countries every month. Valley elementary explores *one new country each month* as students learn about students and their cultures in different countries. Pen pals, video exchange and the willingness to go beyond English language make such projects more interesting, fruitful and exciting. The critical element of what transpires across countries depends upon the teacher and thereafter, the students. Not unlike a student in a busy metropolis attempting to understand the lifestyle of a rural child elsewhere, far and remote as it may be, there is the advantage of crossing not only national borders but also class structures and socioeconomic boundaries. The working class segment or low-income minority groups, at least within large US suburbs have some access to technology, and hence, have also acquired the ability to interact with students from other socioeconomic backgrounds. Students at the Lincoln Elementary in the town of Bellwood may have begun to feel empowered in that they are able to communicate transcending their socioeconomic limitations.

> **Lincoln Elementary School** Contact Name: Mrs. Denise Zemke First Language: English eMail address: denisetarr@aol.com Classroom Grade: 6 Average Student Age: 12 City/Town: Bellwood State/Province: Illinois Country: USA. Comments: We are interested in corresponding with German speaking classrooms. We are located in a suburb of Chicago, Illinois. We are a low to lower middle income minority district that just recently received computers. (not counting the Apple dinosaurs) We look forward to making new international friends via the Internet. Date Submitted: Sunday, September 22, 1996 at 20:32:55 (EDT). (*Access email Classroom Exchange*)

Just as we begin to understand technology's role in minimizing conventional restrictions historically found within classrooms, it may offer to remove traditional barriers or perceived limitations of physical disabilities within a classroom. Disabled students in wheelchairs at the Cedar School are able to communicate, without the restrictive connotations associated with their physical situation.

> **Cedar School** Contact Name: Sammy,Steve,Adam,Marc and Stuart First Language: English eMail address: cedar@tcns.co.uk Classroom Grade: secondary Average Student Age: 14 City/Town: Southampton State/Province: Hampshire Country: ENGLAND. Comments: We all have physical disabilities the majority of us are in wheelchairs. Date Submitted: Thursday, September 19, 1996 at 04:35:30 (EDT). (*Access email Classroom Exchange*)

Geographically isolated communities, far removed from the busy cosmopolitan cities, may often contain and offer unshared cultural histories. Populations dwelling in isolated communities or amidst unique cultural enclaves may become rich sources of information. Bellville Elementary in Ohio "in the heart of Amish country" could perhaps become a source of information about the Amish culture to someone in Tashkent.

> **Bellville Elementary** Contact Name: Bill White First Language: English eMail address: william.white@ecrknox.com Classroom Grade: 4 Average Student Age: 9 City/Town: Bellville State/Province: Ohio Country: USA. Comments: We are a very rural school looking for penpal classes around the world to correspond with through e-mail OR snail-mail. We have lots to share as we are in the heart of Amish country. We are anxious to hear from you. Date Submitted: Tuesday, August 20, 1996 at 11:55:40 (EDT). (*Access email Classroom Exchange*)

If the physical appearance, geographical location, age, gender, color of the skin, ethnicity, or the accent of a person is no more indicative of his or her identity, the medium grants a notion of ethereal anonymity that plays no immediate role in the ascription of conventional identity labels devoid in the `cyberworld'. Albeit, technology has evolved over time to overcome some of the current limitations, it may allow video interaction between kids. Global SchoolNet's *Collaboration in the Classroom* allows video interaction between students in two or more schools in different countries. Dismantling the intangible anonymity, we will soon be able to associate a face to the voice and message.

Many educators suggest collaborative learning over the Internet to understand global issues. If communication can enhance collaboration across cultures and countries, one would assume the arrival of what Yvonne Marie Andres in her article at this site entitled, *"Collaboration in the Classroom and Over the Internet"* calls "telecommunities" (*Collaboration in the Classroom*). According to Andres, "Collaborative learning becomes even more significant when the students who are working together are from different nations with varied

165

cultures, histories, and socio-political beliefs." Andres believes that as the technology improves, cross-cultural communications will also develop.

Following the development of technology, snail mail has been replaced by electronic mail. Email could allow creative "global dialogue among as many children as possible," as seen in case of the *KidLink* Project at *International Kids' Space* (Wheeler, 1992), Slonet's *Kids Online*, and *SchoolNet*. While correspondence allows interactivity between individuals or schools, art, literature, music, poetry, history and other such activities provide venues for discussions on culture. The *KidzPage* for example, offers creative opportunities for teachers who may want to encourage understanding culture through poetry at the elementary level for students engaged in cross-cultural experience. As Al Rogers (1994) notes, in today's world:

> [T]housands of children in dozens of countries around the world are living the reality of the global village in personal, hands-on, interactive ways. Through the medium of networking and telecommunications technologies these students are for the first time learning to think of themselves as global citizens, seeing the world, and their place in the world, in ways much different than their parents.
>
> As students, there is no question that curriculum will change as more and more schools join the net. Students who have the opportunities described here have already begun to make their own paradigm shifts regarding their place in the world, and how to relate to it. As the global market economy grows, these students as adults will have advantages in their experience and mindset over those who were isolated to their own classrooms and communities. (Online version)

Rogers lists stories about online student involvement connecting students within and beyond the North American continent as they engage in discussing issues, concerns and as in the case of the Israeli children in the following passage, firsthand narratives of traumatic experiences:

- The Global Grocery List stimulates a discussion with Japanese students who are surprised that their diet staple, rice, is so much more expensive than in other parts of the world. Students in Japan and America discover principles of protectionist trade policies.
- Students in Europe and America find out from children in Israel what a SCUD attack is REALLY like.

166

- Students in Southern California learn from children in Santa Cruz, California, what they need to do to prepare for an earthquake... lessons learned from bitter experience.
- A student in Cold Harbor Springs, New York interviews Russian Jewish immigrants in Brooklyn. He recruits online acquaintances in Moscow and Jerusalem to interview Russian Jews in those places, and send him the results, so he can compare the stories from all three places in his high school sociology project.
- Students in New York collect relief supplies to send to their online friends devastated in the Florida hurricane. (Online version)

According to Milone Jr. (1995), "Using technology to learn and teach about themselves and where they live gives students a better understanding of their place in the world—and of the technology that will inevitably play a major role in their future" (p. 44). If the exchange of information between students across the Net could influence their thinking about their own place in this world, their relationship with others, and their role in the global village, it is possible to argue that they will grow into adults who are more sensitized to critical issues. We may thus expect a more informed generation that is not only more comfortable with their own identities but also not subject to the conflict and tensions that have existed among their predecessors. Perhaps the current struggle to label or categorize people into specific groups may be unnecessary, as identities evolve beyond ethnicity and race.

One of the issues that evoked strong reaction during the last Canadian census was the categorization of people into various "ethnic" groups. As Gardner (1995) noted in his post-election discussion:

> Some social scientists are even arguing that government should abandon the race question and other race-based social policies. For most Canadians, categorizing others by race is almost automatic. We use certain physical differences as cues—hair texture, eye colour, some facial shapes, and especially skin colour. Each of these features is a product of genetics, but only skin colour is plastered all over the body like a genetic billboard. So differences in skin colour are the ones that cause most Canadians to assume Oscar Peterson is "black" and Jean Chretien "white" (Online).

Perhaps, the most reactive response was from the so-called "South Asian" group that was not indicative of the differences and wide range of identities between

167

members arbitrarily clustered into one large umbrella category. Another category was, "White" in contrast to Chinese, South Asian, etc. that was too broad and not indicative of a corresponding ethnic background of the person. Issues of nationality triggered other sensitivities among people who were born in one country, lived in another, became naturalized citizens in a third country but retained birthright and/or citizenship in a non-resident country. If lineage was considered, some people had parents and grandparents from multiple countries and thus, some respondents were forced to define their identity based on residence.

If the notion of ethnicity during the census attracted such intense emotional reaction among Canadian population, we need to ask what is *ethnicity*? According to Hall (1997a), "Ethnicity is the necessary place or space from which people speak. It is a very important moment in the birth and development of all the local and marginal movements which have transformed the last twenty years, that moment of the rediscovery of their own ethnicities." Hall, argues that rediscovery of ethnicity is always positioned in a discourse and that:

> [it] comes from a place, out of a specific history, out of a specific set of power relationships. It speaks within a tradition. Discourse, in that sense, is always placed. So the moment of the rediscovery of a place, a past, of one's roots, of one's context, seems to me a necessary moment of enunciation. I do not think the margins could speak up without first grounding themselves somewhere. (p. 36)

The *24 Hours in Cyberspace* was a major event of posting pictures & paintings from around the world on international events. Publishing online thousands of images and hundreds of stories in a single day— of people walking, singing, sleeping, working, reading, writing, holding, touching, smiling, crying, etc. A day in the life of a person consisted of hundreds of images from around the world, including the remotest part of the world that became a frozen time capsule in the history of the Internet revolution. These were submitted by both professionals and amateurs, young and old, and from North and South Hall (1997a) describes a similar event hosted in London by the Commonwealth Institute that sponsored a photography competition inviting people in Commonwealth countries "to represent their own lives." The Institute said that this would be "harnessing of a hundred different histories within one singular history, The history of the Commonwealth." Hall notes: "This was a notion of using the cultural medium of photography to explode that old unity and proliferate, to diversify, to see the images of life as a people in the margins represented themselves photographically" (p. 37). This experiment also proved how empowering it was for peoples in the margins.

> Extraordinary stories, pictures, images of people looking at their own societies with the means of modern representation for the first time. Suddenly, the myth of unity, the unified identity of the Commonwealth, was simply exploded. Forty different peoples, with forty different histories, all located in a different way in relation to the uneven march of capital across the globe, harnessed at a certain point with the birth of the modern British Empire — all these things had been brought into one place and stamped with an overall identity... That was an enormous moment of the empowering of difference and diversity. It is the moment of what I call the rediscovery of ethnicity, of people photographing their own homes, their own families, their own pieces of work. (p. 37)

Thus, identities assume the right and express by breaking out of the mould that has consistently misrepresented and forced to be reckoned as an interpretation of the *Other*. Hall (1997b), calls this recovery or rediscovery as "re-identification, re-territorialization and re-identification," and posits it as an action challenging resistance to the margin's exclusion and marginalization (p. 53). It may be true that children of first generation immigrants are faced with resolving their identities especially when challenged by their peer group in school. Lack of understanding about the complex nature of identity may result in conflict and tension in schools. As schools become more international with the diversity of students from various national and cultural backgrounds, more initiatives aimed at developing and nurturing cross-cultural awareness along with exercises resolving conflicts that may arise out of misconception and misunderstanding are needed. Peter Copen, a successful industrialist founded the online *I*EARN* to develop and nurture cross-cultural and international understanding of relationships at the school level. *I*EARN* believes in understanding, discussing, and working toward common goals that are altruistic and humanitarian and deals in issues that characterize the unique relationship between industrialized countries and the developing countries. Other issues include the environment, social justice, and educational awareness. The New York based *I*EARN* encourages participants to "undertake projects designed to make a meaningful difference in the health and welfare of the planet and its people" through exercises that look into the issue of violence[27]. Their intent is to improve the health and welfare of the planet and its people and to address issues such as conflict resolution, cross-cultural awareness, and prevention of violence, at the local, national, and international levels. Strategies of preventing violence at the school level provide a basic understanding of conflict resolution within a wider global context.

> This project is designed to stimulate in-depth discussion of the causes of violence and ways of addressing and preventing it. The activities come from curricula on conflict resolution and violence prevention written by the Massachusetts Prevention Center, Educators for Social Responsibility, and other reputable educators in the field. Topics include Coping with Anger; Alcohol, Other Drugs, and Violence; Cross-cultural Awareness, Public Health Prevention Model; Finding Win-Win Solutions; Communication Skills; The Violence of Discrimination; Warning Signs of Dating Violence; and more. The goal of this project is to promote further understanding of the problem of violence and to take action to make our schools and communities more just and peaceful places. Students and teachers are also invited to add new topics for discussion relative to violence and its prevention.

The connectivity allowed by projects like the *I*EARN* help K-12 students to work collaboratively in different parts of the world, in sharing their understanding of different cultures and their visions for the future. As the fear of the unknown

---

[27] Though linked to over 500 schools in more than 32 countries, membership requirements make *I*EARN* inaccessible to the non-paying public.

creates xenophobia, communication between cultural groups may alleviate some of the misconceptions prevalent in North America and around the world. Direct contact with individuals or schools in different countries allows sharing stories, letters, projects, and other such activities that encourage developing more accurate understanding of peoples and their histories. Similarly, sharing of day-to-day events and activities can be revealing. If art galleries and photographs of things that we do everyday can bring a richer understanding of cultural diversities, the *International Schools CyberFair 97* would perhaps achieve this goal[28]. According to Vinton G. Cerf, co-inventor of the Internet and senior vice president of data architecture at MCI, the *CyberFair* is expected to "fulfill some of the promise of the Internet as a platform for bringing the world's cultures, schools and young people together." According to the organizers:

> Children participating in International Schools *CyberFair 96* will learn what it means to be part of a global community. They will work with groups of children located around the world, each group putting their local community on-line. Children will act as "Student Ambassadors," working with local artists, local business, and the rest of their community to show the world what is special about their place. With local artist and musicians, for example, students can conduct interviews, tape music, take photographs of art, and show the world their cultural heritage. Working with their local chamber of commerce, farmers, or local business, the International Schools *CyberFair 96* students can show the world the things they make and grow.

What the project attempts to do is to highlight local cultural products to the whole world. If teachers can use such projects in their classrooms, they would be able to develop global perspectives. If global educators can complement their teaching with audiovisual markers like the *CyberFair* in their classroom activities, they can ensure the development of a different perspective among their students and among themselves. As Martin-Kniep (1997) alluding to a truly reflective global education endeavor notes that, "Teachers [and students] will view the world from multicultural and global perspectives and will recognize that different people hold distinct views about the world." According to Martin-Kniep:

---

[28] The *CyberFair* ran as an exposition, throughout the year (1996 and 1997).

1. Teachers will understand the role of individual and societal values in the evolution of human history.
2. Teachers will understand the positive and negative role of technology in society.
3. Teachers will examine events and issues by situating them in a context of time (past, present, and future) and space (local, national, regional, international, and global).
4. Teachers will appreciate the relationship between people's language and their culture.
5. Teachers will demonstrate an awareness of the importance of civic and community responsibility in a global society (note rubric on civic discourse in global education).
6. Teachers will develop curriculum and instructional materials that promote the attainment of a global perspective. (p.105)

All the above excepting number 6, could be true for students also. A number of activities and projects reflect the existence of multiple perspectives. If initiatives can reflect Global SchoolNet's objectives of the *Schoolhouse* described as, "a global, multi-dimensional community, comprised of educators, businesses, government and community organizations collaborating across time and space to transform the way we work, live, and learn," more Internet projects could truly address the needs of global education programs. Participation in the Global SchoolNet projects does not require any membership and the project "organizes, manages, and facilitates collaborative learning projects for schools with any level of connectivity. . . from email. . . to desktop videoconferencing." Many schools have joined projects that allow them to get in touch with different countries, and thereby, different cultures. *Slonet Education*, with its *Classroom Connect* allows communication with different schools. Such an exercise is not confined to email exchanges but also includes separate Web pages dealing with literature, writing, languages, science, math, politics, social studies, Arts and Music, libraries and museums, and children's books.

One can employ more than one way to develop a global perspective. As Kris Bosworth at Indiana University notes in the *Teacher Talk* posted at the Global SchoolNet site:

> Global education refers to teaching about interconnectedness - how countries across the world have common economic, political, cultural, environmental and societal ties. These connections influence people locally as well, with elections, the media, disasters, pollution, job markets, export/import opportunities, and wars. There are many approaches to help students gain a global perspective, like starting pen pal programs with other countries or areas of the U.S., reading authors from other countries, visiting special art exhibits or attending other local cultural events, getting people who have been abroad recently to share their experiences, or writing to Embassies for information (many Embassies will send free documents, pictures, and posters).

> Kathy von Ende, a world geography teacher in Kansas, has used international guest speakers to help her students go beyond the facts of countries they study. For example, during a unit on the diverse continent of Africa, she invited four Africans from different parts to talk about their backgrounds. Prior to the guests' arrival, she had students learn about the country and prepare questions. Guests often use activities to interact with the students, such as writing names in another language or teaching different social customs.

> Kathy says, "My students really learn to appreciate different cultures. You just can't get that from the news, or reading, or discussing. In this way, the guests enrich the curriculum for the students." Her students are also learning how similar people are around the world.
> *Teacher Talk*, Volume 1, Issue 2.

Activity-oriented lesson plans attempt to address some of the global issues and involve online interaction with different cultures. The electronic medium offers encyclopedic material for armchair online expeditions in a multimedia environment. Online virtual tours may perhaps be the future of interactive media in culture studies where students see, hear, and research "live" on the Internet. With its "largest, most diverse complex of museums, art galleries and research institutes in the world," the *Smithsonian* offers Research Information System and Smithsonian Tours on any topic of interest. One can explore among many other issues, stories about nature, history and people through interactive *Discovery Channel Online* at *EdLinks* and participate with educators, students and parents around the world in live, interactive conferences at the *Classroom Connect Virtual Auditorium* offered by *Classroom Connect Resource Station*. For those who can afford, global education can be more effective if cultural understanding can be enhanced through direct rather than vicarious experiences. The role of international seminars for students and researchers has become quite popular in the field of international development studies. From schools to colleges, government projects to university seminars, travelling to developing countries as a part of the study is more common in North American educational institutions. As seen in the case of the *Center for Global Education at Augsburg College*, undergraduate students can travel to the *sites of struggle* even as they interact with "people struggling for justice and human dignity."

> The Center for Global Education at Augsburg College is nationally recognized for its work on experiential education in the Two Thirds World. The Center was founded in 1982 to help North Americans think more critically about global issues so that they might work toward a more just and sustainable world.
>
> SHORT TERM INTERNATIONAL TRAVEL SEMINARS: The Center for Global Education takes learning adults around the world on short-term travel seminars, bringing them into encounters with the peoples and situations of Mexico, Central America, the Caribbean, Southern Africa, the Middle East, and the Asia/Pacific region. These one-to three-week educational trips bring North Americans face to face with people of other cultures -- people struggling for justice and human dignity. Since 1982, the Center has coordinated over 350 seminars for more than 5,000 participants - many of them tell us their travel with the Center has truly been a life-changing experience! Up to 30 different travel seminars are offered each year, most of them open to the public.

While one might question the affordability of such travels, some courses offer close to the actual experience through action research slides, pictures and even videos[29].

Just as short-term travel seminars are prohibitive in cost, overseas student placement, as in the case of *AIESEC Online*, is also not very cheap. Nevertheless, for those interns who can afford residing in another country for a given time it would enable them to live and learn among different cultures. As a "dynamic global association of students which works to contribute to the development of countries

---

[29] An alternative is for instructors to spend time overseas, working at the grassroots level, documenting the activities in pictures, journals, and videos that can then be brought back to the classroom as Dr. David Baine from the Department of Educational Psychology at the University of Alberta does.

and their people with an overriding commitment to international understanding and cooperation," the non-political, non-profit, student-run, independent, educational association engages in experiential learning.

> Values: Belief mutual respect for cultures and equality of people. Vision: fulfillment of mankind's potential. Purpose: To contribute to the development of our countries and their people with an overriding commitment to international understanding and co-operation. Means: Creating opportunities for exposure and interaction between young people of different cultures and nations. Assisting people in acquiring skills and knowledge through management education and practical experience. Offering people the opportunity to interact with their social and economic environment.

Similarly, for those who are not students or researchers, the option to travel as a tourist is an appealing option. In distancing oneself from the tourist perspective of viewing the developing world, the *Third World Traveler* challenges the potential traveller with critical questions pertaining to human rights, environmental protection, and respect for humans for what they call "responsible travel." The goal is to "provide alternative travel information about Third World countries, support responsible travel, make tourists aware of the human rights situation in Third World vacation destinations, and provide opportunities for action on behalf of Third World human rights." The Webmeister at the site writes: "Third World countries are fascinating, [yet] they are usually not free. People in most countries in the Third World have few of the rights to which we are accustomed. ... Rulers are usually military officers or representatives of the country's wealthy elite, supported by the military." The host then raises the issue of people who criticize the government "may be imprisoned, tortured, and killed for having political beliefs in opposition to those of the rulers." He suggests that not visiting the countries will isolate them and the issues that concern them. "The thought of vacationing in countries where torture and murder are officially sanctioned, repels some travelers," he notes. Nevertheless, it is possible to travel responsibly, to meet with the people who suffer, to understand their problems, and to join them in peaceful protests. The Webmaster argues:

175

> Before we go, we need to get the truth about abuses of human rights, absence of women's rights, and restrictions of civil liberties. If we cannot get the facts through traditional channels, we must search for other sources of information. At minimum, this effort will make us more enlightened individuals and will differentiate us from uninformed "tourists". At best, the endeavour may improve the lives of people in the Third World.

Despite his intentions to raise crucial issues, the writer makes assumptions that are stereotypical. The notion that most third world countries "are usually not free" reflects the "know-it-all" approach in the West toward issues that are distant. There is a comparison of "rights" with the assumption that many third world countries do not offer the freedom to which "we are accustomed." With Nepal and the surrounding areas as an example in this case study, mention is made of the house arrest of opposition leader and Nobel Peace Prizewinner, Aung San Suu Kyi. The uncritical comparison of countries ignores differing aspects of geography, political structures, histories, and contextual issues. Suu Kyi is in Burma, operating within a political context different from Nepal, i.e., fighting a totalitarian government, which does not tolerate elections while Nepal, having gone through a massive `democratization' process in 1989, has had the monarchy losing its absolute power to an elected legislature. The indiscriminate comparisons between countries that do not share similar issues or problems, is quite uncritical and inappropriate; it only perpetuates myths and misconceptions about the developing world. In essence, the condescending approach to helping *those other* poor countries achieve Western perspective of freedom may actually harm the good intentions of the writer.

Perhaps this raises the current controversy surrounding the sanctions against Cuba. With the Pope visiting Cuba and issuing a formal request to the United States to remove trade and economic embargo against the last bastion of formally acknowledged socialism, critics including the Pope have argued that such sanctions only hurt the poor. Yet, despite the disinclination by the Conservative politics of Thatcher and Reagan, the ostracism of South Africa facilitated the dismantling of

176

apartheid in a pariah nation state. The debate is whether one would support the tourism industry to sustain an oppressive government even as direct contacts with the population are maintained (to understand their struggles) or to isolate the country disengaging the offending regime and let the country's poor suffer in their sequestered fight for justice.

If support for the various grassroots movements in their struggle for freedom and justice in the South has to be effective, our institutions in the North will have to educate the public. This is especially true in the case of educational institutions that have the knowledge workers engaged in international co-operative projects. The increasing involvement of educational institutions in the North dealing with international issues allows activists and scholars to address global issues without having to travel. These activities not only help analyze and act but also serve as venues of public education by disseminating valuable information to the student population and the general public. As seen in the case of the University of Alberta's *International Centre* with its annual International Week consisting of ongoing conferences and presentations from resident researchers, activists, and visiting scholars representing their home countries, culture can be learned from lived experiences. One could formally engage in the academic exercise of culture studies by referring to the available global education courses and programs at The *International Centre: Directory of Resources for Global Education* home page. In its objective, the Centre intends:

> [T]o educate the University of Alberta community about the issues of the developing South, providing a look at a reality generally far removed from the experience of those who live in the wealthier North. A major thrust of the program is to promote international students as "living resources" on campus and to increase the level of global understanding on campus by exploring issues in development. Programs offered include Southern Exposure in which speakers pass on first-hand information about global development challenges.

177

7.3. Action through Collaboration

If the fight for freedom and justice in the different parts of the world has to be successful, people will have to join hands in solidarity. The fight for democracy is one in which there are sites of struggle everywhere in the world, some of which in the North will function as a support for people's struggles in the South and some of which will not. The effectiveness of engagement for global justice depends on the connectivity between activists around the world. With technological development in its incipient stages in some developing countries, access to the Internet is almost impossible for grassroots struggles in remote and rural areas in many areas in the South. Yet, the Internet connections offer the connectivity for organized struggle in the case of well-established and funded institutions in the South. *Amnesty International* has established links with many such individuals and bodies in the South. These contacts in the South serve as essential conduits to the dissemination of firsthand information that would otherwise be unavailable to activists in the North. Educators can refer to Internet sources like *Third World First Group* to gain more understanding of issues relating to global inequality at an informational and practical level. Especially at the level of dissemination, sites like the *Third World First* reflect the intent to "...challenge and change perceptions, and promote awareness amongst students and the general public about the real causes of poverty and underdevelopment in the South (a.k.a. the 'third world')."

> Third World First looks at issues of global inequality at an informational and practical level, comments and other links much appreciated... We firmly believe in the power of information, as recognition of problems is the first step to solving them. Hopefully these Web pages will inspire you to take action on some of the issues outlined.

If action is the intent of a knowledgeable person, the transition from acquiring information to the praxis level (action and reflection) can be possible through

178

well-established connections with people (individuals and groups) who subscribe to the same objectives. If human behaviour can be influenced by experiences of the individual, the role of communication and exchange in facilitating those changes can be vital. By disseminating information, the *Edinburgh University Third World First Society* attempts to recognize problems and follow through with action to resolve the identified problems. Since change depends on establishing connections, accessing appropriate information, understanding the issues, and making an effort to act accordingly, not unlike *The North-South Institute*, the *Worldwatch Institute* is another representative of one such site serving as a conduit for global educators. Believing in the power of conscious effort towards change, the Institute addresses critical issues like environmental pollution, human rights, globalization, and privatization.

> The Institute believes that information is a powerful tool of social change. Human behaviour shifts either in response to new information or new experiences. The Institute seeks to provide the information to bring about the changes needed to build an environmentally sustainable economy. In a sentence, the Institute's mission is to raise public awareness of global environmental threats to the point where it will support effective policy responses... The Institute's outlook is global because the most pressing environmental issues are global. Given the earth's unified ecosystem and an increasingly integrated global economy, only a global approach to issues such as climate change, depletion of the stratospheric ozone layer, the loss of biological diversity, degradation of oceans, and population growth can be effective.

Hilary F. French, in her article at the *Worldwatch Institute* site observes:

> The rapid pace at which the world is becoming more tightly knit--economically, environmentally, and culturally--is one of the most distinctive features of our time. As recently as a decade ago, industrial and developing countries almost seemed to exist on different planets. yet today the distinction is eroding rapidly, as the two worlds are drawn together by a global economy that shows little regard for national borders. And increasingly, industrial and developing societies contain pockets of one another. The developing world has its rapidly modernizing industries and wealthy elites; the industrial world has its underclasses, locked out of its general prosperity.

If "information is a powerful tool of social change" and does influence human behaviour in regard to the information, the analytical content offered by *Worldwatch* might after all instigate and challenge readers to think and act. While much of the information distributed challenge and question the existing situation in and around the world, the *Worldwatch Institute* is mostly engaged in provoking readers towards action that would attempt to redress the wrongs within the global village. As the *Worldwatch* recognizes, with its integrated global economy sharing the earth's unified ecosystem, environmental sustainability is closely linked to the various peoples and their living surroundings. In the case of many indigenous groups, cultural identity is directly linked to cultural sovereignty and the environment. Environmental sustainability is directly dependent on cultural survival and to understand the struggles among aboriginal peoples and other agrarian societies, we need to become aware of relevant issues. Web sites such as *Cultural Survival, Centre for Study of Indigenous Peoples,* and *World Conference on Indigenous Peoples* contain information and links to issues of autochthony. Students may learn about Australia and its people, their culture and its survival being linked to the environmental stability (*The Kid's Locker Room*). Similarly discussions at *The Kid's Locker Room*[30] and *Just for Kids* challenge us to consider the relationship between human survival and the sustainability of fauna and flora including the Koala's future.

7.4. Information: Useful Facts or Misleading Stereotypes?

In order for us to comprehend, analyze and then act as global citizens, we must be able to access information that is current and unfiltered by conventional media. The Internet perhaps provides this option of distributing information bypassing traditional censorship and newsworthiness as deemed by subjective intervention and control. News items about different countries and events in various places become sources of information for students as they cull out ongoing events and news items that relate to issues and concerns that are global at

---

[30] Links to over 100 Australian schools and over 5,000 Australian Web sites.

Yahooligans! If students access "Around the World Countries," "Politics," "History," and "Entertainment," sites like *Yahooligans!* provide a definite departure from the usually inward-looking, locally focused prime time news on Canadian television. While the Web sites are monitored for unacceptable material such as hate, crime, and pornography, contributors who are neither journalists nor "professionals" from around the world freely post many items. This offers the freedom to share individual and personal experiences that would not be subject to authentication by "professional" editors. Albeit, unedited material can also cause problems with uncritical and opinionated stereotype information presented as facts.

In the dissemination of information relevant to human rights, democracy, politics, culture, or just the daily news, the main media in many countries filters information by choosing, selecting, sanitizing and excluding subjects that do not cater to the immediate broadcasting needs. Countries fighting news media censorship have resorted to ingenious methods of dissemination. Despite the relative freedom of press in India, unlike the free print media, the state controlled television news broadcasts are insipid, politically influenced, and rigidly controlled—not to mention highly regulated. Fighting this unfair censorship is the highly popular journalist-influenced *Newstrack* video releases that take pride in "delivering the important news the state broadcast conveniently omitted." The online equivalent to the *Newstrack* is the more global-centred *New Internationalist* with its motto, "The New Internationalist Magazine tells the whole story... So you get the whole picture." Giving opportunities to feature the silent voices is a symbol of resistance that endeavors to deal with, "The people, the ideas, the action in the fight for world development."

The New Internationalist (NI) magazine exists to report on the issues of inequality and world poverty; to focus attention on the unjust relationship between the powerful and powerless in both rich and poor countries; to debate and campaign for the radical changes necessary within and between those nations if the basic material and spiritual needs of all are to be met; and to bring to life the people, ideas and action in the fight for world justice.

In Germany, similar attempts to disseminate "free flow of uncensored facts," especially on race-related and human rights abuses within the country has resulted in *German Alert*, a site that supports *Amnesty International* in its objectives. The monitoring not only includes the illegal activities at large but also includes police atrocities in Germany.

21 April 1997

Nazis Beat, Slash Italian Youth in Anti-Foreigner Hate Attack . . . Bishop Assails Government on Forced Deportation Policy . . . Germany, 'World Champion' at Spying On Its Own Citizens, to Monitor Internet Usage . . . German Prosecutors indict CompuServe Chief

Notification Service

Neo-Nazis, Greens, Anarchists Seek to Disrupt 'Love Parade'

BERLIN -- Neo-Nazis, ecologists and anarchists are actively attempting to disrupt this weekend's Love Parade, where one million youths from all over the world are expected for a gigantic rave. The latest threat against the event comes from the neo-Nazis, more than 30 of whose residences were raided after authorities received a tip that they planned to set off a bomb in Tiergarten park where Love Parade is being staged... Autonome threats to distrupt Love Parade -- based on assertions that the event is an "Americanization" of Germany -- dovetail with protests by neo-Nazis, who go on to complain that Love Parade will bring too many foreigners to Germany.

Bonn Claims Soldier Execution Video was 'Not Politically Motivated'

BONN -- The German government added insult to injury as it claimed Monday that soldiers who taped themselves "practicing" executions and rapes were "not politically motivated." But the Defense Ministry, acting as international protest at the incident spread, fired a soldier who took part in the mock atrocities... The incident is but the latest in a series of scandals involving the German army. Soldiers giving the Hitler salute, off duty soldiers who ganged up to torture foreigners in Germany and officers who glorify the Third Reich have combine to create heightened concern about what is really going on in the Germany military.

182

By spreading the details of such activities overseas, activists are thus able to update and inform other human rights activists in different countries; this not only provides the needed ammunition for their counterparts but also keeps domestic atrocities in check for fear of international retribution. While technology offers a viable conduit for efficient flow of information, one must also beware of dissemination of disinformation over the Internet. Recognizing the origin of the source perhaps allows confirming the qualifications of the information. Al Rogers (1994), considers the free flow of information over the Internet as a vital part of human rights activism. He notes that, "In contrast to this managed flow of information, however, the global Internet of networks is giving millions of people direct access to information in ways the world has never before seen. Information of every sort flows freely, across national borders and around the world, directly from `where it's happening' to where there are `inquiring minds who want to know.'" Noting how the Internet facilitated the August 19, 1991 coup d'etat in Moscow, Rogers describes the developments surrounding the event:

For the first time in over a thousand years, Muscovites raised the barricades and defied the powers behind the coup. Boris Yeltsin, president of the Russian Republic, issued a decree of defiance, proclaiming the leaders of the coup to be illegal and seizing authority within the Russian Republic from the central government. Within hours the following message containing Boris Yeltsin's decree, in both transliterated Russian and English translation, flashed around the world, directly to tens of thousands of computers on college campuses, businesses, homes, and schools:

To: NEWS.GENERAL

From: dvv@hq.demos.su (Dmitry V. Volodin)

Organization: DEMOS, Moscow, USSR

Subject: Yeltsin's decree

Date: Mon, 19 Aug 91 21:20:13 +0300 (MSD)

Please redistribute this as wide as possible the following in stripped Russian and an approximate translation to English. It'll be fine, if this reaches world information agencies. Thank you.
Dima

**** **Message in Russian**** ****

This message came directly from Moscow to the people of the world... unfiltered, unedited, without the benefit of selection or "commentary," "interpretation," or embellishment. (This kind of internetworking transmission is substantially different than radio or television broadcasting, which require expensive transmitters: anyone with access to a personal computer and a phone line can accomplish the same thing as our Moscow "correspondent.)

The nearness to what is happening, the direct contact with people who suffer indignation, and the possibility to hear their voices without state intervention, makes the medium extremely powerful. Noting that this is quite different from the conventional "news" that could be "less real" Rogers provides an example from the Bosnian calamity:

Date: November 26, 1991 11:22
Subject: Appeal for Vukovar

Translation courtesy of Tomislav
****
Subj: APEL ZA VUKOVAR IZ VUKOVARA !!!!!!!!!
****
How can I start a story of death and desire to live?
How can I describe millions of feelings in plain words?
How can I concentrate when a packet of death explodes nearby every few minutes?
How can I ask for help from someone whose face I cannot even imagine?
How can I ask in the name of thousands of people, and whom
can I ask, when all the appeals and cries for help to stop
this insane bloodshed have been unanswered?

Death has become the most important aspect of life in this
devastated city. She follows us in every step; she is an
integral part of every thought, of every word that is being
said. Separated from our wives, mothers, sisters, and
brothers; in the constant presence of terrible massacres of
our closest friends; deprived from the most basic needs;
degraded to the level of the cattle awaiting to be
slaughtered we live in damp cellars with no electricity,
running water, toothpaste, soap, diapers for the babies;
with no hope of resting even for a moment, because dreams on
improvised beds are only the horrible repetitions of the
cruel reality.

Can anyone who has not experienced even a little piece of
Vukovar's reality understand the bitter feeling in every
single one of us? Can anyone explain to him/herself and
accept us as savage reality that maybe tommorow they will
not see their families anymore? In our twisted world there
are no lies. There is only one truth; the truth about life.

Life in Vukovar today is the fight for every doorstep, for
the remains of our hopes, of a town that in the morning mist
resembles the site of a Hollywood horror movie.

We are not asking for charity, we are only asking for life
with basic human decency. We are asking for a chance for our
children to have their children. How would the West react if
2,000 of their children were confined to damp cellars with a
threat of imminent death for everyone who dares to go out;
with only one skimpy meal a day and uncertainty of how long
such state will persist? Can you imagine something like that
in London, Paris, Washington, Berlin, Vienna?

We may be separated by thousands of miles, but are our
hearts separated that much? Let us bring negotiators to
Vukovar! Let anyone come up with a single argument for the
war when surrounded by dying babies! Let us gather all the
children that have lost their parents, whose chance to walk
side by side with their fathers and mothers has forever been
lost. No institution will ever be able to replace the care
of the parents.

Vukovar is not just a bunch of shattered buildings; it is a
live organism that breathes. Vukovar has got its own
bloodstream, its life that is being taken away from it. Its
flesh is being torn apart; its bones are being broken. And
while the city is defending itself in a spasm, it is being
attacked by people to whom it represents only a point on the
map.

This message is directed to all of those who love life; to
all those who can appreciate the little things that make
life; to all those who have ever seen a smile of a baby; to
all of those who still care...

STOP THE WAR IN CROATIA, GIVE VUKOVAR A CHANCE!

There is a nearness that is far more touching to the above narration than all the government statistics; while these are necessary, the emotional connection in stories told are far more powerful. The faces behind the numbers and events become real and the challenge to question the need for a political war against the innocent appears less convincing than ever before. The events, the people, their experiences, and even the places themselves acquire their own reality; they are no more cities on a map reported during the evening news. Delia Venables (1996), describes how and why the Internet can be a powerful "medium of protest":

The Internet was designed to survive a nuclear attack - and now it is being used as a protest mechanism for anti-nuclear campaigners to bombard President Chirac to protest against the resumption of nuclear tests. Two students in Japan started a "chain email" urging their friends and colleagues to multiply the letter and to send it on to their friends and colleagues, and the result was 40,000 emails which were presented to President Chirac on the 50th Anniversary of Hiroshima. There is an irony here in that President Chirac had long since disconnected his email address and the emails had to be printed out and presented in physical form...

Another version of Internet protest took place on the same issue, with leading academics and lawyers from more than 50 Universities across 40 countries combining to present a lengthy closely argued memorandum on the legal aspects of the resumption of the tests. This protest originated at Melbourne University. Friends of the Earth currently have, on their pages, statements and advertisements along the lines of "Mahogony is Murder" which state that this particular trade leads to atrocities. These ads have been banned by the Advertising Standards Authority for printed use, but it is by no means clear that their remit applies to internet also. There are various watchdog groups which are setting up Internet pages with information about civil rights issues. Two such sites are intending to name Western companies which sell electronic instruments of surveillance to governments with poor records on human rights. These sites are run by Privacy International (a British group) and Electronic Privacy Information Center (a USA group). I understand that these organisations are loosely linked with Amnesty International who carry out similar "tracking" activities.

In the above "chain email" incident, according to Venables, the overloaded system crashed resulting in the return to conventional means of dissemination. Even as various sites offer direct connection to experiences and information about events and the daily lives of people, governments and international bodies have their own organized bodies of information in place. As these are mostly for dissemination rather than activism, such sources remain rich in research materials for global educators. At the bureaucratic level, the *World Bank* home page with its exhaustive and comprehensive information (data, proceedings, news releases, policy papers), programs, projects, details and updates of research and other assignments around the world is mostly administrative. Besides policy decision-making, statistical analysis, project implementation and trend analysis, it offers voluminous statistical reports similar to the UNICEF Web site that contains the annual report of *State of the Children* releases. Some online service providers have extended their mandate from the distribution of news to the more activity-based interactive exercises engaging students. Nairobi's *Kids Only* by *Africa Online* (AOL) has a *Global Classroom* page that registered schools can access. Not unlike the AOL project, there is a multi-pronged initiative to link many of the ex-colonies to the Information Superhighway in order to utilize the developing technology and to be a part of the *third wave*.

Despite the promising opportunities for distributing information without censorship or monitoring, the Net can also pass on unedited, non-refereed and non-authenticated information as fact. For example, the *Honolulu Community College* is represented on the Web as a teacher-training institute with its voluminous resource material for teachers. With the topic on teaching ESL to non-English speaking adults ("How people Learn") the writer has innumerable stereotypes and culturally inaccurate advice for ESL teachers.[31] The teacher educator at the Community College recognizes that "Native Hawaiians, Samoans, Filipinos, and Southeast Asians are all minority population groups under-represented in higher education in Hawaii. Cautioning to "Hold all judgments; i.e. be careful about interpreting the culturally different student's behaviour, especially if unfamiliar with the culture," he reminds that as teachers, "we should treat each student as a unique and individual person. These communication tips are offered in the spirit of help. Take what makes sense and is valuable to you. Leave that which you don't want." Following the preamble, Brown's tips then evoke a string of stereotypes:

HAWAIIAN
> Hawaiians make up 12.25 percent of the total state population in Hawaii and are the fourth largest ethnic group behind Whites, Japanese and Filipino. Hawaiians are a minority in their own homeland and are slowly loosing their identity as an ethnic group...

---

[31] From "Cross-Cultural Communication in Education; A Focus on Ethnic Minority Populations. Under-Represented in Higher Education in Hawaii" by Richard Brown, Apprenticeship Coordinator, Honolulu Community College.

Many programs are in place to assist Hawaiians and help preserve the Hawaiian culture. Individual teachers can help by understanding the frustration and low esteem with which Hawaiians regard themselves and their place in society. They have relatively few role models in the school system, so you as the teacher must be the bridge to their future.

Hawaiian students not only tend to sit in the back of the classroom, they will make physical contact with the back wall, if you let them.

SAMOAN

Children, around the age of 5 years are raised and controlled by older siblings, allowing parents freedom to participate in religious, social, and cultural events. *Discipline and punishment are dealt out to children with physical abuse. This may be a reason for the violent nature of some Samoans.*

Unlike other Pacific Islanders and Asians, Samoans do not work well with groups. Packaged instruction or competency-based training may be better suited to these individuals. Students are never praised and *don't know how to react.* They are totally controlled by adults in the family and *expect strict control.* Establish a set of rules and standards and stick to them; if you don't you will loose control. *Samoans are not accustomed to speaking up or asking questions.* Students expect to be told what to do in every case and generally is not a self starter. Samoans do not usually participate in classroom discussion. They are accustomed to the apprenticeship method so maybe teaming in twos will facilitate... *Samoan students don't usually make eye contact.* If this is the case, you are probably in control. *If you are getting a lot of eye contact, you may have a problem.* [Emphases, added]

FILIPINO

Don't underestimate Filipino students' *ability* because they have an *accent.* They are very capable and should be subject to the same standards and expectations as other students. Filipinos do not feel comfortable being singled out in class. *They will not respond well in class discussions.* Students prefer to work on collaborative projects and submit input by joint effort. Students are *uncomfortable when praised.* They prefer to stay anonymous within the peer group. *Don't praise in public,* but do let the student know you appreciate good work. Teachers are considered an authority figure by students. Therefore, *they will not question any action by the teacher.* Students will not ask a teacher for help or ask questions. They normally go to other students for help as they feel the teacher will be offended that the student did not "get it" the first time.

Asian cultures in general adhere to strict social status structuring. Westerners expect eye contact when talking to groups or individuals. Because you are an authority figure, *Filipino students will not look directly at you because it is their custom not to do so.* This is especially true when you are reprimanding them. Don't worry, you are not being ignored. [Emphases added]

SOUTHEAST ASIAN

One important thing to realize is that unlike other refugees, the Southeast Asians are not arriving as an intact family unit. In some cases one parent will arrive with one or two of the oldest children or any part of the family that could get out of Vietnam, Cambodia, and Laos under any conditions. Amerasian children, in some cases, arrived in the United States without any other family members. These children were *rejected from one culture* and are about to be introduced to a new one as far removed as possible from anything they have experienced in the past.

188

They are not used to independent thought and action. You will see them group together often if not in every case. Use this to your advantage and encourage group projects over independent study or projects.

They adhere to a strict social order and will consider the teacher an authority figure. *Don't expect eye contact when you engage in conversation.* Also, don't touch students, especially on the head, this is considered rude… *Don't compliment them in public*, it makes them seem conceited to their peers. [Emphases added]

To assume that all Hawaiians lack role models; tend to be undisciplined; and are unable or are required to maintain an "acceptable" physical posture is misinformation. The issue of differentiating between *discipline* and *abuse* has been an ongoing debate in North America. Even within the continent, the Canadian definition of abuse can be quite amusing to a Texan who believes in corporal and capital punishment. To link the assumption of abuse and then generalize that most Samoans are violent is preposterous. Brown is confined to his own interpretation and understanding of issues like group versus individual work, eye contact, praise and punishment, activity (asking questions) versus participation, customary authority figure versus facilitator, independent thought and action versus meaningful activity, and, cultural rejection versus political disruption. It is even amusing to suggest that "If you are getting a lot of eye contact [with a Samoan], you may have a problem." Brown expresses a genuine concern about the aforementioned groups as minorities needing assistance and yet falls into the trap of assigning his own limited thinking to cultural nuances. I am positive that Brown would be puzzled if I were to make the suggestion that his intent is disjunctive with his prescription in that it is riddled with stereotyping, misconceptions, and assumptions. In cases like these, one may want to agree that some of the misinformation is passed on unknowingly but they still remain that— misinformation. It is vital that teachers in general and global educators in specific guard themselves from such cultural lapses. In fact, one of the causes of xenophobia is the dissemination of misconceptions that lead to enduring structural violence. If information is not critically assessed, global educators may become victims of stereotyping. And unless global educators address causes of violence, the critical element of an effective global education is lost.

One grave aspect of misrepresentation by the educator at this site is the tacit claim to speak on behalf of peoples and cultures that do not have their voices heard. The writer represents so obviously `one set of people talking about other sets who are deemed not to be listening'. Thus, not unlike the old anthropological or sociological analysis in which the `subject' was assumed not to have access to the `knowledge' being generated, the writer develops his or her own understanding of reality; he, assumes their silence and relies on it to maintain his/her image of the other. Thus, the Internet could also become a conduit for culturally normalized racism as the uninformed continue to transmit the "truth" about the *Other*—the silent voices that cannot defend themselves or be heard on the Internet.

7.5. Culture on the Net: From Silent Voices to Voices that can be Heard

Historically, the West met the East in the territory of the colonized. As King (1997b) notes, the first encounter between Europe and non-Europe (developed/developing societies; capitalist/pre-capitalist economies; white/non-white; one culture/many cultures[32]), occurred in "what was to become the colonies, not the metropole; in the periphery, not the core; in non-Europe, not Europe, whichever conceptualisation we prefer. The first globally multi-racial, multi-cultural, multi-continental societies on any substantial scale were in the periphery, not the core." (p. 8). Now that the Internet is the powerful medium that

---

[32] Used by King to remind us the labeling of the "Other".

190

allows the interaction between the North and the South[33], the territories are neither occupied nor to be occupied. These are without borders, without ownership, without physical constraints and definitely not for gaining ownership. Nevertheless, in this ethereal world, one must be cautious of looking at the *Other*.

There exists an area of planned and organized cultural disclosure on the Net that can be identified as a move from silent voices to voices that can be heard. Histories that have been misinterpreted or never been told by traditional sources are now offered on the Net for consumption by the public through online exploration. Some of the more prominent sites like the Jewish sites and the Afro-American sites allow presentation of their history and culture through pictures, sounds and interactive games. Taking the North American example, historically, the "silent voices" of the blacks in the United States have been oppressed, distorted and deliberately suppressed by dominant forces. The *AFRO-America@*, attempts to right this error at its Web site by offering a rich source of historical narratives.

> February 24, 1997 Web posted at: 12:15 p.m. EST. From CNN Correspondent Brian Nelson
>
> (CNN) -- The World Wide Web offers plenty of opportunity to expand your knowledge of the history and culture of African- Americans. For art and history, start at AFROAmeric@, a site maintained by the Afro-American Newspaper Company of Baltimore. The site's art exhibit features African-American works on display at the Baltimore Museum of Art. The works range from the 1800s to present day, and are accompanied by information on the artists.

Celebrating the Afro-American history and culture online has resulted in a number of interesting and rich Web sites that are linked to each other and to a host of other relevant sites. A good historical perspective to the evolution of Afro-Americans within the North American culture provides a solid source for

---

[33] The terms are conventional but "since the 1950s, different terms have been invented (almost entirely by "the West") to map, in Roland Robertson's terms, the global condition: First/Second/Third Word, North/South, developed/underdeveloped/developing, core/periphery/semi-periphery, and so on" (king, 1997b, p. 8).

researchers investigating the various aspects of culture. Black history (culture, music, slavery, etc.) has been written in the voices of non-black historians who have had the power to legitimize knowledge and content based on their own biases. Hall (1997a), describes this recovery of history by the margins as follows:

> They [the margin] have to try to retell the story from the bottom up, instead of from the top down... You could not describe the movements of colonial nationalism without that moment when the unspoken discovered that they had a history which they could speak; they had languages other than the languages of the master, of the tribe. It is an enormous moment. The world begins to be decolonized at that moment. You could not understand the movements of modern feminism precisely without the recovery of the hidden histories. (p. 35)

Afro-Americans and black Canadians have always celebrated February as the Black History Month. This has allowed community groups, educational institutions, media and other organized coalitions to engage in the dissemination of activities pertaining to various African cultures. Unless the histories are told to our children, they will be unable to relate to the individuals with various histories who are a part of the community. Despite the fact that we are what Pinar (1993), calls "multicultural, multiclassed, and multigendered," the exclusion of African American history in many school curricula is not unintentional and such institutional racism "deforms" white students as well (pp. 62, 67).

It is online initiatives such as *A Celebration of Black Culture* that attempt to redress this lopsided education for the marginalized that do not have free or unlimited access to the mainstream media. Established by media and computer company giants, the *re-presenting* of Black History attempts to regain the cultural heritage denied and relegated to the margins.

> February 24, 1997 Web posted at: 12:15 p.m. EST   From CNN Correspondent Brian Nelson
> Biographies are plentiful on this site, and a time-line examines the long history of African-Americans in America. Time Warner's Pathfinder Celebrates Black History through the Ages in an artful manner with a virtual tour of the famous Savoy Gallery, home to the work of some of the best 20th-century artists. The site also holds a retrospective on

photographer Austin Hansen's six decades of work in Harlem and other special features. MSBET, Black Entertainment Television's cyber-collaboration with Microsoft, launched A Celebration of Black Culture in February to coincide with Black History Month. But the site's creators say they consider every month Black History Month.

The site offers Images of Freedom -- a gallery of art with weekly features curated by Dr. Henry Louis Gates, director of Harvard University's W.E.B. DuBois Institute. The site also features in-depth looks at the civil rights struggles of the Fifties and Sixties and space for debate on the continuing struggles of African-Americans.

Biographies, historical expositions and galleries that exhibit pictures, paintings, stories, music, history and the evolution of Afro-American culture remain a powerful source of information for educators and historians. In allowing the youth to discover and explore the ancestral contributions to the present day democracy, the "back to the roots" movement instills respect and self-esteem among minority groups. Similar initiative, not limited to a single month, includes the *Britannica Guide to Black History*. The Internet has allowed the marginalized and the misrepresented minorities to assert their own ways to dispelling the myths and re-writing the history as they see it true. Hall (1997b), describes this process of recovery as a process where "the margins begin to speak. The margins begin to contest, the locals begin to come to representation" (p. 53).

It had to do with the fact that people were being blocked out of and refused an identity and identification within the majority nation, having to find some other roots on which to stand. Because people have to find some ground, some place, some position on which to stand. Blocked out of any access to an English or British identity, people had to try to discover who they were... In the course of the search for roots, one discovered not only where one came from, one began to speak the language of that which is home in the genuine sense, that other crucial moment which is **the recovery of lost histories**. The histories that have never been told about ourselves that we could not learn in schools, that were not in any books, and that we had to recover. (Emphasis added) (p. 52)

As Afro-Americans who have been denied their history but now have moved from the margins to the centre, their hybridity offers them the ability to rectify this historical discrimination through re-presented stories and histories. As Bhabha (1995), explains this:

193

Hybridity is the sign of the productivity of colonial power, its shifting forces and fixities; it is the name for the strategic reversal of the process of domination through disavowal... Hybridity is the revaluation of the assumption of colonial identity through the repetition of discriminatory identity effects. It displays the necessary deformation and displacement of all sites of discrimination and domination. (p. 34)

Those who have no freedom to move from the margins to the hybridized state do not have the liberty to assume the rectification of the representation of their past or the present. While freedom to nurture and distribute information about various cultures is an indication of liberal democracy, it is unlikely that regimes controlling the everyday lives of people in less democratic situations would offer the privilege of criticizing their rulers. If one looks beyond the continent, with restrictions on what can be posted on sites regulated and owned by rulers in the Middle East, a form of sanitized but colorful representation of Arab culture is promoted by the tourism industry in the Middle East. With cultural artefacts, the *ArabNet* contains enormous amount of information on countries principally from the Middle East and Africa. A number of countries are represented including Algeria, Bahrain, Comoros, Djibouti, Egypt, Iraq, Jordan, Kuwait, Lebanon, Libya, Mauritania, Morocco, Oman, Palestine, Qatar, Saudi Arabia, Somalia, Sudan, Syria, Tunisia, United Arab Emirates and Yemen. With a host of awards from Magellan, NetGuide, NBNSoft, Web of Culture, and Microsoft Network, the sites deal with culture, art, commerce, food, tourism, business, commerce, news, and directories. With over 1865 pages, the ArabNet is "The online resource for the Arab world in the Middle East and North Africa." Naturally, the sites stay away from political, religious, educational, sociological or historical issues. For now, issues of human rights and lack of political freedom in some of these religious states and sheikdoms remain the responsibility of groups residing overseas or the *Amnesty International*. Nevertheless, due to the voluminous characteristics of the Internet, information can flow freely through personal email from these countries. The threat of the fax machine to some of these closed nation states is insignificant when compared to the intrusion and influence of the electronic mail. The *third wave* is perhaps the most powerful and disabling development in the history of sheikdoms.

One of the "silent voices" besides the North American black is a group of people that constitutes more than half of the world— transcending color, ethnicity, language, religion, socioeconomic status, geographic boundaries, and state citizenship, namely, the women[34]. One of the ways to delve into the achievement and struggles of women is to offer their voices through history. Specifically targeting K-12 students, the *Encyclopedia of Women's History*, invites and posts unedited writings of students on female role models in history. Partly maintained by Portland Jewish Academy's 5th grade, the site invites students to write about the world's women who have impacted history, living or dead. This not only encourages students to research on women but also allows them to share their own understanding of such struggle with others over the Internet.

7.6. The Struggle for Democracy and Human Rights

Organized political groups usually have well-established agenda that enables them to be focused in their struggle for what they believe is right or desirable. Freedom, social justice and equity are identified as fundamental rights in a liberal democracy. Representing "the largest socialist organization in the United States," the *Democratic Socialists of America*, offers critical analysis by

---

[34] More on the feminization of poverty will be dealt with under the succeeding section on human rights.

195

looking at inequality, democracy, empowerment, gender and cultural relations for "building progressive movements for social change while establishing an openly socialist presence in American communities and politics." As the host describes:

> At the root of our socialism is a profound commitment to democracy, as means and end. We are activists committed not only to extending political democracy but to demanding democratic empowerment in the economy, in gender relations, and in culture. Democracy is not simply one of our political values but our means of restructuring society. Our vision is of a society in which people have a real voice in the choices and relationships that affect the entirety of our lives. We call this vision democratic socialism - a vision of a more free, democratic and humane society.

Considered "Leftist' in its political persuasion, members of the Democratic Socialists call for an egalitarian and democratic society— one that is socialist in nature and realizes the political beliefs of its members. While the socialists may call their vision of a more just and equitable society as "democratic socialism," the need to achieve such a society is beyond labelling. Notwithstanding political affinities, the hope for a "free, democratic and humane society" has not been much different from the visions of peace educators; the only difference has been the suggested processes that achieve this end. The need to allow "silent voices" remains a basic issue among empowerment (Critical) theorists.

The intricate relationship between peace education and global education becomes obvious at the *Institute of Global Education*. Its educational broadcasting station, *Radio for Peace International,* catering to over one million listeners, the Institute is a non-profit United Nations Non-Governmental Organization. Based on campus at the University for Peace in Costa Rica, the projects deal with peace and disarmament.

> [The] goal is to help co-create a world where peace and food sufficiency are a way of life, where environmental responsibility exists, where social justice prevails and where an individual achieves the highest degree of self-realization within a community of cooperation.
> Defusing Terrorism: Pioneering Educators on the Firing Line April 28, 1995
> RFPI is a short-wave station broadcasting from Costa Rica devoted to issues of peace and peace education, conflict resolution, social justice, human rights, the environment and cross-cultural understanding. RFPI has been concerned for several years about the

196

growing number of programs broadcast on short-wave stations in the US that are racist, anti-Semitic, anti-UN, and promote hate and/or violence and the overthrow of the US government. These programs are produced by militia groups, the National Alliance, Christian Identity groups and various other violent groups on the Far-Right. In response to such programming, James Latham, Station Manager of RFPI, decided in February of 1994 to expose and challenge this growing phenomenon with a program titled the Far-Right Radio Review.

Radio for Peace International can be found on shortwave frequencies 15.05, 7.385, 6.200, and 9.400(24 hours/day).

Issues of environmental sustainability are intricately linked with social justice and peace. Peace education not only addresses issues of militant and terrorist activities but also explores, as the name suggests, to analyze and resolve the tensions that caused violence to begin with. Again, the dissemination of information using traditional media resources including the radio is an efficient means to public education. Raising critical issues relating to the pain suffered by the marginalized over radio can be most effective in reaching out to those masses that do not yet have the Internet. With its presence on the Net as a site for advocacy, *Radio for Peace International* for example, deals with the issues that affect children in the developing world:

"Thailand's economy has done well in recent years, ranking as one of the 'mini-dragons' of Asia. Yet, within Thailand, many families remain so poor that their children are sold into prostitution. Thailand plays a key role in exporting raw materials, yet the denuding of Thailand's own forests has left great scars across the countryside and disrupted the traditions of cultural minority groups."

"By personally meeting with a wide variety of resource people whose lives are shaped by these issues and developments, you will gain a firsthand feel for what is at stake for them as their countries undergo great changes. *Particular emphasis will be given to hearing from those who are often in more vulnerable situations—women, children, cultural minorities, and refugees.* The style of the seminar is intensive and includes encounters with people and organizations representing many social sectors, as well as opportunities for group reflection, analysis, and collective learning. Reflection on the role and response of U.S. citizens will also be a component of the program. Meetings with international resource people and visits to markets and traditional tourist sites will round out the itinerary." [Emphasis, added]

In offering rich insights into problems that face the vulnerable in developing countries, readers may begin to ask more critical questions. For a global educator, global issues imply a host of concerns. This is reflected in the case of the *Institute for Global Communications*. With four of the major issues for global educators, the Web site is dedicated to education and action through links with *PeaceNet*, *EcoNet*, *ConflictNet*, *LaborNet* and *WomensNet*.

> **Our Mission**: To expand and inspire movements for peace, economic and social justice, human rights, and environmental sustainability around the world by providing and developing accessible computer networking tools. IGC Special Projects include: The EcoJustice Network, Asian Community Online Network, African-American Networking, and The JusticeNet Prison Issues Desk.

With its focus on the environment, justice, women, peace and conflict resolution, the IGC provides the networking for action and the "five online communities of activists and organizations are gateways to articles, headlines, features, and Web links on progressive issues." IGC's PeaceNet encourages people to "dial locally, act globally" to collaborate on peace issues and is "the best-known and most efficiently coordinated computer effort for peace and protection of the environment" (LaQuey & Ryer, 1993, p.13). The LaborNet is "a community of labour unions, activists, and organizations using computer networks for information-sharing and collaboration with the intent of increasing the human rights and economic justice of workers." The site "seeks to increase awareness among the U.S. labour movement of the different computer networks available to them, and to assist them in coming online through training and technical assistance." The IGC for example, takes up activism for what it believes is the right cause, as is seen in its Web page footer: *"NetAction: Don't be soft on Microsoft! Join the Consumer Choice Campaign."*

The fight for human rights may take specific issues of concern that may emphasize women, children, aboriginal, religion, race, ethnicity, political affiliation, or geographical region in turmoil or repression. While it is understandable that fight for human rights is possible in countries that recognize democratic processes, struggle for freedom, and freedom of expression, many countries in the Middle East have remained private property of Sheiks, Sultans, Emirs, Kings and other forms of monarchies and do not tolerate dissension. Some countries have elapsed into religious fundamentalism with the state usurped by extreme ideologies as seen in Afghanistan, Indonesia, Iran, Yemen, Somalia, and to some extent, in Pakistan. Reacting to such changes and the ensuing human rights violation, exiles and their overseas supporters have established many initiatives to fight oppression. *Human Rights in Iran,* "a net-based community of individuals committed to campaigning for the improvement of human rights in Iran," deals with human rights violations and reports of actual stories and incidents of child abuse, capital punishment, abuse of women, and abuse of writers including journalists. One way of making the site interactive was to provide venues to post information, write to people, and communicate with other human rights sites. It is only through some level of direct intervention and dissemination of information on atrocities committed can a perpetrator be forewarned of eventual consequences besides encouraging the citizens to continue their struggle for human rights. The following excerpt highlights a number of human rights violations:

F. Mossayebi- IHRWG
(IHRWG) is a net-based community of individuals committed to campaigning for the improvement of human rights in Iran. IHRWG's aims and objectives are contained in its general irhwg charter which also sets out the structure of the group and the domain of its activities. The group has no political agenda, and makes no judgment on the legitimacy of the authorities in dealing with them, nor does it takes the religious or political beliefs or personal attributes of individuals into consideration when it defends their human rights. The group is run by a eight-member Steering Committee elected from amongst the membership for a term of one year.
IHRWG'S APPEALS, PRESS RELEASES, & CURRENT CASES: Click on the highlighted or underlined text to see the content of the document.
Defend The Rights of Iranian Children (Released: September 23rd, 1995)
Defend The Rights of Iranian Women (Released: September 6th, 1995)
Defend The Rights of Iranian Women (in Persian)
STOP STONING TO DEATH ! (Released: July 31st, 1995)
Urgent appeal for stopping the execution of political prisoners (Released: June 21st, 1995)
Defend The Rights of Iranian Workers! (Released: May 1st, 1995)

Please stop punishing the victims... letter to Sen D'Amato (Released: April 12th, 1995)
In support of 134 writers (Released December 19th, 1994)
In support of 134 writers (in Persian)
Call for investigation on the death of Mr. Saidi Sirjani (Released: December 1st, 1994)
Saidi Sirjani (Released: July 25th, 1994) [sic]

The *Human Rights in Iran*, not unlike other human rights sites hosted by *Amnesty International*, derives momentum and support from letter-writing campaigns. The importance of letter-writing campaigns is emphasized by a number of activists. For example, Professor Edmundo Garcia, a special envoy of International Alert and a resistance leader under the Marcos regime in the Philippines, described the importance of letters of support from the international community outside the country. Addressing high school students in Victoria, Canada, Garcia described his struggle for democracy during his imprisonment in the Philippines. Suggesting two ways of student involvement in preventing wars, Garcia noted that:

> [it] might be very helpful if students wrote to young people in countries at high risk of war, in order to build a network of youth supporting non-violent conflict resolution... They should write, not to tell others how to solve their problems, but rather to say that they, as young people, believed that youth of the world must come up with new ways to resolve conflict without to resorting to war, and to ask what initiatives were being [pursued] by youth in [the war torn country] that could be supported from outside the country [sic]. (Ashford, 1996, p. 179)

Perhaps the most well organized and famous international organization engaged in human rights monitoring and advocacy is the *Amnesty International*. Being an "independent worldwide human rights movement working impartially for the release of all prisoners of conscience, fair and prompt trials for political prisoners, and an end to torture and executions," *Amnesty International* continues to make its presence felt, not only in the countries of oppression but now also on the Internet. With actual pictures and stories of struggling people, the *Amnesty Gallery* is a powerful venue for the distribution of events, episodes, policies, and other important activities to people across the globe.

Child labour has always remained an issue for human rights advocates and bonded labour has been identified as another form of modern slavery. With children being used as cheap and forced labour, crime and prostitution thrive among innocent children. Fighting this menace is the *International Child Labour Study Office* created in 1993 in response to US Congressional mandates. Focusing on the apparel industry, prostitution, and other such sectors, the ILO program aims at the elimination of Child Labour[35]. By focusing on the perpetrating countries and the support they have from the US and other governments in the industrialized countries, some pressure and ongoing restrictions may have had some results. Yet, history has shown that the United States and Canada have conveniently ignored human rights violations in India, China, Indonesia, and the Middle East during trade agreement negotiations. In fact, China remains the "most favoured partner" and enjoys preferred treatment with low trade tariffs. It is imperative that we also differentiate legitimate child labour from illegal or unjust enslavement. Contributing to the family labour force through child agricultural labour has been a part of many agrarian societies and it could be undistinguishing to criticize a legitimate and perhaps, a necessary way of life. One must differentiate between appropriation of cheap labour in industries owned and operated by capitalists and agricultural labour force that is a traditional way of life. The definition of a "child" is also an issue that cannot be ignored. Definitely, a non-economic actor, a middle-class Canadian/ American/ European child with no economic responsibilities is not the same as a family of many children subject

---

[35] At first it produced two major reports on international child labour. The first report, "By the Sweat and Toil of Children: The Use of Child Labour in American Imports," published in September 1994, reviewed the countries and industries that export to the United States products produced by child labour. The second report, "By the Sweat and Toil of Children: The Use of Child Labor in U.S. Agricultural Imports & Forced and Bonded Child Labor," released in 1995, examined children working to produce agricultural products exported to the United States and children working under forced labour conditions, such as bonded (or slave) labour and forced prostitution.

to the economic and cultural roles. The US Congressional mandate ignores this aspect of developing countries and is another example of Western interpretations of how "labour" should be defined. A critical global educator would raise issue to statements and descriptions that do not highlight our own cultural biases in our understanding and analysis of peoples and histories different from ours.

On the one hand, governments have been hesitant to link international trade with human rights; on the other, federal and provincial departments have been established to deal with human rights violations that are alleged to occur within the country. The *Alberta Human Rights Commission*, the official home of the provincial government's department of Community Development under the main body, Human Rights, Citizenship & Multiculturalism, offers information on human rights, multiculturalism, women's issues and employment equity. With Fact Sheets, information on various forms of discrimination and harassment, the Department offers publication containing various reports. The available information makes it possible for people to understand the process and lodge formal complaints with the Commission. Whether it is discrimination due to being an aboriginal, visible minority, physically or mentally challenged, or being a woman, the Department established procedures allow recourse to the victim. Similar bodies exist in every province of Canada; these provincial bodies work in close cooperation with the federal human rights wing, the *Canadian Human Rights Commission*. It is essential to remember that the lack of political neutrality and autonomy of human rights commissions makes them powerless enough not to challenge government structures. For instance, the Alberta government has refused to heed recommendations by the *Human Rights Commission*. Thus, global education pedagogy needs to highlight issues of neutrality among bodies and Web sites representing government initiatives that may supposedly be construed as objective and powerful.

Besides the government undertaking for equality, justice and fairness, women's groups also have initiatives that are more international and pro-active as seen at the *Feminist com Activism*. With issues that include family life, social world, activism, email messages to political leaders, conference proceedings, alerts and warnings, laws and bills, human rights and education, and political debates, the *Feminist com Activism* is a powerful link to and for women, especially in countries where women do not have the freedom and support to fight for their rights. The Monthly Updates; Outrage of the Month; Call for Action; Equality Now Action Alerts; email the President; Conferences; voting; campaigns; contacting the Congress, government departments and ministers; and using The Electronic Activist to deal with issues are all powerful resources for women and men who believe in justice and equality.

When international human rights bodies for women do not meet the individual needs of some groups of women in unique problems and limitations, more culturally relevant and appropriate initiatives offer stronger support to the cause of women in such countries. The *PACAWOM*[36], committed to the advancement of women in Pakistan, is an endeavour by an international group of individuals. Issues for discussion have included problems of Pakistani women and helping women's organization in Pakistan. Realizing the power to fight from outside the country, the hosts note, "Living abroad, we are in unique position to assist these organizations. We believe that if we work together we can make a difference." With topics such as *Profile of the Pakistani Woman, Political Struggle for Rights, Some poems by Pakistani Women Poets, Stories of Rape*, and *Reports on Status of Women in Pakistan*, the *PACAWOM* has some powerful writings that will touch and encourage all lovers of freedom.

---

[36] Despite the name of Pakistan in its title, *PACAWOM* deals with issues affecting women from all around the world and especially from Asia and the Far East region.

No nation can rise to the height of glory unless your women are side by side with you. We are victims of evil customs. It is a crime against humanity that our women are shut up within the four walls of the houses as prisoners. There is no sanction anywhere for the deplorable conditions in which our women have to live. You should take your women along with you as comrades in every sphere of life. Founder of Pakistan, Quid-e-Azam Muhammad Ali Jinnah, speaking at a meeting held at the Muslim University Aligarh on March 10, 1944.

The journey of my life

begins with home,

ends at the graveyard.

My life is spent like a corpse,

carried on the shoulders

of my father and brother,

husband and son.

Bathed in religion,

attired in customs,

and buried in a grave

of ignorance.

from Goodwin, Jan: "Price of Honor," Little Brown and Company, NY, 1994.

One of the authors was able to contact the hosts at the University of Calgary who were delighted to discuss the implications of issues posted at the Web site. In having to offer information and insights into women's rights, violence against women including *War Against Rape in Pakistan*, planned parenthood, women's health, empowerment of women, formal proceedings of conferences on women and call for action are only some of the many activities *PACAWOM* deals with. Lived experiences of women who survived the trauma of violence constitute some of the most insightful and most touching narratives at the *Profile of Pakistani Women*. The following excerpt (edited at length for space), is taken from the

"Women of Pakistan: two steps forward one step backward" by Khawar Mumtaz and Fareeda Shaheed[37]:

> It is impossible to describe that composite of various averages, the Pakistani woman, for the simple reason that like all other stereotypical 'the's' which pass for reality, she does not exist. In Pakistan as in other Third world countries it is perhaps even more difficult to identify the average woman than in the industrialized countries because the uneven penetration of firstly colonial rule, and subsequently, capitalist mode of production, have meant that a Pakistani woman's life can have remained petrified for centuries, or have been radically altered by the cataclysmic events of her people's history. Depending on her geographical location a Pakistani woman can find herself in a tribal, feudal or urban environment. She can be a highly qualified and self-confident professional, or self-effecting peasant toiling alongside her men folk; she can lead a cloistered life cut from all decisions and information in the urban lower-middle class ghettos of respectability or in the wide expense of nomadic regions, or she can be a central figure of authority in the limited circle of influential women in government and business circles. There are large regional and class variations in the role of a Pakistani woman... [sic]

> ...An indiscreet word with with a member of the opposite sex to whom one is neither married nor betrothed, for instance, can result in severe punishment. A woman has no say in any aspect of her life, including her own marriage, and once betrothed, belongs exclusively to her husband's family. To all extents and purposes she is an alienable property, and once the bride-price has been paid, she cannot be returned, whether in a state of divorce, separation or widowed. These women are invisible, not just allegorically, in that they have no voice and are ignored by statisticians and scholars alike, but literally one rarely sees a girl of over six or seven years old either in the countryside or in the urban centers...

> ...From this class hail many women who have worked their way up into the upper echelons of government, who have become doctors, scientists, chartered accountants, who have risen to the position of deans and heads of trade unions, who run their own businesses and who have entered the field of politics. Like their counterparts in the industrialized world these women have broken new ground and entered exclusively male domains...

---

[37] Zed Press, London, 1987. Also refer Sabeeha Hafeez: "Metropolitan Women in Pakistan: Studies," Renaissance Publishing House, Delhi, 1990 [1st published 1981].

205

...Most of these women bear the double burden of housework and outside work. Consequently, they are first to rise and the last to sleep. They must light the fire, prepare breakfast, have the dishes washed and the house cleaned before setting out on their 'working' day. After everyone else has collapsed in bed, these women are still cleaning, clearing and preparing for the following day. Not only do these women have longer days than the rest of the family, but being the last to eat, they eat less well and suffer from anaemia and malnutrition. Sandwiched between these 'extremes' are the small-town and middle class urban women whose numbers have grown in recent years. These women come close to what could be called an average Pakistani woman. They truly represent the clashes and paradoxes of Pakistani society. In some ways they have the best and in others the worst of both worlds. They are encouraged to pursue higher education but discouraged from entering into careers. Some of them attain some level of financial independence but are not free from patriarchal social customs...

As stories on women's lives in many countries makes mirthless reading, embedded in these anecdotes are flagrant violations of human rights.

According to Roman (1993), the Western feminists or the "first-world women" have represented the "third world women as *passive victims* or romanticized, exotic `others'... resulting in binary oppositions" which some note as "Western cultural imperialism within feminist scholarship." Refuting the argument that the subaltern cannot speak, Roman suggests that we examine whether "privileged (European and North American) white groups are willing to listen when the subaltern speaks" (pp. 76, 79). Recently, there has been an argument for shifting from *identity politics* pertaining to the reduction of public issues of women's movement to individual identities competing among hierarchies of oppression" to *coalition politics* that shares common concerns among differentially oppressed groups (Roman, 1993, p. 76). Roman advises that, "Instead of focusing our attentions almost exclusively upon racially oppressed groups of women and men as either heroic icons or victims of racist practices and

206

structures, we need to study the enactment of power and ideologies in a relational way" (p. 78).

But does the move to coalition politics suppress or distort voices and stories that are "heroic and victimized"? Perhaps it is so that the *Human Rights Global Report* engages in an ongoing initiative on revealing and representing the ones who have no recourse for redress. According to investigations by the *Human Rights Watch* in some countries women are:

> held in custody or detention are deprived of more than just their liberty; they also have their physical security and dignity violated by male jailers who torture and degrade them. Such abuses rape, sexual assault, beatings, abusive strip searches, and the use of degrading language by guards toward women prisoners are facilitated by the power of male guards over women prisoners and by official tolerance of such abuses of authority.

> In any given year, thousands of women and girls around the world are lured, abducted or sold into forced prostitution and involuntary marriage. In countries where Human Rights Watch has investigated trafficking Burma, Thailand, Nepal, India, Bangladesh, Pakistan we have found that police officers and other government officials facilitate and profit from the trade in women and girls. For a price, they ignore abuses that occur in their jurisdictions; protect the traffickers, brothel owners, pimps clients and buyers from arrest; and serve as enforcers, drivers and recruiters.

> Human Rights Watch investigations in Kuwait and Russia document violence against women workers that includes rape and other forms of sexual assault beating, kicking, slapping and burning. In Russia and Poland, we have documented how public and private sector employers fire women in disproportionate numbers and refuse to hire female employees because they prefer to employ men. Although discrimination on the grounds of sex or maternity is prohibited under international human rights laws and barred by the domestic laws of most countries, it is nonetheless routinely tolerated by many governments.

> Domestic violence is one of the leading causes of female injuries in almost every country in the world. Human Rights Watch investigations in Brazil, Russia and South Africa show that law enforcement officials allow such violence to go uninvestigated and unpunished. At every turn, women who attempt to obtain legal protection for domestic assault are turned away, told that their problem is a "private" matter. Laws exempt marital rape from criminal sanction; police refuse to arrest men who beat their wives; prosecutors fail to charge men with domestic assault; and judges accept "honor" defenses that allow wife-murderers to walk away unpunished.

> States frequently use violent and discriminatory means to carry out policies that regulate women's sexual and reproductive lives. In Turkey, police, state doctors and school authorities have forced women and girls to undergo gynecological tests to check women's hymens when they are accused of "immodest" behavior. In Ireland the government restricted the right to free expression in its efforts to suppress information on abortion

services abroad. Polish women are denied equal protection of the law when the state fails to stop doctors and prosecutors from refusing to provide women the necessary documentation to obtain an abortion within the limits of that country's 1993 abortion law. When these abuses are committed in the name of tradition, culture or religion, the international community has been particularly timid about raising protests, making a mockery of the fundamental principle of the universality of human rights. (September 3, 1995 *Human Watch Global Report on Women's Human Rights*)

As Toh & Floresca-Cawagas (1990) observe, "A wealth of evidence has now emerged to confirm the structural inequities and sexist/patriarchal domination suffered by billions of women globally. As the well-known statistics indicate, women are `half the world's people; do two-thirds of the world's working hours; receive one-tenth of the world's income; and own only one-hundredth of the world's property'" (p.153). Implicating the seemingly innocuous bulwarks assumed to protect women and the marginalized, Toh and Floresca-Cawagas note that, "Culturally, the weight of patriarchal traditions including those embedded in religious/ spiritual institutions and structures, have also been a major factor underpinning the injustices and peacelessness suffered by women worldwide" (pp.153-154).

If protection of human rights and strengthening of democracy is our intent, the international body of *The Global Democracy Network*, comprising of 1,000 Members of Parliament in 119 countries offers under the Parliamentary Human Rights Foundation (PHRF) initiative offers a host of information. Aimed to better "utilize modern communications technologies—especially computer networks— as tools to assist democratic institutions and to provide the Internet community with a source of information related to human rights and democracy," the network provides human rights reports, multilateral documents, U.S. State Department documents, Report on Israeli Settlement in the Occupied Territories, Rethinking Bretton Woods, Law, and Media. More importantly, the option to get in touch with the respective departments through email offers a new level of communication without the conventional barriers of cost, distance, lack of privacy and access, and dangers of crossing traditional boundaries in some countries. In using technology to go beyond mere communication, a powerful tool is made available for activists who may have the added advantage of advice from supporters overseas. In offering access to documents pertaining to law, governments, projects and commissions, people searching for information on historical precedence relating to issues relating to human rights may benefit enormously. According to the GDN mission, "The Global Democracy Network is bringing the tools of the 1990s, computers and communications, to finish the job of strengthening democracy and empowering the individual to become a talisman of freedom. Thus, the promise of the Information Superhighway will be realized for all peoples of the world." If distributing specific information on human rights violations around the world and also presenting official or government policy documents for analysis can encourage activists to strategize and act, the GDN mandate is put to good use.

Within the rubric of human rights and struggle for democracy is one group of largely marginalized and ignored people excluded in the communal discourse of antiracism initiatives. Relegated to the periphery are the various indigenous peoples in India, the Philippines, Canada, United States, Australia and other countries who have remained excluded from the equation of rights and justice. Lost in the melee are the voices of people from what some call the "Fourth World." In their struggle for rights, the unheard autochthonous people have had to assert their own initiatives. Asking challenging questions about history, development and justice for indigenous peoples is only a part of the Australian aborigines and their ongoing plight with issues of oppression and racial discrimination— an approach evident at *Action for Aboriginal Rights*:

Action for Aboriginal Rights PO Box 300, Malvern, 3144, Victoria, Australia.

"If you have come here to help me, you are wasting your time..... But if you have come because your liberation is bound up with mine, then let us work together." [Lilla Watson, A Brisbane based Aboriginal educator and activist].

These pages are designed for students(and other searchers) looking for information on current Australian Indigenous issues. The views collected and presented on this page are collected by Action FOR Aboriginal Rights.

Face the Facts: Questions and Answers About Aboriginal People and Torres Strait Islanders

Produced by the Federal Race Discrimination Commissioner 1997 in response to the "One Nation" agenda.

Reconciliation: what is it? If reconciliation is to mean repairing the past, then we (white Australia) aren't taking it very seriously.

We should: • Give back the giveable - such as available land; • Restore the restorable - such culture and language centres; • And then, when we have given back the giveable and restored the restorable, we can give money as reparation and restitution. This will not revive the dead or relieve past pain, but it will do some real good in the present and future. [Quoted from Colin Tatz's speech, Reconciliation Week, Sydney].

Want to DO Something? Who to write to.. For a list of addresses: to make your opinion heard, and to give your support .

Active Action: for info about actions you can take, including demonstrations, and groups you can join...

LINKS for our list of indigenous, Australian websites, General, Media, Native Title Documents, and World Indigenous links.

Explanatory article on extinguishment and why it shouldn't happen.

Press references : Where to find recent articles on Indigenous issues, from Australian newspaper websites.

Perhaps, the notion of helping or even sharing the struggle for liberation may be less appropriate than becoming aware of the issues important to the aboriginal cause. The genuine desire to better understand the things, which may be of value to the struggle as knowledge, may be far more ethical and appropriate than the condescending approach to "lending a helping hand" to the ones who need to be "empowered." In dealing with aboriginal land rights, race culture, politics, and other such issues affecting the Australian aboriginal people, similar indigenous groups around the world may benefit from the lessons learnt in Australia. Other similar initiatives include information on North American indigenous people at *First People's Homepage* at SchoolNet, the *NativeWeb Homepage, The Electronic Store, Settlers in Support of Indigenous Sovereignty, Yukon Native Language Centre, Cultural Survival, Centre for Study of Indigenous Peoples,*

World Conference on Indigenous Peoples, The Village: Indigenous Knowledge and *Aboriginal Literacy Foundation.*

It is true that aboriginal peoples share some of the human rights issues with other marginalized people around the world. While the concerns are very similar, many aboriginal struggles are linked to immediate issues such as logging, deforestation, displacement, land treaties, property encroachment, self-government & autonomy, and the right to natural resources (fishing, hunting, and agriculture). Non-aboriginal concerns usually surround issues like xenophobic attacks, immigration policies, refugee status, and employment equity. Discrimination, prejudice, and stereotyping remain common concerns between the aboriginal peoples and other marginalized groups (visible minorities, women, and low socioeconomic migrants).

Reflecting the multi-disciplinary nature of human rights, a multi-pronged analytical approach with debates and discussions at the international level may have far more implications for developing a public education initiative on issues of cultural imperialism. Perhaps these discourses may include issues relevant to ethics, relationship between the international organizations and the developing world, politics and education, and international aid and health care as seen at *Intellectual Capital*. Literature (books) and more formal writings (reports) offer venues for such analysis.

Volume 2 Issue 12 March 20-26, 1997
Public Forums, discussions, updates, commentaries, etc Speak Out!; Education and Policies; Schools and Technology; Educational Reform; Education and American Politics; Moral and Ethical Issues; International Politics; UN and the developing world; Medical Ethics; Economics; and Book Reviews.

A report on what effect the Internet will have on education; Charts & Graphs: Federal Financing & SAT Scores; Polling Place: Does Clinton Have the Answer?; A Political Pop Quiz; Nadine Strossen urges less propaganda in the late-term abortion debate; Anarchy in Albania; In John Fund's opinion, it's time for the United Nations to deal with Albania, before it's too late; Cloning the USA in Europe; Peter Jay questions whether it is in the

United States' best interests to promote a strong European Union; Report from the
Supreme Court; Cyber Report: Was It a Decent Argument?; Coverage of the Supreme
Court arguments on the Communications Decency Act; IC Interview: Finances, Finances,
Finances; Remnick: Book Review: Dave Johnson reviews Resurrection: The Struggle For
a New Russia, the new book by David Remnick; IC Book Forum. Visit the Forum to
discuss the public policy and political books that you are read.

While it is not obvious in the above, some of the readings suggest that one must

beware of the usually critical but quite conservative and rightwing ideas offered in

these articles that are mostly from an American emphasis and viewpoint. Albeit,

opportunities exist on the Internet for a body of any political persuasion to submit

its ideology for mass consumption— along with the expectation that we read them

with critical objectivity. It is for this reason perhaps that the *New Internationalist*

and *North-South Institute* offer their own understandings and interpretations of

international relations and human rights violations.

7.7. Racism and Anti-Racism

Not unlike groups of activists having established their presence on the Net

for the common good, so have groups that prescribe extremism in terms of

violence, hate, and crime. This in turn has demanded some control over what can

be posted on the Internet. As one of the first groups dealing with the substantive

issues relating to the Internet, *Computing Professionals for Social Responsibility*

(CPSR), does not have any control over what is available on the Net but deals

with the social, physiological, legal, educational, political and economic

implications of technology. While the *CPSR* has assumed the responsibility of

some ethical issues on the Net, it does not have the authority or the jurisdiction on

issues of censorship, hate groups, sex and crime on the Information

Superhighway. Sex, crime and racism have very close connection in that they thrive on violence and hatred. Having discussed the menace of pornography elsewhere, I shall now focus on hate groups on the Internet[38].

A number of strategies have been used by hate groups to legitimize their presence on the Net. Using the pretexts of victimization, historical injustices, eugenics, theories, literature, politics, religion, pseudo-scientific explanations, personal "experiences," music, art, and a host of other such arguments, hate groups present their beliefs to their readers in an attractive and palatable package. One of the most powerful arguments used by these groups is the notion of freedom of expression and the right to "defend their race." Mixed with a potion of seemingly rational arguments and misconceptions, the hate groups provide an incendiary mix of emotions to instigate or influence an unsuspecting novice.

While most hate-related initiatives are white against non-whites, the *Black Panther* is a good example of a hate page managed by the blacks. In almost all cases, Anti-Semitism remains a major component of hate sites. The Anti-Defamation League Annual Report on CNN Online (1996), reports that, "the cyberspace is giving old-fashioned bigotry a new lease on life.. [and that] push-button prejudice is thriving" on the information superhighway. This is true with the proliferation of unmediated Web sites immune to local laws. Thus, hate groups like the *Ku Klux Klan* (*KKK*) have begun to use the technology quite effectively to spread their beliefs. With its mission statement, "To be born White

---

[38] Finding a pornographic site on the Internet involved only one step: using a search engine and entering the word S-E-X. Hate sites were relatively more specific in terms of their search words: Aryan, Skinheads, KKK, Zundel, Aryan Nations, Hitler, etc. While pornography was far much easier to find with just three letters, entering the site required payment. In some cases, the site just did not exist. In contrast, once a hate site was found, hundreds of related sites could be reached through hypertext links. Thus, hate sites remained far easier to access but more difficult to find while pornographic sites were easier to find but difficult to enter.

is an honor and a privilege," reflecting the sentiment behind the group's philosophy, the intent of the *KKK* is quite clear in the graphic preamble:

> End the Invisible Agenda to Destroy the White Race. The world's oldest, largest, and most professional Whites' civil rights Organization. Thank you for stopping by the Knights of the Ku Klux Klan's World Wide Web page.

> As this page has been censored multiple times, it is difficult to ascertain how many people have actually stopped by. The page started a year ago on geocities. The left wing terrorists (ADL, Simon Weisanthal Center, SPLC) wasted no time in putting together a hate campaign to have it removed. These enemies of free speech were successful in having it pulled from www.geocities.com. The page then migrated to www.usawatch.com. Again, the left wing terrorists had it pulled. Now the page has come to rest at this ISP who says, "the content is unregulated." They also have the blue ribbon for "free speech" right on their web page. Well folks, they talk the talk so we'll see if they will walk the walk. Only time will tell if this ISP is really committed to free speech. If you have a probelm with the page, you are encouraged to complain because your opinion does not matter anyway. The Knights of the Ku Klux Klan are bringing a message of hope and salvation to White Christian's of the world. Our Imperial Council is comprised of the finest White men in America. The Knights of the Ku Klux Klan are the direct descendant of Mr. David Duke's Klan. Beware of imposters... [unedited for spelling & grammar]

Claiming to be a non-profit and religious organization, the KKK seeks the protection and freedom to operate as a hate group. Interestingly enough, the *Simon Wiesenthal Center* is considered as "left wing terrorists" and their rights campaign is noted as "hate campaign." Most of the hate groups demand the right to disseminate hate and propaganda under the freedom of expression. Political figures like David Duke remain at large without being prosecuted only because of the lax freedom and rights in the United States; not to mention a very strong underground support of racists and ultra right wing groups in America. And it is even scary to realize that during the Louisiana governorship in 1991, David Duke garnered 55% of the white vote (Pinar, 1993; Roman, 1993).

There is a clandestine specialty segment in the music industry catering to hate crimes. Three men associated with hate music (Resistance Records, a white supremacist group based in the United States) were arrested in Toronto (The Canadian Press, 1997e). In this case, the long arm of the law does appear to have jurisdiction beyond boundaries when conventional products are in question while law enforcement may be more difficult in case of hate sites based in another country. Diamond (1997) notes that, "Even if Canada adopts stringent laws concerning the Net, what do we do if the bigot lives in California or Belgium?" This is exactly what has happened with the *Zundelsite*, a typical hate page with all the trappings of credibility. Very anti-Semitic and intent on disseminating holocaust denial articles, Ernst Zundel alleges a hidden agenda at the government levels. Security, politics, history, and propaganda are the main ingredients of this site. The focus is on re-writing history and proceeding to deny Holocaust, as we all understand. The appeal is for freedom of speech to be anti-Semitic.

> The Zundelsite:"Did Six Million Really Die?"
> "In a Struggle to Free Us from the Lie of the Century! "
> Ernst ZŸndel: "I am no gun-toting warrior! I am a militant pacifist!"
> Ernst ZŸndel takes on the Canadian Spy Establishment in "CSIS Exposed!" and "SIRC Exposed!"
> The ZŸndelsite / Nizkor "Holocaust Rebuttal": The Page You Do Not Want To Miss!
> Now you have a choice. We do not recruit; we convince. Truth has no need of coercion. We invite your support and submissions. If you approve of our outreach on behalf of truth in history and can afford to help us, please send your donation.
>
> Given the repressive Canadian government that penalizes free expression of politically incorrect ideas and opinions as "hate crime" at the behest of special interest groups, I need to claim protection. With precedents set guaranteeing free speech, I am posting the article below:
>
> Mission Statement: The ZŸndelsite has as its mission the rehabilitation of the honor and reputation of the German nation and people. Specifically, the ZŸndelsite challenges the traditional version of the "Holocaust" - an Allied propaganda tool concocted during World War II - that is not based on historical fact but is a cleverly used ploy to keep the German war time generation and their descendants in perpetual political, emotional, spiritual and financial bondage. The evidence and editorial comments placed on the pages of the ZŸndelsite do not argue that atrocities did not happen during World War II on all sides, or that some Jews caught up in the maelstrom of the largest war in history unfortunately died. When 75 million men on both sides are put into uniforms, trained with guns and bombs and given orders to kill each other, atrocities are bound to happen. They happened on both sides to soldiers and civilians. Many, many people died - of all nationalities. Millions died during the war, and many more millions died.
>
> For relentless Holocaust promotion, on the other hand, contact Nizkor. For another Jewish point of view, contact the Simon Wiesenthal Center (tm).

Amazingly enough, there are links to the *Nizkor Project* and the *Wiesenthal Center* Web Sites for "relentless Holocaust promotion" or "Jewish point of view."

The mission statement is accompanied by a posting of disclaimer that partially reads, "given the repressive Canadian government that penalizes free expression of politically incorrect ideas and opinions..." to reflect the need for developing a victimization base for positioning as the oppressed. Gary Prideaux, a University of Alberta linguistic professor has become a witness for the Canadian Human Rights tribunal in an attempt—first of its kind in history, to remove hate sites available to individuals accessing the Internet in Canada (Tobin, 1997, B6). Of course, Zundel's lawyer has challenged the Commission's rights and jurisdiction on his client's rights to freedom of speech (Wattie, 1997, A3).

The issue of censorship on the one hand and the right to freedom of expression has become one of the most contentious issues relating to the Internet. This is especially true among journalists who fear for their rights to news autonomy. The Editorial in the local daily commented:

> There is no greater challenge to free speech in our country than Ernst Zundel. Oh, how tempting it is to try to stomp on him and shut him up... [Zundel] is one of the most appalling men in Canada... The Internet is an anarchistic, international medium... [it is] a free space, for good or ill. It is awash in trash and bad information, which readers must challenge and reject. On the other hand, it brings information into repressive regimes like China... There are situations where the state may rightly limit a person's right to way hateful and wrong things... But to shut down an Internet site for the first time, as the Human Rights Commission is proposing to deal with Zundel, is not acceptable in a country where free expression has constitutional guarantees. (Editorials, TEJ, 1996)

Despite Zundel being a Canadian resident, his site is posted by an admirer in the United States, which in turn is mirrored in a number of other countries. This again highlights the international nature of the Internet. For example, *Skinhead Graphics,* another hate site contains hundreds of offensive pictures that are extremely disturbing and violent. The site has been banned in Germany and Canada but remains accessible to anyone. Vulgar, cheap, hateful, crude and offensive, the site can be viewed in its entirety. Between November 20, 1995 and March 6, 1996 (the day this site was accessed for this study) there were 19227 visitors at this Web site. The site had posted pictures posted of Skinheads attacking Chinese and a group of aboriginal women as a part of a poster-naming competition where the most offensive title would win the prize. *Be Wise as Serpents,* another hate site with literature, graphics, cartoons & publications from Zundel's Publishing house SAMISDAT, remains beyond the arm of the law by mirroring the site in different countries. This simply proves that Internet censorship, unlike censorship of television, radio and newspapers, may not work. Yet, some Internet Service Providers have attempted in vain to clamp down on hate sites as in the case of its infamous subscriber *Stormfront.* Having begun to feel the heat of Internet Service Providers on them, the *Stormfront White Nationalist Resource Page* has a footnote at its site claiming discrimination. With its theme, "White Pride Worldwide" the site is dedicated to being anti-colored and anti-Semitic. As most such hate sites can only exist either as political or religious bodies, the *Stormfront* is highly political and crude with diverse collections of pro-Buchanan and Vladimir Zhirinowsky writings or activities. Some of the contents include David Duke's racist "journalist's travelogue observations" on his visit to India; ranting on anti-censorship; "history" of white race, Boer resistance in South Africa; "definition" of racism and other such topics.

Stormfront was the first White Nationalist site on the Web, going online in March 1995. It was followed shortly by Reuben Logsdon's "Cyberhate." This precipitated an organized hate campaign by the Simon Wiesenthal Center and similar groups to pressure our providers into yanking our accounts. Since then, despite the best efforts of Rabbi Cooper and Company to censor "objectionable" ideas, dozens of new sites have appeared. It's becoming difficult for me to keep up with all of them, but I'll try to keep this list updated with the most substantial of the new entries, along with any URL changes for the old ones.

Please don't ask me to link sites at BHI's Geocities. This company offers free web pages, but it's adopted a policy of censoring pro-White pages as soon as it finds them. Listing them here would only hasten that process. America Online also falls into this category.

My Indian Odyssey: Former Louisiana legislator and current U.S. Senate candidate David Duke describes his racial awakening in India.
What Is Racism?
The Conspiracy to Erect an Electronic Iron Curtain
Louis Beam on Internet censorship.
History of the White Race

217

As more and more Internet Service Providers begin to censor anti-social Web sites, the online dissemination of hate literature begins to take heat. As we see above, America On-Line (AOL), a major provider seems to have taken some action to curtail hate literature on the Internet. Many of the items passed on, as "facts of history" remain propaganda material masquerading as research or factual records from "learned people." The links between hate sites are exhaustive, well established, extensive and very systematic. In fact, David Duke's article on India tries to pass off as an objective view of the country but contains statements full of hate, misinformation and rancour. Claiming legitimacy of knowledge by misrepresentation is not really unique to the Internet. Philippe Rushton has been earning his livelihood as a "scientific researcher" disseminating absurd information as fact in the print medium.

Quite common to many hate promulgators is the use of offensive and vulgar language. This is perhaps not only to intimidate and shock people but also to entreat for the support of a like-minded group of youth. Complementing this rudeness is the presence of crude and distasteful pictures that are not of humanly acceptable behaviour. The preamble to some groups as in the case of *Skin Net* is quite obvious:

> Warning, this web page is not for the racially weak at heart. It is white power skinhead oriented. If this offends you **DO NOT ENTER**. This page contains material and or links to material that may offend some.

If hate has to be "bought" by gullible youth, it needs to be passed on as legitimate knowledge and must appear as a political struggle or resistance for democracy, survival, and the future of a given group or race. *Politically Incorrect* is an example of how topics at some hate sites are quite diverse and exhaustive. A considerable amount of material is passed on as legitimate knowledge and the ability to link factual history with propaganda is quite impressive. *Race and Rape* or the *Jewish Conspiracy* dwells on themes that try to discredit races by producing seemingly research knowledge. As expected, people who have already believed in the concept of racial superiority would support this cause. In keeping with its desire to appear legitimate and knowledgeable, topics at *Politically Incorrect* include, "Holocaust or Hoax?" "Race & Rape in America," "The Black War on White Americans!" "South Africa Rape Report," "Something Queer on Campus," "Race, Evolution & Behaviour," "Hate Crime Hoaxes in America," "Occupied America," "Immigration and American Identity," "The Truth Shall Get You Fired," "A Natural Law of Race Relations," "Kipling: The Wrath of the Awakened Saxon," and "Dysgenics." The accuracy, the source, the context and many other aspects of quotations remain questionable. Eugenics as a prop to explain genetic differences has remained the oldest crutch by pseudo-scientists even from evolutionists to genetic engineers. Whether racism, discrimination, knowledge, information or analysis, there is an impressive façade of academic front to all the trash that exists on the Internet. Unsurprisingly, racists like Rushton parading as academic researchers remain figures of admiration and source of information for the racist movement.

As many extremists believe, the promulgators of hate have strong positions of being persecuted and having been treated unjustly. Most such movements have strong historical and political precedence to building on its existence and legitimacy as a just cause for social justice. The attack on opponents of hate is diversified (radio, TV, literature, etc.) and the Internet provides a powerful venue for those seeking information on sources of hate and crime. Religion, as always, remains a crutch for hate and crime.

219

In this incendiary web of violent repository appear politics, violence, religion, crime and hate— all intrinsically linked with acts of cowardice and malice. There is an intense emotional involvement among hate-mongers, which may influence young minds to act inhumanly. An element of helplessness along with a challenge provides the cinder for unsuspecting minds to take arms against the imaginary oppressors. Unsurprisingly enough, Timothy McVeigh remains a hero to the hate groups. The "struggle" is linked with traditional Scriptures, in the following excerpt at the *The Watchman*:

Requiem for s Witch Doctor

Excerpt from the issue released after the Oklahoma City bombing. Revelations 18:21-24: "Thus with violence shall that great city Babylon be thrown down and shall be found no more at all...and in her was found the blood of prophets, and saints, and of all that were slain upon the earth. White man, this is your final call: there is nowhere else to run or hide. Either fight, die, or prepare to turn your daughters over to the mongrelized descendants of dusky two-legged beasts. The choice is yours.

There is a warrior-like appeal to battle call where new recruits are made to feel helpless, instigating them to take action to defend their rights. Hate groups use religious literature to justify illegal activities and resort to appeal through fine art, emblems and music. *Paintings of and by Hitler* is one such resource centre offering offensive insignias and other hate literature as is the *White Power Brainwash TV* that focuses on music and television as a medium of "propaganda by anti-White activists." Condemning whites dancing with blacks on MTV as anti-White propaganda, the *Brainwash TV* is dedicated to convincing young minds about the danger of integration.

Have you seen the hosts of these new MTV shows.... freaks like Kurt Loder who look like they are on their death beds dying of AIDS! Or how about that piece of trash Jenny McCarthy? And of course they have to have "correspondants" from around the world that almost always are non-whites.

Have you ever witnessed one of their so-called dance programs? Or how about their dating shows such as the current Singled Out? These shows are a barrage of beautiful white girls draped over niggers and other non-whites! Even the Mtv hosts are usually paired in black and whites. And have you ever seen these "Free your mind" segments and commercials? Now if you asked me, if Mtv was "truely" interested in having their viewers "Free their mind," then they would show an accurate and fair portrayal of all sides and views to allow them to make up their own mind. They always portray the minorites as the victims and the white race as the oppressor. The "Free your mind" programs always seem to paint a rediculous picture of our movement. What kind of message is being sent to our kids? If you think about these statements, whether you agree with my ideology or not - you should begin to question their motives.

I personally know alot of people who have banned their children from watching these programs, but I think the opposite should be done. I think the kids should be shown this outrageous behaviour - followed by family discussions. Mtv and the "Powers that be" have found a sure-fire way to brainwash the youth and this must be countered with positive pro-white programs. [**Unedited for spelling errors**].

As music is the bastion for reaching out to young minds, MTV is a main target of attack. The intent is to present anything non-White or `black' as uncultured, violent, and vulgar in racist language.

Karen Mock, National Director of the League for Human Rights of B'nai Brith Canada writes in her article *Hate and the Internet*:

The Problem of hate did not begin with the Internet; so although stamping out offensive sites would be an ideal solution, how feasible is it, if new ones will invariably appear to take their place? The best way to attack the problem is to offer an even stronger counterbalance. It is important to remember that just as hate can be transmitted over the Net, so can good education and positive messages of tolerance. (Mock, 1997, p.2)

In total agreement with Mock's suggestion, one can argue that hate can be counteracted with love and understanding through peaceful initiatives. If hate-mongers have achieved an organized presence on the Internet, so have the anti-hate movement with their no less-developed activities on the Internet. *Links to Extreme Nationalists* consists of a long list of hate groups as links, posted for information by anti-racist groups on the Internet. Why would one want a response to the hate groups and more importantly, why do we need hotlinks to such sites? Without the right and wrong aspect of the issue, resistance and contestation online is indicative of the human interactions through ages; it has just been extended into the technological phase in the development of an electronic or "virtual society."

221

In this battlefield of rights and wrongs, believers and detractors engage in verbal diatribes.

> People say that we should just ignore right-extremists, that we should give them no attention at all. Ignore them? And then what? Let them grow in peace? Some people also say that they grow in number because of the negative attention they get, but at the same time they fail to see the resistance that same attention provoke. I believe that people need to know what is going on, and they need to understand what threat these groups pose. I also believe that without a voice speaking against this menace, we'll end up in a far worse situation. Let us learn from the mistakes done by our fathers who fought for the freedom that we now dwell in. Extremism, no matter if it is right or left, is wrong and will not work in a real society - simply because there is no room for a different opinion under such a rule.

To some, allowing extremism and terrorism on the Net can not only nurture but also facilitate their existence. Unless resistance is established and hate stopped at the human level, perpetrators will assume the right to spread and continue their inhuman agenda. Rather than suppressing their voices through censorship, one might argue for a rational exposition of their follies, their beliefs, activities and implications. *Nazism Exposed-Fighting the Nazi Menace*[39] with its exposé on hate groups offers links and some insight into this aspect. This is the Webmaster voice:

> Nazism, fascism and extreme nationalism are today at the highest peak since the destruction of Hitler's dictatorship in 1945. Today, all over the world, fascists and extreme nationalists win millions of votes on their simple racist solutions to the very complex problems of the society. In the streets, Nazi boneheads are spreading fear by using murderous violence and terror. These fascist groups blame the cultural and ethnic minorities for the problems in our society. These individuals, and their political leaders, are a threat to our democracy, and to everything that is decent.

> This page was created to spread information about the activity of Nazi, fascists and extreme nationalists in Europe and on the Internet. It was created because it is my belief that these groups would only grow in number if they are left for themselves. We can no longer hide our head in the sand and pretend that they don't exist, and we can not accept that people are being murdered because their skin colour, culture, religion, appearance, sexuality, way of life or way of thinking are different. These extremist groups must be stopped!

---

[39] With links under different sections such as, Electoral, Political, Individual Groups, Organizations, Personal Pages, Magazines, News, and Music, from countries like Italy, Austria, Germany, Norway, Denmark, France, Finland, Sweden, Russia, and Belgium, this site is one of the most exhaustive link sites to hate groups.

> Many people have written email to me with support to this project, but there has also been some rather nasty letters sent to me. On this page you will find a collection of the worst ones, and you will also find some good [and bad] quotes here.
>
> Links to Extreme-Nationalists on the Net
>
> Organizations in Europe
>
> This is my on-growing list of Nazi, fascist and extreme-nationalist organizations, magazines and groups in Europe.

> Here's your opportunity to do something about fascism on the net. The Call For Votes [CFV] on rec.music.white-power has been sent out. Read all the instructions carefully before you send your 'no' vote.

In assuming an active role of exposing the Nazi propaganda, one concurs with the objectives of initiatives similar to the *Nizkor Project* or the *Simon Wiesenthal Center*. Electronic voting may be another rational method of voicing opinions about what should be freely allowed on the Internet. In the above call for votes, I was able to spread the information around and participate in the electronic voting. By raising awareness about hate groups and hate sites on the Internet, it not only warns the readers but also prepares them to respond and react to hate on the Net. For those educators who need such information for their classroom teaching, a number of resource sites exist including, *The Anti-Racism Resources Home Page* with its long list of anti-racism resources and links categorized by race and ethnic groups, the *Antifascist Web!* consisting of writings by Antifascists from Cyberspace (all over the world) along with innumerable links, and the *Hate on Net* with its long annotated list on hate groups on the World Wide Web.

Fighting against hate groups requires support and collaboration, not only among the average person but also among high profile individuals who are role models for the young. *Artists Against Racism,* run by a non-profit Canadian organization and geared toward youth, engages artists (painters, actors, musicians, poets, writers, etc.) to work towards prevention of racism through education. They

223

also engage in the dissemination of information, providing teacher resources, distributing letters, and discussing historical evidences. According to their theme, the organization "is a monumental, educational campaign for schools and communities across Canada and around the world (featuring posters, billboards, public service announcements and videos) where artists serve as role models for youth." Its mandate is *"Prevention through Education."* Attempting to "educate youth about racial tolerance in schools and communities around the world" over the Internet, the writers also provide pointers like, *Combatting Racist Incidents in Schools or Communities* and *Networking* (ie. "Links to other anti-racism groups who also report on racists so you can find out exactly what they're up to"). An initiative without the high profile artists is the *Crosspoint,* "Net's biggest collection of links in the field of Human Rights, Anti-Racism, Refugees, Women's rights, Antifascism etc..." that has links to other interesting and relevant sites including, *Indigenous Peoples Resources*, and *Jewish Resources.*

Of all the initiatives established to fight the Nazi menace on the Internet, it is *The Nizkor Project* that offers one of the most effective resistance ventures online; most hate groups love to hate the *Nizkor Project* with an intense passion. Countering racist groups and Holocaust deniers, arguments are made attacking each and every point offered in Zundel's position.

> We are often asked *Why do people deny the Holocaust?* The cynical truth comes to us by way of an obscure extremist group: "The real purpose of Holocaust revisionism is to make National Socialism an acceptable political alternative again." Nizkor is not a single collection of Web pages, but a collage of projects focused on the Holocaust and its denial, often incorrectly referred to as Holocaust "revisionism.". Nizkor's dedicated volunteers provide and maintain the following...
> Showcased collections of information about the Holocaust and its denial. Here you will find Nizkor's responses to the most frequently perpetrated denier myths regarding the Holocaust.
> Those who call themselves "revisionists" repeatedly pose such questions as "What proof exists that the Nazis practiced genocide or deliberately killed six million Jews?" - and their responses to such questions can be misleading. The 66 QAR feature provides factual refutation of these denier myths.

Nizkor is committed to maintaining a listing of other sites on the Internet which relate to the Holocaust.

In presenting actual survivors, their stories, pictures, and consequences of hate, *The Nizkor Project* is able to challenge the Holocaust deniers. *Nizkor* is a Hebrew word meaning, "We will remember." Ken McVay, the Director of *Nizkor Project* estimates that only about 150 individuals in Canada are actively engaged in posting hate propaganda on the Internet (Mock, 1997). Yet, it is a growing phenomenon, especially on the Internet due to its anonymity, legal immunity, non-accountability, lacking of monitoring and uncontrolled access. In keeping with the presentation of historical fact relating to the Holocaust, *The Museum of Tolerance*, based in Los Angeles offers voluminous evidential information. By raising issues of Holocaust, racism, and prejudice, the museum aims to raise awareness through education.

It also appears that *The Simon Wiesenthal Center*, as a non-profit foundation dedicated to the Holocaust survivors and human rights, has become a formidable opponent to the hate groups. Educating towards peace and understanding, the Centre remains a cause of extreme discomfort among hate groups. Believing in the power of technology, the Centre believes in the dissemination of information for subsequent action. As the header states: "The incredible power of the Internet is bringing about significant changes in the way people from around the world communicate with each other. It is the Simon Wiesenthal Center's goal to facilitate discussion about how these changes impact our society, especially with regard to the spread of anti-Semitism, racism and bigotry."

Similar to the game exploring issues relating to hate at the Alberta Human Rights Home Page, the *Simon Wiesenthal Center* has an online survey on "Hate on the Internet." More importantly, the Centre has mechanism for reporting incidents of hate by people wanting to give account of hate crimes using the established hotline, for allowing their staff to use these reports to continually monitor world-wide hate groups, and finally, planning effective strategies of action to deal with the hate-mongering. Amidst this spate of hate and resistance to hate, there appear incidents and stories of promise and hope. One of the most exciting features at the site is the *CyberWatch—On Alert!* with its renegades from the hate groups testifying and sharing their experiences with the online readers. "The Making of a Skinhead" at the *CyberWatch* site features one such experience:

> Thomas James (TJ) Leyden is a self-proclaimed former skinhead and a fifteen-year member of the neo-Nazi, White Supremacy Movement. Due to his recent and profound change of heart, Leyden abandoned the skinhead movement in an effort to redeem himself from the violence and hatred of his former lifestyle.

> In an unprecedented chain of events, TJ decided to contact the Simon Wiesenthal Center with his story. His biography presented below has been the subject of a recent feature in Time Magazine, NBC Evening News, and The Los Angeles Times. In addition to revealing the routine activities and beliefs of white supremacists, Leyden's story discloses the tactics neo-Nazis use to recruit new and young members. As TJ himself was once the target of skinhead recruitment, he now gives advice on how to recognize and avoid the groups' advances. Leyden's firsthand knowledge of the activities of neo-Nazis and hate groups provides the online community with an invaluable resource to combat their ominous message of hatred and intolerance.

It is stories like these that not only warn young people but also describe in detail the clandestine strategies employed by the hate groups to malign and spread misinformation and hate against different groups of people. It appears that in contrast to other anti-racist groups, sites with Jewish sensitivities have taken on the hate groups in a more organized, successful and effective way. As times have changed, to the consternation of the hate groups, even their hometowns that have in the past sprouted histories of hatred are changing for the better. A former Ku Klux Klan hotbed in Georgia has elected its first black mayor.

> STONE MOUNTAIN, Georgia (AP) -- By the light of a blazing cross, the Ku Klux Klan proclaimed its 20th century rebirth on the granite mountain that gives the town its name. For decades, white-hooded Klansmen flocked here for annual gatherings, and Confederate heroes are sculpted into the side of the

mountain. Today, the mayor's office once held by an imperial wizard of the Klan is about to be filled by a black man, who also lives in the former KKK leader's house. (CNN Online News, November 16, 1997)

Some experts argue that despite isolated cases we see above, the racial divide has only deepened in the 90's. Brian Aull and colleagues (1996, writing in their article posted at *Artists Against Racism*, note:

> In many ways the Black-white situation is worse today than in the 1960's. According to the 1988 Committee of Cities report (in the U.S), the polarization between these communities is much more pronounced now than in the 60's [as] "There is greater despair, less hope and less opportunity to escape from poverty and misery" among Blacks now than in the 60's. An underclass has emerged that is growing in size and anger. Cut off from the mainstream of America, it has created its own set of mores, laws, and economies, one of which - drugs - has caught the attention of the nation's leadership, because its poisonous tentacles are infecting the mainstream of the nation.

One recent case of hate crime through email at the University of California raised a number of issues relating to freedom of speech. According to authorities, the University surveillance video captured Richard Machado e-mailing 60 Asian-American students:

> "As you can see," the alleged message began, "I hate Asians, including you. I will hunt all of you down and kill you. I personally will make it my life career to find and kill every one of you personally." As a result, Machado, a newly naturalized U.S. citizen from El Salvador, is being prosecuted -- a case that raises questions about how far free speech can be taken in cyberspace. "If you threaten somebody's life in a way that a typical listener will think that you're serious, that's constitutionally unprotected," said Professor Eugene Volokh of the UCLA School of Law. But in court papers, Machado's attorney, who declined an interview for this story, argued that the federal law being used to prosecute his client is, in effect, criminalizing e-mail. (CNN Online News, November 9, 1997)

According to constitutional experts, excluding direct threat of violence, "The constitution protects all sorts of opinions, really bad ones as well as really good ones -- communist advocacy, Nazi advocacy, bigoted, racist, sexist material..."(CNN Online News, November 9, 1997). In Geneva, the United Nations sponsored a weeklong meeting of government officials, human rights activists, and Internet service providers from 148 countries to discuss international treaty banning racial discrimination.

Concerned at the growing use of the Internet for racist propaganda, international experts are debating how -- and whether -- to combat the spread of computerized hate messages. Binding global controls on the Internet are unlikely, officials said Tuesday, since the technology is changing faster than rules can be made, and because of free speech protection in the United States... It is widely agreed that the Internet offers an open platform for racists and white supremacists, although nothing has proved this leads to a related rise in racist incidents. Much of the problem stems from the United States, where groups such as the Ku Klux Klan, the Aryan Nations and skinheads base their Web sites. Under the U.S. Constitution, which guarantees free speech, these groups are permitted to post their views on the Internet, which can be accessed by people in other countries. (CNN Online News, November 11, 1997)

Despite such international proclamations, domestic racial conflicts in North America have not abated. In 1996, Texaco Oil Company in the United States was embroiled in a race related legal conflict involving senior management officials who had exhibited racist behaviour toward Afro-American employees. The issue began after the disclosure of secret tape recordings on which Texaco executives allegedly belittled black employees and plotted the destruction of evidence. After word of the tapes surfaced, Texaco was faced with a civil-rights boycott. An ongoing reader feedback at the CNN Interactive site ensued.

7.8. Struggles and Counter-Struggles[40]

The black response to white supremacist ideologies with degrading stereotypes and "assaults on black intelligence, ability, beauty, and character" was to fight for self-recognition by resisting the misrepresentation through re-presenting their visibility without the historical distortion (West, 1993, p. 17). Yet, West considers this process of "demystification" tends to become reductionism, in that it may assume one-factor analyses (crude Marxism, feminisms, racialisms, etc.) suggesting instead a "Critical Organic Catalyst"

---

[40] In cases where email and URL addresses of correspondents listed specific names, these have been deleted. Actual names have been changed to their initials. Pseudonyms remain unaltered.

228

involving "openness to others—including the mainstream" that maintains "group autonomy" rather than "group insularity."

The CNN Interactive Feedback posted unedited letters from subscribers and readers on the Texaco race issue. As expected, writers represented both sides of the debate.

CNN Interactive Feedback
You said it...

Tuesday, November 19, 1996 20/11/96 8:04:28 AM
TOPIC: *Jackson: Keep pressure on Texaco until culture changes*
Let me begin by saying that the Texaco executives were wrong for what they said. I will boycott Texaco, but not for the reasons that the Rev. Jackson thinks tha everyone should. No, I'm going to boycott Texaco because of reverse discrimination! Mr. Jackson, you are doing nothing but hammering a huge wedge in the already stressed fracture between African-Americans and all other Americans including the other minorities such as Spanish, Asian, etc. If I were one of those other minorities, I would be pretty upset that my African-American Texaco co-worker just got a 10 percent raise because he got his feelings hurt! I am an Italian American so I am considered white, but I can assure you that the next time an Italian joke is told in my office, I'll take Mr. Jackson's path and sue the hell out of my employer! I just hope that Mr. Jackson is there to lend me a hand, will you be behind me Mr. Jackson?
T. P.

Here, one can see an issue dealing with racism/anti-racism and the ongoing debate as to who stands for those who belong to neither of these institutionalized race divide (the Italian who is responding here). A view from another historically marginalized member from the Italian origin, the comment here, is a challenge to Jackson's boycotting of Texaco. This should remind us that there is not just a monolithic group of clearly identifiable *silent voices* but a number of diverse groups of *silent voices* that vie to be heard in their struggles for justice and equality.

As the call for boycott strengthens, another voice wonders why racism in its various forms should even become an issue.

> I am an American, working for my company in England and cannot believe this situation concerning Texaco and the Jesse Jackson condemnation. The English cannot understand our unreasonable attachment to racial subjects. I dare say, each one of us has, at one time or another, told a joke, used an accent, mentioned someone with their race or nationality emphasized, etc., including Mr. "racist" Jesse himself. It appears... they find this an opportunity to blackmail a successful company for their own gain ... I will attempt to purchase Texaco gas at any opportunity, as they have attempted to resolve this situation. I wish we could have a reverse boycott and attempt to purchase all from Texaco.
> M.B.

I am surely tempted to believe that this person never belonged to the marginalized groups of people and hence, never understood the implications of discrimination. As to his proposed defiance of the boycott, events following the Texaco incidents proved that it did work. With the subsequent revelations of confirmed racist comments and policies followed by senior management at Texaco, a legal settlement ensued.

Another writer supports the black community in its struggle to fight the systemic racism she recognizes in corporate America:

> I strongly empathize with the outrage felt by members of the black community towards the revelation of conversations of Texaco's senior management. Unfortunately, their mindset is the fairly typical of corporate America. Frankly these revelations are the best argument I can think of for keeping affirmative action alive. They will only do the right thing when they are forced to-by the government or by the bottom line.
> E.Z.

For those who do not comprehend the implications of systemic racism, the notion of organized resistance can appear as "extortion":

> Any financial losses Texaco faces in the near future will not be due to Jesse Jackson's pathetic boycott, but rather from longtime customers like me who are turning our backs on Texaco for caving in to extortion brought on by Jackson and the NAACP. But, surely the press will tote their ridiculous boycott as a devastating financial blow to Texaco. Don't flatter yourselves guys. I hope Texaco learns a valuable lesson from all of this and sets an example for other large corporations in fear of similar schemes. You cave in to the racist extortion of the NAACP, you lose customers! I'm sure Texaco's shareholders are reminding them of that fact right now.
> J. B.

Joining the debate is another person who argues for a coalition that is inclusive and representative of the marginalized groups. Insightful is his comment on how selectively different are the responses and reactions of critics when different kinds of *voices* are heard; Jewish, Japanese, and Afro-Americans:

> It is long past due for all aspects of society to fully address the existence of and effects of racism and or discrimination on black people in particular. Black people have for the last 500 years plus been considered to be the lowest form of humanity. The revelation of these problems at Texaco are not, repeat not and aberration. As far as corporate America is concerned, This is for the most part the norm. Certainly, in the last five years efforts have been made to start up diversification programs. However, real dialogue about how past discrimination has affected black people has for the most part been shelved. My personal experiences and conversations with other African- Americans, particularly black men, reinforce my views that a true coalition of government, private and business organizations needs to be formed as a permanent body to investigate past and ongoing problems. Also, I question why other groups can seek to address problems that have affected them in the past (i.e. , the internment of Japanese during World War II, and the Jewish holocaust) and no one seems to have a problem with this. However, when black people discuss problems caused by the effects of slavery, discrimination, and racism still being experienced by our people today, we are being divisive. A call has gone out for these problems to be addressed. The principles that this country was founded on requires that they be addressed . . . Then and only then can we have true reconcilement and forgiveness.
> M. H.

There is a price to pay when supporting resistance, as the following writer notes:

> I wonder if the Rev. Jackson realizes that the boycott of Texaco is also hurting the minority owners of Texaco gas stations throughout the country.
> g. m.

What the writer ignores though, is the fact that there are many Texaco gas stations operated by white owners who decry racism at the Texaco headquarters and yet suffer economically from the boycott; emphasizing that sensitivities, morals, ethics, and justice cannot be defined by the color of one's skin. As a postscript to the issue, the discrimination lawsuit against Texaco Inc. was officially settled for an historic $176 million, the largest race-discrimination settlement in U.S. history in November (CNN March 26, 1997).

Struggles and counter-struggles occur on an ongoing basis between racists and anti-racists; the difference being that while the former prescribe hatred and violence, the latter either commission re-education and rational arguments or not unlike the hate groups, engage in hatred and violence. At the *Micetrap's Hate Mail* we witness an ongoing conflict between the three identified groups of writers. The Webmaster writes:

> Although most email I receive is positive, I can usually expect to find a few emails opposing my web site. Some threaten me, but most are just ebonics-filled garbage. Due to the fact that my dedicated supporters harass them so much, most users on my last hate mail page have to delete their accounts almost immediately! I highly encourage all of you to email these people with your comments and viewpoints.

Not only is the host aware of the opposition but also prides in his supporters harassing people who wrote in to complain. Yet, not unlike the *silent voices*, the supremacist groups also have their detractors who feel that the site does not represent true "resistance."

> From: ALPHA
> To: w.w.p.
>
> After viewing this web page I have to say it is one of the WORST pro-white web sites on the internet. You should do the people of the White race a favor and REMOVE it. The correct address would be whitetrash.com, for I have never seen such an assembelance of shinhead stupidity and ignorance anyplace. You and this webpage are a INSULT to those who are seriously working for the future of the White Aryan race.
>
> If you are a sincere White man, get your head out of your #@* and make a REAL web page, if not, just do the Aryan people a favor, shut it down!
>
> bxxxxxx@hotmail.com
> I expose Alpha as the JEWISH-like scum that they are, and will continue doing so until they are off of the net for good!

One of the most violent acts of cowardice from an opponent of racism emphasizes what one should never do to overcome hate— using hatred to remove hatred:

> From: JK
> Hey You Fxxxxxx Nazi Bastard... I got one thing to say to you Biotch - I sent a bomb to your fxxxxxx house! Hahaha, you weak fxxxxx - you are dead!

Unsurprisingly, the racist recipient of the threat responds:

This was probably one of the dumbest people EVER to email me a threat! Not only did he send this illegal threat directly from his personal account but after my ISP contacted his internet provider he sent me numerous apology letters and accidentally forwarded me a copy of an email he sent to his service provider containing his phone numbers!

Having been reprimanded for uttering a threat, JK regrets his approach:

Dear sir:
I wish to apologize for my "threat" to you earlier this week. In no way did I or do I intend to carry out such a threat. As you may have guessed, I disagree with your opinions. However, I am an advocate of the First Amendment and your right to express your views without consequence of threat of bodily harm. For my actions, I am truly sorry. I will not contact, harass or threaten you again.
Sincerely,
JK

This obviously did not win the admiration of the hate group representative:

I find it rather comical how quickly people are "advocates of the First Amendment" once they are threatened with lawsuits and the loss of their account!

Dear Mr. M.
I received your message regarding my bomb threat to a white supremacist. I have written an apology to the original recipient and assured him that I had no intention of carrying out such an action. But that still does not excuse what I did, so I wish also to apologize to you. I am sorry that I used your services as a vehicle for such hateful language, and I assure you it will not happen in the future. I am an advocate of human rights and the First Amendment, neither of which were upheld by such idiocy. I am fascinated by this new technology, but I realize that it does not absolve me of responsibilities. Nor does it grant me immunity from laws regarding threats and harassment. I am truly embarrassed and ashamed. Please accept my apology. I can be reached at xxxxxx until 2 p.m., and xxxxxx afternoons and evenings (work).
Sincerely,
J. K.

[Response] Is this loser a geek or what? If you have some spare time on your hands, why not drop him a line and ask him why he did such a stupid thing? Perhaps you may want to explain to him your differing opinions, also.

Another writer seeks to rest the debate with a comment:

From: M.
BASTARDS!!!!!!!!!!!!
YOU ALL MAKE ME SICK!!!!!!!!!!!!!!!
THERES ONLY ONE RACE THE HUMYN RACE

Let us for a moment, look at the first statement regarding the notion of one race. The idea of one single "human race" has been laid to rest at the genetic level. Dan

233

Gardner (1995), in his article, "When Racial Categories make no Sense" reminds us of the scientific evidence in the early 1940s that "the racial map of human beings did not match what they were learning of human genes. Early on, it was seen that there was no gene that was unique to a race, and so there was no "black" or "white" gene." Gardner continues:

> "Race has really lost its significance as a concept," says Prof. Lewontin. Indeed, Prof. Sapp expresses the widely held view that "'race' shouldn't be used in [the study of] human biology because it is so tied up in political and cultural meanings." But the problem remains: Even if race has become meaningless to scientists, it is very real to practically everyone else. "Society's belief in the existence of races creates what social scientists call a social reality," says California State University sociology professor Yehudi Webster. The reactions of the public to the O. J. Simpson verdict—harshly split between black and white—are a reminder of that social reality, if any is needed. **Biological race is dead; social race is alive and thriving**. [Emphasis added] (Online).

One cannot dispute that social reality still exists in that color plays a significant role as much as any other visual clues to the "difference" in a person such as gender, disability, or features that are not part of the dominant pool. The critics who vehemently decry affirmative action or employment equity recognize the "visibility" of "visible minority" which constitute "social reality" of discrimination but question the classification of the group "visible." Historically, if hate groups have believed in the racial purity based on the biological determinism developed from social Darwinism ("Struggle for Existence" and "Survival of the Fittest"), race identity is now implicated by "social reality" more than biological makeup. Critics argue that raising "race" issues can only aggravate and highlight sensitivities. As Gardner (1995) describes:

> Most social scientists and government policy-makers are well aware that our racial categories make no biological sense. But they continue to pour out social policy that uses the race categories of the "social reality." Canadian employment equity legislation, for example, is designed to help those who are "non-white in colour or non-Caucasian in race." The race question was placed on the 1996 census for the purpose of creating the visible minority data for employment equity to function. That is the sort of government policy that infuriates Prof. Webster, author of "The Racialization of America." The addition of a race question to the Canadian census is, he feels, "an act of promiscuous stupidity." (Online)

Defining racial categories for people with multiracial lineage could become a traumatic experience. Would it be possible to place oneself within a particular category (visible or non-visible) based on his or her own reckoning of their identity based on "social reality" rather than genetic makeup?

Despite the fact that there is an element of pity on the part of the following writer for the hate promulgators, his/her caustic approach to setting the fact straight does more harm than honor to the cause of anti-racism:

> From: C.B.
> Just when I though I had witnessed the sickest of the sick, when it comes to the web. I find your filthy page. This has to be the most concentrated page of ignorance that I have ever seen. Aryan has become a dirty word because of you and your terrible message upon your people. If you want purity so much why is it that no land on this earth is 100% white. No race has vanished from the earth through rape. Rape has only mingled the races further. Your retarded message only contradicts it self. You all should heed the words of the most Intelligent White man every to be "Stupid is as Stupid does" How I pity your children and their children after them. May the spirit of the world have mercy on your souls and bodies.

JR in the following, uses a calmer and more sensible approach over bitter and rancorous invectives in response to hate:

> From: J. R.
> I was dissapointed to see that I was not included on your hate mail list. I e-mailed you several weeks ago concerning the **mis-information on African-American accomplishments** your sight was propogating and the blatant ad hom aim (sp?) attacks against various racial groups your sight promoted. The new design of your sight looks a lot better and a great deal more professional. **It's a tragedy that you waste your obviously bright minds on such senseless ideas.** [Emphases added]

Obviously, as the following passage proves, it does not appear to have influenced the hater, raising the much-asked question, "Why do we have to establish contact with haters? Why can't we shut them down?" Censorship debate aside (discussed in detail elsewhere), one can only assume that eventually, people will be challenged to think rationally.

> Dr. J. R.
> I am very honored that even my opposition recognizes my web authoring talents. I think it takes a big man to admit talent and skill in work that they despise. But, I think this guy needs to sit back and realize that the African American page is only a joke. Everyone

knows how much the niggers have given to our society! Where would we be today without: excessive crime, drive-by shooting, open-air drug dealings, vandalism, graffiti, gangs, basketball players that can slam dunk, etc ect etc. And just think about how empty our poor jails would be with them! Hahahaha!

More writers fume with hate at the hater but only succeed in eliciting further hatred:

From: xxxxxxxx
Your page is really mean and it suckz.What is the point of it?Your a nazi and everyone else in America is supposed to love you.I don't think so listen half of the people in this country are mixed with another race.If you find one true pure german nazi well your lucky.I think you should move back to Germany where you belong,because you are worthless here.Everyone will overpower your corney whitepower.That page is very offensive and I don't like it.Keep your page to yourself and the KKK.

From: Kramedart@aol.com

Fxxx you you White power... Grow the fxxx up!......whats wrong with you.....every person on this earth is equal!!!!!...why cant you understand that..... So I give a big FXXX YOU !!!....to all you white power inbred fxxxxx. DIE!!!!!!!!! Maybe if everyone screams this enough... suddenly we will all become equal. Or perhaps if Congress would pass a law...

From: Maverick
Regardless of what you guys or any people you have listed in your ant-mail box say, you are freaking ignorant... Do you want to spend your short life hating everyone who doesn't look like you do? What a waste. Eventually you will die and with you dies your ideas-your kids hopefully won't act as you have. Show the world more respect. Show everyone more respect! And most of all, buy a clue.
M.

The hater calmly responds:

It will always amaze me how many people do web searches for topics such as "white power" or "skinheads" and then become enraged after visiting my website. **No one MAKES you come here... you come here on your own!** And not one place on this whole site do I claim to be a klansmen or nazi. So why would I want to move to Germany... to add to their insane immigration problem - I doubt it! [Emphasis added]

The following is a response from a black female who derides the hate group with copious insults and verbal violence. As the response to the diatribe proves, reacting to insults with more insults can only perpetuate the violence and hatred.

Dear honkies,
being an educatid respetable black female I find myself asking why I should even waste my time righting to your ignant inbred, trashy mutha phucking asses...What you need to do is go back to school and get more than 8th grade education and maybe you would

236

realize how fucking stupit you really are. doesnt it really piss you off that you are the minority in this country? And just think its only going to get worse. Soon there wont be a master race because everyone will be mixed. even your little fucking cracker ass children will be marrying and fucking out of your arian race because they will have more intellgence and self respect than their own parents. I can understand why you are jealis of african american people though. Us women have the curly hair your stringy haird wives try and copy with rollers and the golden skin they lay in tanning beds to attain. And ofcourse when it comes to men, well anyone knows how inferyor you are. and its not just the size, you just dont know what to do. I guess its because your used to fucking your hand, relatives, or any fucking farm animal that will do.

[Response] Wow, looks like another looter of the L.A. Riots finally figured out how to turn on their stolen computer. I have never seen so many mis-spelled words in my life... and they are criticizing me?And by the way - "respectable black female" is an oxymoron!

A radio station decides to intervene in the discourse of personal exchanges:

From: KUHF-FM Radio

Subject: this site must be removed

Obviously you never heard of George Washington Carver, William Grant Still, Marian Anderson, James De Preist, Dean Dixon, James Weldon Johnson, Andre Watts, Paul Freeman, Alvin Poussaint, Harry Belafonte, Sidney Poitier, Leontyne Price, Henry Lewis, Sanford Allen, Arthur L. Phillips, Kenneth Goodman, Kenneth Clark, Gordon Parks, George Bridgetower, Samuel Coleridge-Taylor, Jose White, Joseph Bologne, and several thousand others----all of whom (I feel it safe to assume) were of far greater intelligence and imagination than you could possibly hope to boast. All of these people had far better things to do with their time than create obscene websites like yours. I agree---your site must be removed.

Kuhf Fm Member Services Dial 743-Kuhf, , Houston, TX 77054
713-743-5843 Kuhf Fm Radio Station, Houston, TX 77021 713-743-0857

[Response] Although nothing should surprise me anymore, I find it rather interesting that a radio station would/could advocate censorship. And looking at that list of what I can only assume are niggers, I am proud to announce that I have no clue who most of them are!

One of the highlights of this barrage of hateful exchange culminates in a series of hopeful writers who wish to exterminate the other:

From: J. T.
You are so pathetic it is funny. Now I could waste my time telling you how dumb your white pride BS is but I'm sure you've heard it all before . The fact of the matter is you are nothing. You amount to the equivalent of Dog sxxx...FXXX NAZI SYMPATHY. FXXX FASCISM!! Your mind is so small, you are nothing.

From: C. A. L.

> hey, you racist fxxxxxx thug of a moron. Nazi's fxxxxxx ...you ignorant twits need to get enlightened, or better yet: DIE respond if you dare... A SHARP THAT WOULD GLADLY SHOOT YOU DEAD

The saddest part of this conflict is the following observation by the hate group representative in this volley of exchanges, who rightly observes:

> Eeeeek, more threats of violence... don't these guys realize that I am the one that is supposed to be a HATER? Threats like these make me wonder who is really "full of hate."

In fact, one would agree that the hater was more calm and focused than the ones who derided him/her throughout this exchange, raising some serious questions. Instigating the hater and challenging him/her or even worse, censor the site to only be "mirrored" by a host of other hate groups in different countries can only aggravate the situation. As Mock suggested earlier, "hate is in the minds of humans," the hater in this correspondence finally states a seemingly simple but extremely dangerous and truthful saying that reflects the whole issue of hatred:

> Although I will eventually die, my ideology will never die. As long as there is one proud white person left in this world, it will continue. And as far as plastering houses with papers - what a waste of time considering I reach 4,000 visitors a day with my website!

In response to a call from CNN Online for writers to contribute on censorship and hate on the Internet, a number of individuals posted their thoughts[41]. The issue of censorship ties in closely with the freedom hate groups have on the Net.

> BZ- 11:52am Nov 13, 1997 ET (#43 of 52)
> The most dangerous philosophy existing today is Political Correctionism. It attempts to not only change people's actions, but thoughts as well, much as the use of "Newspeak" was to do in Goeorge Orwell's "1984". However, even though Political Correctionism is as evil as Maoism,it's proponents have a perfect right to disseminate their beliefs over the Internet,or anywhere else for that matter,as should any other group.
> --
> EB - 12:30pm Nov 13, 1997 ET (#46 of 52)
>
> To be intolerant of hate is not to be intolerant of freedom. In this case, censorship is appropriate.
> What is freedom without boundries? It ceases to be freedom and becomes irresponsible and often destructive behaviour. Words do hurt, not only individuals, but society as well. We are reaping a harvest of destroyed families, violent communities, etc... because of the seeds sown by the philosophy that morality is a matter of personal preference, no

---

[41] CNN Question: What are your thoughts on this conference as well as Internet speech?

boundries, "Don't legislate morality." The statement itself is nonsense By saying its not right (right and wrong is the essense of morality) to legislate morality we have ourselves created a moral code. A code where its "OK" to hate.

Nigel Maywood - 12:36pm Nov 13, 1997 ET (#49 of 52)

EB,

Legally, it is OK to hate. It is called freedom of thought. Did anyone see "Politically Incorrect" last night? I was sleepy but former Clinton bimbo Dee Dee Myers tried very unsuccessfully to defend legislation against hate crimes. David Boaz of the Cato Institute and Bill Maher grilled her quite well. Boaz asked if the crime for burning down a synagogue is one year, then how can you deny that adding a second year to the sentence for hating Jews is not a thought crime? Bill Maher added: "What would the sentence be if you burned down a synagogue because you LOVE Jews?"

As motives speak for themselves, a violent action such as "burning down a synagogue" cannot be construed as a manifestation of love. If mere logic can be exercised to argue against censorship, it may not be possible to maintain law. Bill Maher is wrong in using logic for the sake of using it since any violent act against another human cannot be explained away as a desirable act. This might bring in the issue of euthanasia which is beyond this discussion. As to the topic of hate, there is an ongoing debate as to whether the government should define "hate."

Scott Munro - 12:37pm Nov 13, 1997 ET (#50 of 52)

Everyone on this board has been concentrating solely on governmental "solutions" to hate speech. I agree, it is not the place of government in a free society to outlaw the expression of ideas, even reprehensible ones. We should remember that, if we allow government to outlaw hate speech, we must accept the government's _definition_ of hate speech. Already, some in the U.S. have equated opposition to affirmative action and welfare with "hate speech," and I, for one, am unwilling to entrust my freedom to the goodwill and common sense of our legislators, (much less to the corrupt and useless United Nations). Personally, I would like to see even equal opportunity laws for the private sector (not for governmental agencies) abolished. Is that hate speech? The answer, of course, is no, but there are many who would say yes.

However, there are peaceable, non-governmental ways to combat hate speech. Pressure ISPs to drop customers who spew racism, and boycott any advertiser stupid enough to sponsor a racist site.
Of course, this still leaves the problem of "What is hate speech?" but I think most people (unlike most politicians and bureaucrats) are smart enough to figure it out. [Emphasis added]

239

Quite eloquently put, the following reader returns to the basic crux of the problem— Hate is in the mind and education is the need for dealing with the symptoms of hate:

T R. - 12:37pm Nov 13, 1997 ET (#51 of 52)

Rather then attempt to stop the hate messages, we should instead stop the hatred. If more was spent on education, then people would be educated not to hate, thus ending messages of those sorts.

Do we ignore hate groups? Not doing anything, as the following reader suggests, is not an option. We may need to differentiate between apathy and interference.

Nigel Maywood - 12:44pm Nov 13, 1997 ET (#52 of 52)

TR

If you force people not to hate, even if it is under the guise of education, you only make the problem worse.
Stupid people are going to act stupid and continue to hate along whatever lines they choose. Best thing is to ignore them - they usually go away. And if they don't go away, oh well.

And I disagree with the poster who thinks that most people on this board are focusing on governmental solutions to hate speech. I see some but not that many. And I also believe that most Americans are against regulations on free speech. The problem is that the fools in Washington don't seem to agree. The solution to the problem is to vote those fools out of office.

A very interesting position is posited by MM— Why not allow the hate groups their own space to present their voices? This will exclude them from occupying more visible spaces in other people's lives.

MM. - 11:10am Nov 13, 1997 ET (#37 of 53)

The Net should allow and foster hate groups to further their views. Why? I dont want their views being shouted at me when I walk to work, I dont want their views being scrawled on the walls where I live - let them have their place. Then, if someone wants to see and hear their views they can go seek it out on the web. No one goes to the hate sites unless they want to. But more importantly, what is the nature of 'hate' speech? Something that you and I collectively dislike? In WW2 was anti-German speech 'hate-speech'? (You'll recall great slogans like 'The only good Jerry is a dead Jerry') Or anti-Japanese speech? Anti-Italian?

Point is, 'hate-speech' has always been part of our society, and recently, 'hate-speech' is the same jingoism thats simply not main-stream. Not cool. Not Politically-Correct. When the day comes that I need to express my hate-views against whatever evil oppression I see I

240

want the right to express it as I please. And so, while I personally despise the bile that Supremecists and Anti-Semetic groups vomit, I have to recognize their right to speak it, because my day may come too.

MM's argument that people "seek out hate sites" is compelling and opting for less intruding violent actions over physical violence may appear alluring. This again highlights the issue of dealing with hatred in the minds of the perpetrators rather than clamping down on their medium of dissemination.

This is so well articulated in the following four messages:

B. Elmore - 11:24am Nov 13, 1997 ET (#38 of 53)

The way to combat misinformation has always been with correct information. The Internet is a microcosm of the world at large-- stopping 'hate messages on the Internet' is no different than stopping hate messages in the world at large. Trying to shut up people like this never works; **it only turns them into martyrs** and sets a dangerous precedent for the time when what is right and true is in the minority.

When someone spreads lies and hate, the proper response is to say in the same forum that they're wrong, and to point out in detail exactly where and why they're wrong. This takes out all the teeth out of their message, for what defense is there against the truth? [Emphases added]

TG - 04:38pm Nov 12, 1997 ET (#2 of 53)
truthful journalist, B.A. Walter Cronkite School of Journalism '96

Hmm...

Free speech is never a threat to anybody but would-be dictators.... **Racist speech is not a threat as long as we are free to speak out against it.** The obsession with race was caused by government intervention, and yet the liberals propose more government intervention. [Emphasis added]

KS - 11:00pm Nov 12, 1997 ET (#7 of 53)

Having just completed a documentary video "http://www.accelerated.com/Fusion" about a racially motivated murder that occurred near UC-Irvine, the site of a recent hate email incident, I have had considerable time to formulate opinions about hatred in our communities. While I feel that laws against hate are important in that they establish a community standard of intolerance towards hatred, **I also feel that legislation is possibly the smallest factor in changing peoples perceptions of the world.** If people are truly concerned about hatred on the Web, let's do something about it and lead by example. As with any new, undefined medium, there are good and bad potentials for what the Web will become. In my opinion, we, users of the Web are the one's who can make the most profound impact in the debate over hatred on the Net. The only way to effect lasting

241

change of people's opinions is by providing Web users with information about the hatred that exists in the world and on the Web, and by being open to one another, being willing to learn about and empathize with one another. Legislation is only one piece of the pie. If people are concerned about hate, let them lead by example. KS.[Emphasis added]

SB - 11:04pm Nov 12, 1997 ET (#10 of 53)

While I dislike seeing all the hatred that pours through some people's computers, I have to say that they have a right to free speech. What we need is more education so that people know better than to believe the crap that comes on the Internet. What we don't need is more government control.

Teachers as global educators need to recognize the issue of free speech even as they educate students about not visiting Web sites of hate groups without understanding the background to such resistance movements. Teachers must provide the necessary guidelines to browsing hate sites and encourage critical thinking among their students rather than preventing them from being exposed to undesirable Web sites. Having experienced the actual effect of hate sites, the discussions and implications surrounding censorship, it is my understanding that education remains the best strategy for dealing with hatred. Initiatives like, *The Nizkor Project* and *The Simon Wiesenthal Centre* are doing exactly that—challenging misinformation and re-educating the public. One of the positive aspects to the hate groups on the Net is that they provide, for their own reasons, links to the anti-racism sites, offering opportunity for people to gain insights into the issue.

Amidst this contestation involving struggles and counter-struggles, it is imperative that we ensure voices of rationale are clearly heard and that in cases of children and young adults, there be a critical analysis of the ongoing debate. Censorship to screen hate sites may have to be confined to local ISP providers and parents who may want to use appropriate software filters. A prepared and informed teacher may be able to use the existence of hate to stimulate discussion and challenge his or her student to the implications of violence in society.

Chapter 8: Sharing Experiences

8.1. Conversations

The conversations surrounded the following questions:

- What relevant sites have they discovered and what relevant issues have they explored?
- What did you find on the Internet that was relevant to cultural issues that were global?
- How do they feel as to the content and presentation of the issues?
- Did they interact with other users over the Internet by involving in Usergroup/Newsgroup discussions? If so, what was their experience?
- Do they feel that the available sites contribute to the goals and objectives of global education?
- What is their reflection on the pedagogy (rather than the content) and how would they use the Internet as a tool for pedagogical process? [Appendix].
- How much of this has influenced their understanding of cultural issues?
- How representative (in terms of the cultural aspects of various people) was the information on the Internet?
- What were the different cultural issues they saw relevant to this discussion?
- To what degrees were these available on the Internet?
- How would they use the Internet as a tool in dealing with issues relevant to global education?
- How did they find the sites? How was the access?

As the group completed the Orientation and first focus group session, the following observation was made in the Journal:

Why do I get this feeling that everyone in this group thinks computers are great and will assist in solving many problems in this world? [Albeit] a couple of them are wary and critical about the technology itself. [In fact, by the end of the session I had noted] Half the group do not have easy computer access; a couple do not own connectivity [connection, i.e., access]; one is really new to this mumbo-jumbo; one is pretty good with the techno-jargon. Balanced group!

Sites

Ron[42], specializing in instrumental music, initially found 22 sites relevant to his area of interest—*racism* and *antiracism education*. Using search engines like Webcrawler and Yahoo, Ron found Canadian sites like *Artists Against Racism* and international sites that addressed Holocaust and anti-Semitism. Ron found that:

As well as "revisionist" sites, there were a few "anti-revisionist" sites ("promoting the way the history books say it happened"). One latter type of site is based in Vancouver. The whole library site is made accessible and they claim to take a critical and analytical approach- posing arguments and questions to people. They also respond to email queries.

Ron did not send email to this site in Vancouver. "I haven't sent anything yet, but I'll try to find a couple of sites listing newspaper clippings and I was thinking of writing to *Artists Against Racism* for some pamphlets to use in some of my classes." Even if Ron wanted to send an email, he would have been more willing to contact the antiracism sites rather than racist sites. In fact, he did contact a few site hosts via email.

---

[42] All names of participants have been changed to pseudonyms.

Ron did not find any chat boards and during the initial stages of the project had not yet talked to Chat groups or other browsers. "I'm still not familiar with that aspect of the Web. I have read a couple of views where there are a couple of Chat groups are devoted to these types of subjects. So, I'm working on trying to find some of this." Referring to the *Aryan Nations* home page, Ron noted that, "Some of the anti-racist sites have links to racist sites for education but the racist sites do not have links to the anti-racist sites." While this is true in many cases, it was found that some racist sites did have links to the anti-racist sites. According to Ron, "Germany is a hot site for racist/anti-racist sites."

Nalini, a graduate student in International Education, initially found 8 sites relevant to her area of interest—*Social Justice* in general and *human rights* in specific. Of the several sites explored by Nalini, some related to peace education and some specific to social justice. Sites relevant to the Ogoni issue were of specific interest to Nalini. Nalini used the search engine Excite to search the Net. One of the main concerns for Nalini was the static nature of many sites which could "have more frequent updates of site information." Initially, Nalini considered herself a 'novice'. [Hence], I could also email people directly about issues. I am using someone else's email account. Found some publications on Ken Saro-Wiwa."

Since Nalini was caught up in her own work, she did not find any new sites of any great significance following the first conversation period. This, she said, was "due to lack of access time and also my own work." Nalini did return to some of the sites she had visited initially but as she comments, "One of the problems with sites is that often the updates are minimal and sometimes, there is no change in the content. Some sites do not exist anymore [when you go back to see them]. When bookmarks are followed, some of the sites do not exist anymore.

Not having the equipment at home makes it difficult. Did not interact with anybody else."

There appeared to be some caution in how Nalini felt about the usefulness of the Internet as she noted that while, "The initial excitement is well-founded, to expect that I would have every needed information available on the Internet was not a realistic expectation." According to Nalini, as in any medium, "misrepresentation [of facts] could be possible." Having browsed for other sites in the area of social justice and human rights, Nalini felt that "the Amnesty site was by far the biggest source of information," noting that she had enlisted on their email and activism sites.

Waheed, an After Degree student in Secondary Education, found sites relevant to his area of interest—*Peacekeeping* and *Conflict resolution*. Waheed started off with the position that he preferred only resource link sites. According to him, "One of the problems regarding prescriptive vs. descriptive sites is that I have a natural inclination towards resource-based sites that allow you to come to your own conclusion on things like these as opposed to the type of editorial sites—people trying to convince you." Waheed thought that this was also very true with global education sites, too. While he did not interact with newsgroups or Chat groups, Waheed found sites that were relevant to sustainable development. These sites had links to archives and other Web sites. One such site, "the *International Institute for Sustainable Development* based in Winnipeg dealt with sustainable development and global security. Another idealistic goal and deals with a wide range of topics and policies throughout the entire spear of global development, everything from economic to social to industrial to military to security issues, everything is dealt with here." These Web sites have minutes of meetings, and policy papers from academics around the world. Waheed had positive comments about the IISD site:

> It presents alternative viewpoints. They are not looking for people with one view. They had people both anti-United Nations and pro-United Nations. It tended to be towards the pro side, but I got the sense that it was because there is much more academics who support the work of United Nations... This is much more mainstream (in contrast to the fringe) and much more critical analysis of things with elements of prescription but it was done within the sense of recommendations as opposed to demands. The site also contains innumerable abstracts. Secondary teachers and researchers would find this useful; I just loved it.

Waheed also found another site that he felt was balanced and mostly objective. The site *Project of Peacekeeping- United Nations,* considered "good" by Waheed, attempted to convince readers about American intervention overseas. According to Waheed, this site had

> a specific goal in mind; it is an American site convincing people to support and increase American involvement in United Nations and its various subsidiaries; in particular, multilateral conflict resolution. Very pro-United Nations and very pro-peacekeeping, anti-American [believing] in gun-toting diplomacy. They were critical of American invasions of various countries and were unhappy with Desert Storm. They liked the idea of going to Bosnia. Lots of graphs and charts and maps. Focus is on successes and not failures... The primary information was presented straight from the horse's mouth as it were. These included lists of policy papers form the United Nations, bulletins from peacekeeping forces, and press releases. So you could use [the available material] to support whatever you wanted to support.

For Waheed, the negative aspect of the site was that it would not emphasize the failures of the United Nations. Waheed, perhaps, is recognizing the fact that "computing also offers pluralism, different things for different people" (Greenberg, 1996, p. 108). The Internet promises multiple offerings, different perspectives, and different ways of thinking even as it allows the consumer to select and critique what is appropriate. This is the freedom available to the reader rather than the editor who decides to screen material for appropriateness.

Gunadasa is in the diploma program specializing in Adult and Higher Education. His area of interest—*Culture and Education* was initially chosen as it was considered relevant to the discussion of global education but it eventually became clear that Gunadasa was mostly interested in the administration (as management) within the context of culture. (e.g. Educational online services dealing with administrators. "How do they view educational administration?"). Gunadasa was interested in exploring how administrators around the world dealt with culture and questions like "How did German administrators operate within their idea of technology (use of computer technology)?" and "How do different cultures deal with technology in their school systems?" Gunadasa had to be reminded to consider the definition of global education and the need to focus on the area within the cultural realm for this project. Perhaps the wide nature of Gunadasa's interest resulted in accessing fewer sites.

Ron found more sites following conversation one: "[S]ome great new ones; couple of them that were very interesting and I found, different types of sites that were more interactive." With the area of interest being antiracism, Ron was able to explore and interact with other people on the Internet:

> There is one site that deals with national civil rights museum and a couple of other places have online two or three various exhibits, displays and information on some topics. One site has an open discussion group on racial harmony- racial disharmony. It's similar to a Chat-group. It's an e-mail discussion group, posting answers and questions, so and so forth.

Fifty percent of sites that Ron recorded were relevant to his area of interest:

> I have been able to find through a couple of other search engines, like master lists, resource pages that are just lists of links, some of them by their name, I thought were little more on the boundary of the topic and so, I haven't pursued them too thoroughly yet. Probably about half of them had information relating to the topic.

248

For the most part, it has been quite objectively based. I found more sites lately- with more people having individual Web pages. They were opinion-based and the one in Oregon, the antiracist homepage, is one of the main [link site] resources... It's got 50 or 60 linked sites and they are linked to anti-racist sites. Some of those are linked to racist sites to show the other side of the coin.

Ron was able to request information on resources and other relevant materials using the on-line connection:

I posted in a couple of places and there was one site in discussion- *Just Cause On-line*. It is actually quite exhaustive with news clips, classroom resources that are available, poses questions, offers information, has good and bad, like things that are good happening in the U.S. and the world that are working against tolerance. And there's also an area of special items. People like myself are doing research projects or interested in classroom materials. There's one grade four teacher who was doing a unit on prejudice and was asking for materials. So, it is really good for that and people respond quite quickly. So, I just put a little notice up there and I got some things back- suggesting different sites to go to. One of the sites was advertising a community-based program to identify and eliminate or re-direct racial tension or agitation. So, I received a couple of those and couple of ones I had not heard before. A lot of people were very supportive, very willing to offer information, very open as well.

Did Ron have an opportunity to get involved in any discussion with the hate sites? While Ron had not communicated with the hate groups, he did not rule out the possibility.

I haven't yet had any discussion groups on the hate sites. I just browsed a couple of them quickly and I'm probably gonna get a little more into those now that I have a bit more time on my hands. But a couple of white supremacist pages, and "white pride"- the other type of hate came up lots. So, I haven't done the [email correspondence] yet. Haven't quite taken that risk- making myself known. But, I'm sure I'd say we're looking at information for research- whether they'd try to offer best arguments as they could... So, everybody is very open and helpful.

However, Ron did use email to communicate with groups and individuals from anti-racism sites. While Ron had the intent to contact anti-racism sites, he was hesitant to engage the racists in an email debate. The challenge of communicating without engaging in a violent confrontation with the racists remains. In spite of Ron's findings, it was found, as in the case of Zundel's hate page, hotlinks from racist sites to anti-racist sites. Zundel states, "For relentless Holocaust promotion, on the other hand, contact *Nizkor*. For another Jewish point of view, contact the *Simon Wiesenthal Center*" and Zundel provides both anti-racist sites as hotlinks where one could click on any one of them and be taken to the respective sites.

Despite the German ban on hate sites, Ron came to believe that Germany was a "hot site" for racist/anti-racist sites. While estimates abound, it is impossible to confirm Ron's assumption due to lack of sufficient information regarding this aspect of the Net. Thus, in the Cyberworld, the physical origin of the host site remains unimportant; the virtual world represents what it claims to do.

Nalini's problem with the static nature of sites without frequent updates was a legitimate concern. Except for news sites (e.g. CNN, ABC, NBC, MSN, Globe and Mail), constant updates remain unlikely. Some sites, such as the *KidLink* were unchanged even after six months. Despite her little or limited technological background, Nalini had begun to "communicate directly" with people on common interests. She became a part of activism by enlisting on Amnesty's human rights site. She had begun to feel the freedom and the need to participate through the electronic forum. Yet, Nalini's initial excitement about being able to access voluminous information eventually faded since she also found the increasing possibility of "misrepresentation of facts."

Waheed's concern was with the prescriptive nature of sites including global education sites in that he did not want to be "preached at." He loved the site that was pro-UN, with "recommendations as opposed to demands." Believing

250

in the US intervention for peace but decrying violence and American invasions. He did recognize the lack of criticisms against the UN. Between Gunadasa and Ron, the former was unable to find relevant sites while the latter had 50% relevant sites. Hence, it was obvious that the success of a Web search was dependent on accurately identifying the area of interest and defining appropriate descriptors; Ron was able to do that successfully. In fact, Ron was able to establish online communication with other educators and obtain advice and referrals regarding curriculum resource materials.

By this time, the browsing had started off at a slow pace, more than the act of finding actual sites was the amount of time needed to spend on the Internet in just finding one's way around (despite having acquired various computer skills). The Journal:

> For every relevant or suspected to be relevant site you have 20 irrelevant or inaccessible sites! This is time-consuming; nobody is going to believe how much time this thing takes! [I reasoned] No wonder, some of the participants are not doing much!

Nevertheless, it was evident that there were many sites available for global education educators. The urge to "*be optimistic*" on this aspect of Internet was undeniable. In fact, some excellent sites that dealt with human rights, women's rights and aboriginal rights along with some pornographic sites were discovered; this was, of course, not unintentional:

> Browsed through some really "dirty" sites linked to the first few sites. But, the search words keyed in asked for these sites; it wasn't accidental. Most sites do have more than one screen with repeated cautionary notes and posted disclaimers warning people of potential displeasure. While access is not difficult, only those who are intent on browsing these sites would be entering those areas.

It was the unravelling of the hate sites that was surprising and it evoked some strong emotions:

> Began browsing hate sites and this is very disturbing (despite the fact I pride myself in being an objective unemotional researcher). Some sites are outright rude, nasty, horrendous and absolutely obnoxious to a non-white [or any] person. Compared to the pornographic sites, the hate sites are extremely easy to access and widespread. It seems like an understatement that the liberty of speech is being trampled wilfully as people claim academic freedom to do anything on the Web. If posting bomb-making instructions and pedophilia is illegal, why can't hate groups be kicked out? There is this ambiguity as to anti-censorship; I myself hate censorship. This is a difficult area.

If there had been an option to vote for or against censorship at that time, it would have to be for censorship; perhaps, our thinking was less logical and more emotional. Yet, a small part of goaded towards defending freedom of speech over censorship. Back to the Journal:

> The easy access to various hate group sites just amazes me! Why can't the local ISP determine which sites are accessible in Canada? When it comes to hate groups, they could inflict considerable damage on young minds. Some sites are outright crude, vulgar and absolutely uncultured and inhuman!

Access to the Site

Ron thought that the sites were easily accessible while "antiracist sites were fewer in number." This may have been due to the search words because one of the authors did find quite a few antiracist sites. At the school level, Ron felt that "Schools control access to areas on the Web" and thought that it is good in that it will provide differing perspectives [for students] while a certain level of maturity is required for kids to access the undesirable sites."

In terms of actual accessing time, Ron found that just one or two popular sites took a little while longer. He felt that, "most of the sites had very good access in terms of downloading, information, articles, and pictures" and that the sites, "tend to be fairly pleasing to the eye with graphics, text and pictures. They are fairly user-friendly. Some are harder to find than others. I started with a search engine and it took 3-4 different sites to get to the specific one."

While Waheed found that the sites were "user-friendly but pretty ideological," Gunadasa tended to be distracted with the smaller details of technology *per se*. Despite repeated prompts, Gunadasa remained more concerned about the presentation of and access to a site than the content of the sites: "People should be more careful about designing a Web page. Lot of gibberish. Perhaps there should be a rule to set up a Web site. What is the relevance of a Web page? [One should] restrict number and size of graphics [on a Web page]. Gunadasa felt that it took long to access sites, commenting that there were "a lot of irrelevant sites. Firstly, too long to load up. If a site takes more than 30 seconds, I move on."

Following the first conversation, Ron was able to get a better feel for accessing sites. As Ron described this:

> I didn't have trouble with any of the sites. I didn't have long wait at all for information. People are adding graphics to the background of page and it increases the download time a little bit. But it never takes more than a minute or two to load the whole thing and all the text comes up right-away and so I can read while any graphics are being loaded. So, no, I haven't experienced any real time delays. Occasionally, I saved a couple of pictures, like a couple of pictures from rallies and riots that got out of control and a couple of little posters. There's one where the sites had thumbnail sketches of poster they offer, like anti-discriminatory posters- so I downloaded a couple of those.

The access issue is partly dependent on the user; if one was unwilling to wait for more than 30 seconds as in the case of Gunadasa, the WWW can become a frustrating wait. Ron was able to deal with this aspect more creatively by reading the text even as the graphics were being downloaded. The irrelevance of a site, as experienced by Gunadasa, was perhaps due to the use of inappropriate descriptors. Journal entry:

> While some participants have voiced their partial skepticism (replacing their initial enthusiasm and belief in technology), not one of them would deprive themselves of the advantages offered by technology! While there seems to be an inherent understanding in the limitations of technology, a cautious hope and belief in its usefulness remains among the participants and, for now, in me.

Overall, there seemed to be an acceptance of the limitations but the willingness to get around it.

Personally, having gained some experience in understanding what patience is all about during the Internet journeys and based on those experiences, one could consider the following as some of the current barriers to using the Internet:

(a) *Affordability*: The struggle to keep up with constant upgrades, more memory hungry machines, larger hard drives, faster modems, better monitors, and newer software besides obsolescence make living with technology quite expensive.

(b) *Access*: Excluding expensive ISP's, high-priced ISDN lines, the busy telephone lines make it very difficult to gain access to sites. A minimum of one-hour wait and 200 tries are normal with the University of Alberta connections.

(c) *Connectivity*: It does take a long time to establish connections with some sites giving it the better suited name, *World Wide Wait* instead of the *World Wide Web*. This is especially true if the Web page is graphic intensive.

(d) *Search Terms*: Each search engine handles it own descriptors for a term; hence, one could end up spending many hours in unsatisfactory searches. Following a slow access and download time waiting for graphics to appear, one realizes a few minutes later that the site masquerading as a global education site was only a promotional site.

(e) *Error 404!*: This is a term for sites that do not exist anymore or have moved. Even discovering this could be the equivalent of going through a long sequence of voice message answer system only to discover that the lines are busy.

(f) *Download time*: This is the amount of time it takes to download a site or contents of a site to the local machine. In some cases, one would have had to sit for 3-4 hours waiting the site to download, only hoping that the connection would not be lost. Having discovered *ArabNet*, the downloading of the site resulted in 75 pages, 451 graphics, 1 hour and 25 minutes downloading, we lost 37 graphics retakes due to being disconnected by the University of Alberta. Optimistic as ever, another 3 hours were spent next week, downloading the site.

Global Education

Ron felt that some sites did contribute to the aims of global education in that the sites, "do aid the cause of antiracism-in a global manner." In trying to understand the definition of global education, Ron "spent a lot of time reading over all that information [given by the researcher] to define it more for myself." Many of the sites were inter-linked to other related sites as Ron described:

> These sites are not the sole elements for any of the groups that they are related to. They are an expansion from the grassroots— paper passing-out, newspaper advertisement, so on and so forth. So, none of the sites that I have come across so far [is] exclusively that orientated. So, they do offer a variety of mediums in which to pursue, like the antiracist centre in Norway. They do promote general human rights, equal opportunity and they do offer assistance to discriminated persons, in terms of monetary [assistance] or advocacy.

As to whether the sites Nalini had accessed contributed to the goals and objectives of global education, she felt that, "They could. It depends on the person who is using it. Usually aimed at higher education or community sites. Haven't seen anything for public schools; perhaps it is due to the type of sites I am accessing."

Waheed remained skeptical about some global education sites.

> With a lot of the sites that are dealing with global education you have a profound left-wing character to them. While there isn't necessarily anything wrong with that, the problem is that they tend to be somewhat extremist in their points of view. And because of their extremism, I find that I am naturally sort of turning off their message... They are very critical and they don't provide any alternative answers.

> *No Man Net* run by Michael Barrett is devoted to development of peacekeeping in Africa as a whole and Somalia in particular... The editorials tended to be very critical and very anti-United Nations; very anti-United States; and very anti-Western- very unreasonable. But the reason that I gave you my own political viewpoint [earlier as the more centre] so you can take it with a grain of salt; I naturally have inclination finding left-wing criticism to be somewhat stringent [and] somewhat strident... By left-wing extremism [I mean] *radical humanitarianism* as opposed to *communism*.

Waheed feels that they are critical, left-wing, extreme in views, anti-UN, anti-US, anti-Western, unreasonable, stringent and strident, radical humanitarianism, and yet provide no alternatives. In fact, Waheed concedes that these sites "turn him off." One of the allegations of global education is that it reflects the Marxist agenda and contains values that are "pro-Soviet, anti-capitalist and anti-American," and yet, "Marxists have played a minimal role in global education (Lamy, 1989, pp. 41-42). Global education, with its perceived "subversive intent" and "with hidden agendas" remains a "radical movement" by the "leftist crusade." This perception may have had an influence on Waheed's understanding of what he believes as "radical humanitarianism." In essence, as the Cunningham/ Tancredo suggest, "Every issue raised by any program of global education...[is] a political issue— of the most controversial sort" (Wronski, 1988, p. 147). Perhaps, challenging traditional and conventional structures may in itself become a necessary ingredient of global education. Waheed's comment also raises the issue of how different is the Internet from the classroom environment. If issues perceived as political or controversial cannot or will not be addressed in the classroom, one could also expect similar reaction to the material found on the Net. One could also wonder whether discussions over the Internet tend to occur between "like-minded" individuals and groups that may exclude dissenters. Unlike the conventional classroom, the Internet does offer the option for visitors to engage in active or passive interaction with the Web site proceedings.

Waheed also found some positive aspects of global education sites. He notes that, "There are some excellent critical essays there that are critical of the way that the United States is handling things but they are done in a very academic sense by respected academics [and] professionals and are being presented in such a way as to support what they are saying as opposed to the type of editorial commentary... So, that is good. And there are links to other useful sites."

Waheed demonstrated at the first conversation that he had some understandings about international relations. As he describes:

> Up until 1989 one tended to look at the Eastern communist totalitarian states versus Western democracy. In a political sense, state controlled economies versus capitalist economies. But now it is becoming more mainstream to look at the developed world versus the underdeveloped world- the North versus the South.

> It is starting to be that while people have historically tended to look at left and right as meaning, left- socialism and right- capitalism, people are now looking in the traditional sense of the left being looking forward for change and right-wing conservatism sticking with the status quo. And in that sense, you are looking at the right-wing people continuing this unequal relationship between the North and South. The North as a sort of Social Darwinistic, patronistic-type of relationship with the underdeveloped countries who are client states- [with] more economic domination than political domination. While I believe that there are problems in that area that need to be addressed, I don't think it's a productive way to address them— to reduce to reductionism. This sort of

257

economic reductionism is the biggest problem, I think, [with its] reducing all the problems in the third world to economics and reducing all problems to the unequal relationship that these several countries have with the West. They sort of deny the fact that there are domestic issues in all these countries making it extremely difficult for change to occur, and they tend to try and transpose Northern developed value systems on these underdeveloped countries... For e.g. In Somalia, there is the system of warlords, the system of dividing the country up into competing almost feudalistic thieves has been around for thousands of years and probably will be around for thousand more. It has become a lot more dangerous because of the advent of weapons of mass destruction... [with the idea of] "Every man for himself." And to blame the West for all this is frivolous in the worst possible sense.

Waheed thought that all sites "did not all necessarily deal with global education...but overall, they did. [For example] the Canadian military (the peacekeepers' home page) deals with pictures and ways to send letters and military reports, downloadable maps, not prescriptive, dealing with plain information, news update, etc." Waheed found few sites that had the term *global education*: "I didn't however, with the possible exception of the first [site] one I was talking about, run across a site dealing with the terminology of global education. [Thus, mostly indirect or implied]. But they are global education." Waheed, with his background in political analysis, refutes economic reductionism. He does not believe in reducing the third world economics to unequal relationships between the North and the South; rather, he would like to include issues that are domestic and local within the South. Waheed's own preconceptions of "left" and "radical" movements probably led him to believe that peace education sites were one-sided. In fact, the *No Man Net* Waheed refers to in his conversation contained legitimate criticisms of US intervention in the developing countries. Waheed's own political philosophy, which he agrees could be limiting his own understanding, convinced him of perceived biases and "leftist" tendencies.

Gunadasa was unable to find any site that was useful for discussion: "Have trouble finding any site relevant to global issues," but left with a promise of, "I will have to explore this further." Hence, for items like, "Have you changed your thinking about global concerns?" Gunadasa was only able to say, "Too early to make a comment on this." When asked about the role of the Internet in developing global identity, Gunadasa reverted to how a Web page should look and the preferred changes in the presentation of a Web page. Despite the introduction and orientation to global issues, Gunadasa remained oblivious to the topic and the critical aspect of global education. Hence, the conversation remained unfocused except for the censorship issues relating to the Internet. Gunadasa was not able to make it to the rest of the discussions. In terms of the methodology of identifying volunteers for the project, participants were made aware of the focus of the study. Based on the responses in the Preliminary Questionnaire, all participants had some degree of familiarity with issues relating to the study. The initial Orientation involved clarification of the focus of the study. It eventually became clear that Gunadasa had understood global education issues as "international" issues and perhaps, this precluded Gunadasa from contributing more effectively. This also raises the issue of the current interests that are termed, "global" that may lack the critical element to issues that are global.

Following the initial browsing and readings, Ron thought that many of the available sites he browsed contributed to the goals and objectives of global education. Ron describes this as follows:

> In terms of global education, I found a lot more sites; the topic itself has been global, because there's information around the world, so, seeing more along the lines of global accessibility also in terms of making people in other cultures aware. Most of the sites I found, of course were, North American-oriented, probably 70%, just because of the greater access to resources here. Those sites I found in foreign countries - many of them were in foreign

languages, which made it so much [more] difficult, because I can't read Norwegian and I only know [a] little bit of French. I can read the French sites, but some of them were from Japan, Norway, Sweden, and Germany. The Simon Wiesenthal Center had all of their information available in several languages. They had it in Russian and French and German and Japanese and Chinese and a couple of other languages. And, they are adding more all the time, to make it more accessible to people in different cultures and different places of the world. And a couple of the foreign sites are in the process of converting their information- like a couple of Norwegian sites had started putting pages on in English so that they can catch people's interest- as well the German sites as well. So, some were in German and some were in English- a combination. That was helpful; it gave you more access there.

Ron also thought that many of the home pages representing the developing world were actually based in North America: "Two of the eight were in North America. So, I think, I had five from the States, one in Canada, one was in Britain and the other in Germany. So yeah! Very much based in North America. But of course, they try to present a universal view. There are a number of web sites from antiracist organizations in Toronto being a big metropolitan centre." Ron thereby arrived at the conclusion that few grassroots sites were from the South. While Ron's search may have yielded this result, many sites have been established in the North on behalf of the initiators in the South due to issues of costs, access, freedom and rights. *PacaWom* is one such site that while based in Calgary, Alberta operates on behalf of the Pakistani women. Conversely, *ArabNet, Africa Online, Deccan Herald,* and *Malayala Manorama* are sites based in the South without any mirror sites in the North.

At this point, it became imperative as to the nature of how one utilizes the Internet and how on the one hand that would affect his or her ability to gain information or on the other, wander aimlessly without specific outcome:

The Internet itself does not motivate a person to pursue global education objectives per se but only provides a conduit and venue for people who are looking for a tool to access and disseminate information. Just having the information is as good as a horde of books in the best library where the person

260

only has to pick the topic and then look for the appropriate sources. One could also roam through the aisles looking for nothing in particular. Browsing aimlessly may result in serendipitous rewards but incidental discoveries remain quite fragmentary for an organized research in any topic. Similarly, a person surfing the Web aimlessly may access nothing in particular. An individual who does access issues of global relevance will have to be sensitized to the issues and be searching for sites that are specific to the topic. A sensitized person may look for it beyond the conventional sources of information, i.e., the library or the book store and go on to the Internet due to its powerful networking.

Perhaps, our previous orientation to global education enabled us to use the Internet in a more conscious and critical manner. Similarly, a teacher exposed to critical pedagogy may be apt to deal with crucial global issues in a discriminating way. The issue of global identity for Ron was more easily dealt with if one used the Internet as a tool:

> I guess, the topic [of racism/antiracism] may help bring people together and in some case may help just polarize people against those who perpetuate what is considered hate crimes or hate literature, or what tends to be really insulting. So, it may make it easier to deal with the problem like discrimination [by using the Internet to] bring people together. It helps to create a global identity or global purpose. [sic]

What Ron is talking about is the notion of "people coming together" in a common language and shared experiences that are familiar to each other and their own identities. Turkle eloquently explains this:

> It's not because of the Internet that we're shaping multiple ways of thinking about identity. The Internet is taking it to a higher power; the Internet makes the issue concrete. The Internet presents a very common experience and lets you play with it, gives you a language with which to talk about it. I haven't been at all surprised by people's thirst for getting online. (Greenberg, 1996, p. 164).

Nalini felt that the Internet had enhanced her thinking as a global educator:

> Some of the sites that I have visited have given me that sense of being connected. Of course, that is one of the underlying concepts in global education- the interconnection. So, connected to people, even though I may

not interact with them, but connected with like-minded people. So, there isn't that sense of isolation. I feel isolated if I am on the Net with racists.

According to Cortes (1983), global education entails exploring the meaning of groups and group membership, group image formation, perspectives, and intercultural communication. In being able to belong to the group is a part of the process of community membership. Nalini felt that the ability to be "connected" even without interacting with others was empowering. The Internet for Nalini has contributed to the removal of isolation among like-minded people— in this case, global educators. In being able to identify and become a part of the corporate body of global activists can in itself become an empowering experience. If this is true, the Internet can be acknowledged as a powerful tool that enables potential activists establish connections across borders. Tye and Kniep (1991) describe global education as engaging in the learning of problems that cut across borders and boundaries and most importantly, as relating to the "interconnectedness of systems" that are cultural, ecological, economic, political, and technological" in nature (p. 47). Thus, the process of connecting to explore issues that are interconnected includes by its nature, elements that constitute an exercise in global education. For Nalini, this is the first phase of establishing contact before moving on to actively exploring and reacting to substantive issues.

Classroom

During the initial stages of this project, Ron described how he would use technology in his classroom. Expecting to contact a teacher in another country or a group of students in another country Ron set up discussions between kids. He felt that "kids may be more comfortable in discussing such topics with somebody

262

in Cuba, Russia, Bosnia, India, and France [over the Net] and that will bounce back into the classroom and generate lively discussions."

During the later stages of this project as a substitute teacher, Ron was also able to incorporate some of the Internet resources into his classroom teaching.

> I am actually teaching health section at my junior high; not my area of expertise but I'm subbing and so I have to teach that too. I'm gonna talk for a day or so about racism and I'm hoping to get some educational materials from a couple of the sites that promote those materials. Like this one [*Artists Against Racism* has] a wealth of educational materials in English and in other languages as well. And they have a serious teacher resource centre. This is in Norway, but they do mail worldwide to those who are interested. You have to pay for postage; but otherwise materials are free. The site has newspaper archives, newspaper clippings, etc.

In Ron's classroom:

> Some of the kids were talking about Hitler, Nazis, etc. in a very casual and flippant way. They did not know the cause of the events but only had some idea as to what it was. They seemed to be kidding and not using appropriate language. I found that a couple of sites I explored with them and would have avoided them. Perhaps the kids were not yet ready for this. The kids were from grade 7 (around age 11). I was trying to be serious without being an opinionated teacher [who was] condescending. This is a racially diverse school [and yet] they were not aware of the seriousness of their activity.

In response to whether he would introduce racist sites to his students in the classroom, Ron noted that he would "hardly" want to include hate groups as examples of undesirable sites, adding, "[I] will have to discuss with the administration. [They] may not want to access the sites. Personally, I would be concerned if the kids go in and [visit] some of those sites." Ron would try "more safe, civilized areas" before venturing out onto the hate sites. "There is the danger of racist sites influencing (converting) innocent kids. I would stick with antiracist groups. Contact people for resources, set up multimedia presentation materials, etc." While Ron had expected to use the Internet for establishing informal twinning between students in the classroom, he found it more useful in obtaining resource materials for teaching. In responding to his student's behaviour regarding Nazis and corresponding language, Ron joined his class in exploring sites that he thought would perhaps address the issue. He did have second thoughts on whether his grade 7 was ready to deal with some of the material at these sites. This exercise may emphasize the need for teachers to visit sites beforehand to confirm the appropriateness for a given classroom (age, topic, maturity, etc.). Ron did realize this and other ethical issues relating to presenting controversial information to junior high students. In order for the global teacher to be effective, it is imperative that there be a fair degree of commitment and understanding on the part of the principal, other teachers, and perhaps the local teachers' association (Case & Werner, 1997; Boston, 1997; Jarchow, 1997; Wilson, 1997). Besides, it is imperative that a global educator allows his or her students the freedom to surf on their own with sufficient warning about how they will have to view and understand the material. This is especially true in cases of students who have access to computers in their homes. It is monitoring, rather than surveillance, that will offer students the safe space to develop their own understanding of issues available on the Net besides the freedom to be innovative in their browsing.

How would Nalini use the Internet for a successful global education curriculum in the classroom?

[It] Depends on the student and the level of expertise. It definitely broadens one's horizon. It also depends on the teacher. When I access countries and see pictures, it is exciting. But there is a time element involved. I had to exit many times before the site [could be] completely accessed due to slow and busy lines. For students, there is the basic country information and it could be very helpful. But it takes time— that is the limitation.

Planning in advance and filling in a particular time frame [could avoid the delays]. If it is busy, the students may access after school but again, they may not have the technology back home. Even then, there may be the need for supervision.

How would Nalini use the Internet for activism (taking action) over merely accessing information?

> At this point, [I use it] only to interact with other people. I would hope that later, I may give my own feedback over the Internet, into the connection… One can create [one's] own home page and put out the information. Information including upcoming activities, publications, other links, etc… I would like to further the women's issues and human rights and [this] can be done through the Internet. The Internet has a place for action (action research) and spreading the word.

One concern for Nalini is that:

> There is a massive amount of advertising. Televisions, movies, radio, and magazines all utilize sponsors. Lot of advertising on the Internet. I do go into entertainment amidst serious work- like entertainment. I have accessed health, entertainment, information about a university in the UK, etc It gives me an element of hope for the future, dealing with more than just myself- opening up to a new world.

> I like the futurist magazine *Utne* (which I subscribe to) and I accessed the *Utne* magazine site on the Web. It can be addictive—especially if I had access to the Internet in my home.

For Waheed, "With the current technology, communications and resource access are the important aspects of research implications for class room teaching… As the Internet matures, the use of technology in the classroom will evolve." For example, how do people elsewhere look at a certain issue remains an interesting aspect for Waheed. As a global educator, Waheed feels that issues such as physical isolation from the rest of the world along with cultural differences remain less of a problem with the intervention of the Internet. He notes:

> I have people from as far as Germany and Australia sending me their opinions through email… One of the problems in education has always been teacher isolation… When you are dealing with global issues, you have more of a problem because you have cultural problems to deal with. You don't see

things through the eyes of the people who are living there and all too often, and the Internet provides a wonderful way for people to communicate with one another and bridge those gaps... With C-u-see-me, it will bring the video into the classroom where you can see each other.

Global SchoolNet's *Collaboration in the Classroom* allows such video interaction between students in two or more schools in different countries. We will soon be able to associate a face to the voice and message. In Waheed's case, the Internet serves as a conduit to "seeing through the eyes" of people living in other parts of the world. The physical act of "seeing" through another's perspective may facilitate developing and appreciating different worldviews. In fact, Ron's experience in the classroom demonstrates this aspect of "developing different perspectives." As Ramler (1991) notes, "Global education involves perspective taking, seeing things through the eyes, minds, and hearts of others" (p. 44) and placing oneself in the "shoes of the other," can be a revealing experience.

A couple of months into the project, Ron had found access to more classroom resources. According to Ron:

> Many of the same sites just provided more examples or they just spoke, say, on instances that may happen in our own country that it would be able to give people in the other parts of the world. So, if that provides a different perspectives for kids in a school that is very multicultural, it would speak to a lot more people because they can place themselves in the roles identifying with victims and the perpetrators- open up their perspective a little more. I spent a couple of days talking to a couple of my health classes, between topics. These resources may have been made available in other ways but the Internet makes it much more accessible and enables communication much more quickly.

While Ron felt that all this information on the Net had not changed his understanding of global issues ("I don't think my view in terms of its value has changed very much since last time. The research is continuing... I haven't come across any mind-shattering revelations"), Ron's experience with the Internet as a resource, appeared to have been enriched:

> Again, like last time, it [the Internet] has helped me become more aware in my own teaching and in other people's teaching as well, and it has made me less tolerant when kids are sort of jabbing each other with what could be considered racial slurs or even gender. Especially in a junior high, the situation where I've been working grade seven and nine with the kids, [they] tend to use that type of language a lot. The users of it are much less self-conscious. So, it's made me much less tolerant and has generated some good discussions among the kids as to how it makes other people feel.

Despite Ron's feeling that his "values had not changed much," his decreasing tolerance for racist comments in the classroom proves a change in his sensitivity. According to Tye and Tye (1993) and Gilliom (1993), this kind of teacher sensitivity to the issues is one of the important requirements for a teacher to become an effective global educator.

Did the browsing on the Internet change Ron's thinking about the world? Despite what Ron feels, has his identity evolved?

> Rather than "change," it has "expanded my horizons" finding other groups with common interests [such as] awareness of racism. About groups fighting for the same cause all over the world- beyond the country we live in.

After having read some articles and discussions on the topic of elimination of racial discrimination at the international level [including] activism, the struggle, and heroic people, this exercise has made Ron "more aware of the problems and the magnitude of this problem in society." When asked as to whether the increase in sensitivity to global issues was because of his experience on the Internet or due to his own sensitivities, Ron felt that it was a combination of both:

> I think my experience on the Internet germinated or brought it on. It increased my sensitivity, because it's a new venue for me to experience that sort of communication, like most people experience the advertisement on TVs and radios, tapes and what not but you know it's coming from a different direction. So, this is like trying to find the right key for some people, so ... I

take it to the next level. And so, from that point of view, the research on the Internet was the key.

Though Ron had become sensitive to issues perceived as global, it was not clear as to how action for transformation and solidarity occurred. These could have been activities such as joining campaign against racism or actions that established solidarity with human rights movements.

As Nalini was not teaching but has been in the faculty, she had some interaction with a student who had had problems with her students. Nalini explains how she began to see the Internet as a part of the solution:

> A teacher teaching in the North has had classroom problems. "All hell has broken loose." She has had to face a volatile community, out-of-control kids, who last year, were great. She has been abused and threatened. A trouble-shooter is coming in [to resolve the problems]. I have been thinking of creative ways of dealing with this traumatic situation. If only they could sit down and work with tools allowing them to be exposed to a wider world. The connection to the outer world would perhaps give them a sense of connection and learning. I began to think, "How would the Web do this for them?"

In attempting to use technology as a tool among physically isolated communities, Nalini has begun to explore an age-old concern of disconnection. Being connected becomes an act of empowerment, as seen with the students at the Lincoln Elementary in Bellwood and the disabled students in wheelchairs at the Cedar School. As geographically isolated communities gain access to the rest of the world, they will be able to share the sense of connection Nalini experienced. Perhaps, the kids in the above situation may be able to share with the rest of the world about their lives in the North. Thus, they may not only improve their self-esteem and self-worth but also enrich the knowledge of people elsewhere, as seen in the case of Bellville Elementary in "the heart of Amish country" in Ohio.

Main Use of Technology at the Present

Ron felt that the main use of technology would be *communication* and *access resources*. For example, "*Artists Against Racism* is a good site that offers information, posters, music, etc. Perhaps whole modules for teachers, sites newspaper clippings, etc." Being a music teacher, Ron had tried to bring in antiracism concept into music by, "Using music to depict increase in violence and dealing with it – making kids aware through a compositional project writing music or acting it out. Finding ways to deal with violence. Music is a powerful medium, it is emotional; attaining some kind of peace through music- definitely among adults. May not be that emotional for high school kids but the possibility is still there." For Ron: "The medium is important, I think. It does play an important role in terms of how it captures person's intention and imagination. I probably have to call it may be 60-40 relationship with the information being on the 60 side. Just because of the power to put so much in front of you given that many people become visually oriented with televisions and computers." Ron describing how he used the information on and access to the Internet in his classroom:

> For the music group, I talked about the conversation one and using it for communication with other people, the discussion, particularly. But of course, I want to contact before hand whoever is in control, the master control, to make sure that it was focused appropriately to the class. Even if it was between one other school and our school. And, I'd have kids, these from a social studies point of view, what idea would be to have kids, pick a group or on the other hand take a racial group and do you research in terms of the history, history of discrimination... More of the sites are now not flashier but better. So, I think, there's a decrease in the hierarchy on the web in terms of master and resource pages... So, in terms of self-organization and self-control, and hopefully, it doesn't become too big, it's still hard to wrap your mind around it sometimes. But once it becomes more organized, I think it will definitely have increased value. I realize last couple of months that some of the sites that I was using before- I just did a little check of the ones I was using before just to see was it changed since the last time I looked at. Some of them had more links to the main upper level pages, and some below them were sub-divided into different areas. So, that was definitely an improvement.

269

And I think that will probably be as it continues. And I'm sure probably some of the other people have found that too that it could be getting more organized.

For Nalini, "The Internet is a great tool but with two major limitations: accessibility and updating of information." Nalini also felt that one needed to be careful in checking out whether "the sites are active and are updated. Critical, [and] not blind acceptance. In my research work, I found the Internet to be very helpful." Nalini still felt that the Internet helped ease feelings of isolation:

When I sat down at the computer, I found that there were others who think like me. Secondly, I was feeling very isolated at that time and [the Internet] changed that. I could connect with other people who were thinking and doing and writing about [the issue I was researching] and just to think how good it would be if those problem kids could have a similar [connecting] experience!

While Nalini agreed that she would go back to the Internet to use its potential as an aid for a global educator, she felt that "the Internet was not indispensable." In contrast to the initial phases of this project where the participant had hesitations and scepticism relating to using technology, the participant had now begun to look for solutions to every day problems with the help of technology. Without becoming a committed believer or a skeptic, Nalini's observation ties in with how one of the researchers had felt at this time. Journal note:

No one can be completely unbiased. I go into this project with some strong biases and opinions... I do feel that there is a legitimate argument on both sides of the issue: computer geeks wasting away their lives at the keyboard in the belief of almighty machine that is a panacea for the everything from efficiency to poverty and then, those Luddites on the other side, who think that this is a curse that artificial intelligence would take over the world! Both are far-fetched and extreme. I go into this project with this understanding and belief.

According to Ron, the Internet helps spread information about community activities, allow email information over the Net, provide a venue for sharing information, and offer resources for teachers. Ron thinks that the amount of information on any given topic is "mind-boggling" and "staggering." In fact, he was "taken aback" by the volume of information. Ron thinks that the Internet will enhance one's sense of global identity, "Assuming that they will have access to the Internet [because it] provides a better interactive medium."

Her experience with the Internet did have an impact on Nalini's thinking and action. As she noted:

> It makes me feel more connected to the world. When one cannot go to these countries, I could at least connect with them over the Internet. The inability to go to these places is compensated by being able to connect; I don't have to go to Nigeria... The Internet is wonderful for people who are physically restricted, either because of economics or health. I am becoming a believer but with some qualifiers. We deal with global education and peace education [and] to hear it and see it on the Internet is validating.

For Nalini, while the Internet could be a tool for empowerment, there was a note of caution: "Yes, but with a qualifier. As in anything, we need to never lose our ability to think critically. It is an emancipator but only to the extent that you are willing to dialog with it... The Internet has been very liberating for me." Nalini felt that her identity of the global citizen had changed in that it had "increased [her] awareness and knowledge and the connection." Greenberg describes how Turkle explicates identity as a moment that "isn't fixed but variable and fluid" — the "liminal moment" when "things are betwixt and between, when old structures have broken down and new ones have not yet been created" (Greenberg, 1996, p. 109). Nalini is in this "state of flux" as we all are, the liminal moment, what Turkle calls "a moment of passage when new cultural symbols and meanings can emerge. Liminal moments are times of tension, extreme reactions, and great opportunity" (Greenberg, 1996, p. 109). Greenberg dwelling on this aspect notes that while such moments are "painful, tough, full of hard choices... they can be exhilarating."

271

After a couple of months into the project, Ron felt more optimistic about technology: "I think [the Internet] will be more beneficial; I was a little bit wary last time, I remember, but I am feeling better right now." Ron's feeling of being more comfortable is very personal— he is not just talking about the technology but relating himself and his experiences to technology. As Turkle (1995) in clarifying her interest in the subject muses, "[T]o understand how ideas move out from a sophisticated technical world into the culture as a whole and, once there, how they shape the way people think about themselves" (p. iii). In the production of multiple stories and the unfolding of multiple selves that Turkle extrapolates, the computer is more than a simple tool for typing— it facilitates in the evolution of your identity that enables in the concept of "you are who you pretend to be... Computers don't just do things for us, they do things to us, including to our ways of thinking about ourselves and other people" (1995, p. 26).

> After having spent some time with technology, Nalini comments:
>
> My hyper excitement [about the technology] has become more balanced and I think I am more [computer] literate... but they change so much. But definitely, it [browsing] is worth doing. Again, if it [were] suddenly taken away from me, I would survive without it. I might miss it, because of some of the stuff you can access, like the connection with the broader world. Time-wise, like I can spend four hours just like that! Given the option, I prefer books. They go where the wires don't and those books won't crash on me... there is something romantic about books.

Nalini's comments reflect Turkle's warning: "We need to be careful. Ultimately, the computer is a machine" (Greenberg, 1996, p. 165). In similar vein, Shenk (1997) had argued that "Computers are neither human nor *humane*" (emphasis, original) (p. 11). A year later, Nalini emailed:

> Monday, June 16, 1997
>
> Hello John,

How nice to hear from you. Things are going well...just plugging away at it and can actually envision a completion of this portion of my experience (the thesis I mean). Must tell you that you handed me a gift when you introduced me to the NET; it has proven to be an asset in my research process.

Sincerely

[Nalini]

If one reads carefully into the change in Nalini's relationship with technology, over a period of two years a remarkable "love affair" has blossomed. It is interesting to note the change among some from scepticism about technology to some qualified confidence in its utility and some waning of excitement among believers in technology—from unrestrained hope to cautious promise. In one sense, the Net remains a paradox of marvellous implement and to some extent, a destructive tool.

Barrier

Ron believes that the Internet can be an important tool in the classroom and feels that, "In terms of communication, it will be important. Many schools have labs and Internet access; a possible project would be writing letters asking questions or giving stories about discrimination; asking guidance materials." Yet, it is true that, "the barrier at the moment is technological resources [and in some cases there is] only one computer in the school. Hence, access is limited."

Ron believes that "for schools, [the technology] is a top priority. Most of the teachers don't know how to use [it] but they have to have it there; just because they see it as a prestige thing; in having technology of the future in their school [and] Mostly, teachers are inexperienced in technology." According to Ron, some of the limitations in using the Internet include, Isolation (cut off from everyday experiences); losing out on emotional and body language and expressions (facial, etc.); lacking traditional communication advantages between people interacting face to face, and very limiting nature of the medium. While the "Unified project over the Net may help... it still is limited interaction." The commonly assumed barriers to technology, according to Ron, "is not insurmountable in Canada."

Waheed still thinks that the Internet is hard to use. "There are search engines, but it takes some time. It is not monitored; there is lot of junk or crap. A lot of people have home pages [that are useless]." He also feels that there is an overwhelming amount of information that needs to be sifted out from seemingly important information.

For Nalini, "There is an element of power [as to] who controls what, i.e., who is pulling the strings. I don't know who controls it [the Internet] now but a wild guess— it could be the technical/technological people. When computers started to be the thing, I had this phobia with computers and I had to take some courses to get through that, to find out that I could work with them and that they were not there to intimidate me. But they have their limitations too... I love it! (Internet) but I also like reading print." As Stoll (1995) pondered, "Ugh! Can't lie the laptop on my chest. A paperback might weigh ten ounces—a pound at most— but this thing weighs five pounds... It's cumbersome, clunky, ghastly slow, and mechanical. The text isn't hard to read, it just feels unfriendly... There are no pages to turn. No dust cover to touch... Come to think of it, I can't read an electronic book in the bathtub, on the beach, or on the subway. Book publishers have nothing to worry about" (p. 41).

A final note on the planned complexities among technologists. Nalini was concerned about the techno-jargon—the language used by technologists to intimidate computer novices and make their "expertise" esoteric. There appears an undue amount of energy and attention spent among many users in understanding the technology rather than the content. The distracting nature of the Internet seems common among many users.

Censorship

As to the question of whether we should allow racist sites on the Internet, Ron felt that the "Level of censorship should be at the personal level- parents, teachers, educators, etc. since it is not possible at the international law."

> Nalini was not very clear on the Internet and censorship issue Not sure! Do not believe in censorship but I believe in respect. Recognizing the complexity of any issue or question- we cannot take a universal approach to anything; we need to look at each one individually. To see offending words on the computer can be quite violating." Someone locally will have to take responsibility to deal with such things on the Internet. Parents, teachers, etc. must take the responsibility to do that. But there can be situations where parents cannot do it.

Waheed is against censorship and "would refuse to censor even if the material is offensive." When probed for reasons, excepting the notion of freedom of expression, Waheed thought that he needed more time to think about the issue of censorship saying, "I really don't know what the answer is."

Gunadasa thought that it would be "impossible" to regulate the Internet and that perhaps this could be done [by consensus] through forums, chat groups, and societies like International Society for Technology in Education (ISTE), (an international group that should recommend, rather than control, what we should focus on)." Gunadasa felt strongly that it was desirable to regulate the Internet rather than controlling it. Nevertheless, he felt that, "It [was] a tough issue. When it comes to moral aspects, it could be easy to regulate. We have to deal with this just like television; some people find it acceptable for their children to watch something that other parents may not find it so. I have the remote control to regulate what they watch. The *Net Nanny* for the Internet can help control what our kids watch. Depends on what is morally acceptable in our society."

> Ron ponders over the good and bad on the Internet:
>
> I think there has been a decrease in people trying to— throughout the Internet being self-controlled... In terms of programs on the computer, programs are available on the computers for parents to decide whether kids can or can't see and cry against government regulations and try and return some responsibility to the people for to controlling themselves. A lot of times, they're talking about in terms of bad people like people who go out there to create or do crimes, sexual crimes or hate crimes. But they're very small percentage of the users and are controllable and police-able by those responsible for the systems— usually those Web-masters.

Ron perhaps raised a pertinent issue of how global educators need to be cautious but not paranoid about the perils of browsing on the Internet. Teachers could resort to advising students about the dangers of uncritical browsing. They could also, not unlike street-proofing the kids, ensure "Net-proofing" their students before allowing them to browse without supervision. Students could be taken to both racist and anti-racist sites along with critical commentary on how the conflict and tensions exist on the Net. Ron had a clearer position on the censorship by the end of the second conversation.

> Yeah! I've got a bit more optimistic on this issue. I've have had a chance to see some of the programs that are available and what not. The Simon Wiesenthal Centre— that's one of the big ones I found that was really a good site to access. It was mainly Holocaust-oriented of course, but was very accessible, had lots of archives, a new page conducting polls in terms of attitude, U.S. Presidential election, in terms of racial harmony, disharmony, and statistics for their own use. Multi-lingual, they had...what they call the *CyberWatch* [censorship software]. If there were incidences of racial disharmony or discrimination, they could be reported [to this site] and those could be passed along to the authorities to be followed up.

276

Ron's thinking on the censorship issue evolved as it did in case of our own understanding of whether to regulate the Internet. The initial shock of having visited some of the hate sites had convinced us that censorship was not only moral and ethical but a necessity. Eventually, having had time to ponder over the issues and read debates over the impossibility of controlling the Internet, we came to the conclusion of local regulatory bodies or mechanisms. More importantly, we have come to the notion of dealing with the people behind the technology than establishing arbitrary restrictions. As Mock (1997) notes, "The problem of hate did not begin with the Internet; so although stamping out offensive sites would be an ideal solution, how feasible is it, if new ones will invariably appear to take their place?" (p. 2). Sites like *White Power*, *Zundelsite* and *Skinheads* have already proven that attempting to censor a site in one country only results innumerable mirror sites around the world, facilitating the mushrooming of more hate sites that are beyond monitoring.

The Internet's Future

In projecting the Internet's future, Ron thinks that it will become more prevalent, more affordable (at least in the industrial world), increasingly common for personal use; assist in the development of virtual technology; and result in more email and chat groups through VR, making it more interactive. Ron also thinks that "the government will not have so much power to step in and control [and that] majority of the users will control the use of technology" Ron parts with a note of caution: "I see a lot of growth; yet, we have to be vigilant."

Nalini felt that the Internet of the future might be more interactive. She was concerned about the isolation aspect of Net users but it did give access to

277

some people who are physically restricted. "Sitting in front of the computer the whole day could make us very physically isolated but the interactive component where you are not intellectually isolated because you are actually accessing the whole world— so, there has to be some balance somewhere in there." Nalini also felt that the Internet of the future would "be more controversial," with "the gap between the rich and the poor widening, it could be available to only the rich. It may serve as a propaganda tool. The Internet can be considered as a 'double-edged sword' and not just a necessary evil. It has the good and the bad." In being able to access and download one whole dissertation for printing, Nalini felt that it was a remarkable tool for researchers and students. Nalini notes that in a society that believes in instant access, the Internet accessibility could be improved and made more affordable. She would also like to see it in more schools.

Waheed envisions that the Internet will change how people think of 'nations.' Accordingly, "The construct of the nation state will be almost unimportant, they will exist, but become unimportant." This is especially true since the Internet has no borders and there cannot be prosecution of individuals in one country when material has been posted in some other country. Recently, "CompuServe in Germany took material off the Net. China is trying to create its own Internet... but in less than 5 years, they will have to give up..."

Waheed feels that while voting and democratic participation will be at grassroots level using the Internet, "There will be increase in calls for democracy because of the Internet [and] people will keep voting for their own personal interest rather than national interest causing confusion and unstable situations [sic]." Waheed is optimistic about the future of the Internet and the people using them in that, "Information will be widely spread, while [in the past] only certain segments of the society had access to information, now everyone will be able to do so." Yet, one needs to heed the caution by Roszak (1986), that to give the reader the illusion of power by gaining access to data is "data mongering." The notion of abundant data "available to every man and woman in their home is supposedly destined to be a liberating force" is tenuous at best (p. 161). On the contrary, as Shenk (1997) reminds us, the increasingly available information will only create a new form of stress:

> With the pressure to deal with digital information that may not be meaningful, we have begun to develop the guilt of not being able to deal with abundance. Yet, we are bombarded with information that cannot be ignored and somehow needs to be assimilated, lacking which, could be considered a deficiency resulting in guilt. This dependency, according to Philip Nicholson causes "technostress" (pp. 43-44).

Assuming that many will have access to the information, this may not be a universal occurrence across countries. It is important to realize that the participants are speaking as voices from the North. The notion that common person in the developing world has or would have access to technology, taken for granted in the developed world, raises a host of questions about perceptions of access and democracy in the North.

Gunadasa was less optimistic about the future role of the Internet. He felt that by the year 2010, the Internet would,

> set up class societies across the world, not just in countries. Access to someone in Africa will be limited and thus deprived of the information that I have access to. Some classrooms may not have access to technology. There could be disparity in access to technology across countries... Eventually, the Internet will be controlled by a few people.

Ron thinks that despite limitations, the Internet would become more popular and useful.

> [T]he Internet can bring people closer together, more resources can be shared in terms of that, which may create more access. And again, it will become more accessible and I fully believe that... It will be heavily regulated [and] censored,

and it will be truly combined world effort with self-policing –showing great personal responsibility [within] the global community.

By the end of the second phase of the Project, there was a sense of satisfaction and confidence among the participants as to their relationship with technology. More interestingly, they were venturing beyond the mere use of technology to apply their skills in becoming better global educators.

The Journal entry:

> The second and final focus group is now over; had interesting discussion. It is easy to see how people who have questioned technology change to be able to use it but cautiously while they consider the limitations critically. More interesting is the way individuals begin to apply their knowledge of the use and implications of technology to problem situations that are remote or happening with their acquaintances. Resolving lack of classroom discipline among isolated aboriginal groups of students in the Northwest Territories by introducing computers and networks. It sure sounds promising!

Personal Change

As to whether this experience had changed her understanding of global issues, Nalini felt that it had, "to [a] certain extent." Raising some strong feelings about access and connectivity, Nalini comments:

> Usually I feel isolated and not connected. With the Internet, I feel connected with someone in another country has similar interest. In the US and in the UK, there are lots of people working on the Ogoni issue. Work is being done at the university level and community level, research and scholarly work being done in this area. Extremely happy to find peace education and knowing that other people are out there, doing similar work. I haven't touched the tip of the iceberg.

For Waheed, it was difficult to measure whether the Internet had really changed his global perspective. "The problem is that I have been deeply involved with the Internet even before the project… The term global education was never a defined word for me but all along, I have been dealing with global issues on the Internet but this project has clarified the definition."

In terms of having developed a global identity, Waheed felt that the world around him had helped him reorient himself to the notion of a global citizen. He notes:

> Until 1988, I have identified myself as a citizen of the "Western world," a very Aryan type of attitude. When I was in Europe, it changed to a "patriotic Canadian." When I returned, I became very narrow, identifying myself as Albertan and Edmonton. Later, [my recent schooling] opened my eyes on issues affecting developing countries. Following that, I edged toward the global citizen; it still is a dominant worldview.

While Waheed does not directly attribute his global identity to the Internet, he has in a sense, become what Turkle calls, "the naturalized citizen of the Net, not a native" (Greenberg, 1996, p. 161). We see Waheed having gone through multiple and evolving identities to become a global citizen sensitized to issues that are critical and global.

In transcending beyond physical boundaries, Waheed feels that nationalism in its basic nature will remain but the Internet will facilitate looking beyond the man-made boundaries of nation states:

> It is tough for people to identify a global community because people need to reach out and touch. Some people require it to be a narrow view, like family while others need an entire civilization to identify themselves. The Internet is taking people beyond nationalism towards global citizenship but there will always be nationalism and regionalism. Environmentalism, for example, is futile to be considered under national concern but religion cannot be considered under at the global level... [sic].

For Ron, the whole experience appears to have had some impact on his life:

> Outside of teaching, probably increased sensitivity when dealing with sensitivity issues, issues of music like sound and silence. We had them try to sit quietly and then record the sounds that you're learning and very few of

them, would talk to a friend for a second. They'd write down that they heard their friend's voice but not that they heard their own speaking. And even the sounds that were around them, the school outside, people walking in the hallway, that are very quiet sounds. A lot of them didn't pick up on these. Then we talked about their abilities and sensitivities to sound and the fact that they were deadened somewhat by popular culture- a lot louder music at the same level repeated at them. We had discussions about sensitivity to other issues as well. It's like being used to medication when I take larger doses to have the same effect. So, the more sensitive they are to things, they are more able to perceive and understand and react to them, like in music...

I was reading a book by a Canadian writer Sheaffer. This book is called *Ear Cleaning* and based on the premise that you have to clear people's ear out of what they hear everyday, so they can be open to the good experiences-musical and otherwise that are important, and he starts the book on talking about noise. How noise is undesirable to the act of communication and then he goes on to talk about silence- nature of sounds- different musical aspects. But you just apply it to another area.

How did Ron use this exercise to raise race issues?

I talked about sounds first, in the classes... I asked them to be quiet... once they were quiet, I said, "Now, you are quiet... Part of the noise was the insults from boys to the girls." And I said, "Just hear the sound of my voice." That is when I was talking quietly [softly]. And, then I mentioned what in music kids would be doing, in terms of sound and we talked about sensitivity. They had just talked about family dysfunction and function in the family... We almost ran out of time. I asked them to go home and think about things that are said to you that are may be insulting or degrading and to make a list of that. Some of them had, whether it was from parents or other kids, some had very extensive lists. And, they had been sensitive to it before and they were sensitive to it now and they were more willing to take action to try to stop it. Like saying, "Please don't do that to me, that's not appropriate," which is a large part of their education in the early grades like 7 to 8 – learning what is appropriate behaviour in whatever society they are part of.

Ron was trying to apply the concept of being able to listen to other's voices over the day-to-day noise that may mask the silent voices of people and culture.

8.2. Focus Groups

As to the *need for global education*, some felt that it provided an increase in knowledge base and that it encompassed more relevant and contemporary topics or issues. As it emphasized the interconnectedness between human beings, global education could enhance global awareness in relation to self and others. They felt that such an exercise facilitated the development of a "global citizen". For some, "not much had changed since the Love & Peace era in the 60's," and as the world had become smaller through the electronic medium (e.g. the Gulf War media coverage) [Time and Space], they felt that the electronic medium might facilitate the development of global education. For some, this could enhance the survival and well being of the planet. All participants agreed that it was vital to learn about different societies and cultures.

The participants felt a sense of interdependence among various nations. Our lives do affect others within the global realm [interactions, interconnections, and interdependence] and we do influence each other and we all are affected by decisions made elsewhere. This inter-connectivity was especially relevant with the example of Chernobyl disaster affecting the global community.

Some participants noted that global education need not always be negative or be used to scare children. They felt that it could engage kids in discovering, understanding, and critically questioning since kids whose action will have an impact on others must be judiciously exposed to critical analysis of global changes. One participant observed that we beware of our intentions, in that, we explore with kids as to why the western nations do not concern themselves with issues elsewhere unless there was any gain for them.

283

As to the *concept of Global Education*, the group agreed that global education increased knowledge and awareness of the global or broad-ranging—intercultural and cross-cultural issues. Global education entailed learning about different cultures, countries, and customs. It implied teaching about the world in contrast to living or experiencing it. In developing a healthy world around us, global education provided an alternative to violence, i.e., conflict resolution and non-violence or peace.

In terms of the *nature of the Internet* and its role in the lives of global educators, some of the participants felt that the Internet was a valuable tool in contrast to the visual and verbal situations in real life. Due to its faceless nature, "there could be no prejudice on the Internet." One could not see whether the person on the other end is young or old, female or male, Caucasian or Oriental or African. To some, this would make the Internet a phenomenal tool to remove barriers. Yet, it is worthwhile to beware of the nature of this so-called innocuous tool that Turkle believes is "no *simple* tool but instead an evocative object, helping us to redefine who and what we are, where we stand in the world of artifact" (Greenberg, 1996, p. 161).

Some participants felt that the Internet provided "intimacy" between schools and/or kids (twinning) while others noted that it still raised the fear of "human isolationism" due to technology. For some, it remained a valuable tool for distance learning (e.g. videoconferencing and being used in some form in the Australian Outback) and provided access to teachers and resources despite the distances and lack of accessibility; others cautioned that it allowed only certain classes and the privileged to access services.

Some of the participants reminded the group that the Internet allows newsgroups that are out of context to exist and hence, we needed to be critical and not take everything at face value. Despite the presence of voluminous amount of information, the Internet may allow conflicting information [messages] and checking for reliability was not only essential but also crucial.

In envisioning the *Internet's future in global education*, the participants felt that the Internet had the possibility or potential for dealing with critical issues and providing greater access in all classrooms (at least, in the developed world). For some, it offered the possibility for individual instruction (e.g. LEARNET in Edmonton Public Schools) and could remove isolation as to the learning environment while for others, it would have to facilitate and not take the place of teaching of global issues.

Not only would it promise greater access and affordability, the Internet could play a role in home schooling in allowing access to education from remote places. It would allow twinning where classes could solve problems with others across countries. One participant thought that the Internet would result in a less paper-based society (environmentally friendly).

While for some the Internet allowed communication across the world, others felt that it could result in the loss of indigenous languages. All participants agreed that the Internet had the potential to increase the disparity between developed and developing world in that the third world countries will lack access and affordability to use the technology. It would allow access to only the privileged in the less developed countries. On the one hand, the Internet offers freedom to communicate and express but on the other, it could be subject to

285

unwarranted censorship. Some participants expressed concern over the possible privatization of the Internet and its decreasing accessibility for some.

In essence, participants envisioned the discrete use of the Internet. Rather than replacing teachers and classrooms, they felt that it would be used during specific class time when issues of importance are being dealt with. Thus, it would be an aid or tool to supplement the teacher's role in the classroom.

Following the completion of the focus group, participants chose specific areas of interest as they planned to begin surfing the Internet. Thus, each of the participants had identified a relevant area of interest to pursue during the Internet search and hence, the second focus group session elicited specific issues and concerns.

During focus group session two, elements relating to the following questions were addressed:

- Why do we have to concern ourselves with global issues?
- Do you think we need global education? Why or why not?
- What area/areas of cultural dimension interested you most?
- In having been a part of this project, what have you achieved for yourself?
- Besides this project, how do you plan to use the information you have accessed?
- [In terms of processes; barriers; resolution strategies; and failures] Has your experience on the Internet had any influence on you and the way you interact at the (a) Personal level (b) Interpersonal level (c) Professional level, and (d) Societal level?

- How do you perceive the current domestic and international events relating to cultural issues as a result of your Internet explorations?
- During your experience with the Internet, what specific aspects of technology encouraged/ discouraged you?

Similar to the first focus group session, the activity entailed dealing with four major aspects of the study, namely:

(1) The Need for Global Education and Our Role in it
(2) Clarifying the Concept of Global Education
(3) The Internet and its Role in the Lives of Global Educators, and
(4) A Vision of the Internet's Future in Global Education.

As to the *need for global education*, the participants now felt that it was a natural outgrowth of technology and the survival of the planet (not just the environment) was crucial to human sustenance. To some participants, this need for global education was not just dealing with survivability but nurturing of life. Some participants felt that global education increases our understanding of various issues and then allows us to take appropriate action; it inspires and allows us to take action at the micro and/ or macro level.

In essence, some noted that global education enhances the connectivity between peoples and increases our understanding of the role we in [the] North take, in maintaining the status quo of the South. It also enables us to actively look for ways and means of expanding what is to "serve the globe" and allows us to reconsider what is just and equitable at the global level. Global education helps create, at least partially, a global vision and culture to unite disparate groups and permits people from different backgrounds to have common experiences and shared goals.

In terms of what the participants had found on the Internet and how they were relevant to cultural issues of global dimension, participants cited a number of *area/areas of cultural dimension* that most interested them. These included: (a) Women's Issues (b) Human Rights (c) Cross-cultural arts (visual and written) (d) Empowerment (e) Peace Education (f) Cultural Identities (g) Anti-racism (h) Cross-cultural Links, and (i) Research and Technology.

Following their browsing and experience on the Internet, participants were positive in terms of the *nature of the Internet* and its role in the lives of global educators. They felt more positive about the Internet being used to expose students to different media in order to encourage learning and communicate with people more easily than might otherwise be possible. Some noted that in allowing two geographically separate groups to collaborate, the Internet would provide unique educational experiences. A few participants felt that if properly used, the Internet could help students be challenged and allow them to learn at their own rate or pace.

As to the *use of technology* for educators in terms of ease of use, relevance, and value of information, the participants were encouraged by the affordability of using technology to access information. Nevertheless, some questioned the relevance and use of information they had accessed and recommended conscious attempts to be critical when viewing sites and their contents. While one participant felt she had been "emotionally touched by the medium," the same participant also felt discouraged with the lack of *direct* emotional context in that it lacked the feel of paper or tactile stimulation. Some participants were fascinated by the process of searching and weeding through enormous volume of information but one participant sensed an element of distraction due to what he called, "Web Tangential Syndrome" (WTS[43]).

For many, the Internet was an experience in itself while others remained convinced that while the Internet was a valuable source of information, books remained a major source of accessing knowledge and information. Many realized that they would have been able to access information much more easily if they had up-to-date equipment.

In envisioning the *Internet's future in global education*, the participants felt that in the year 2010, the Internet would facilitate and broaden the horizons of understanding—reducing nation state boundaries; it would quite possibly connect the world where boundaries are transcended. Some felt that the Internet would continue to impact the knowledge level of individuals: "Children know more than me now or when I was a child in the 50's. So, in a way, things have already gone beyond what I ever imagined." Some participants envisioned that technology would provide access to enhance each other and not just themselves; it would perhaps link most classrooms in the industrialized countries by computers and become an important tool among skilled and knowledgeable teachers. Yet, others caution that technology would become unaffordable and hence, limited in terms of access and ease. One participant believed that technology would bring the promise of Virtual Reality, creating an intense and effective addition to the learning environment and allow Virtual Classrooms; accordingly, development of Virtual Reality Sensory equipment would enable communications in an artificial

---

[43] Web Tangential Syndrome or WTS, as used by one of the participants, is the proclivity to digress browsing for relevant and many a time irrelevant but interesting sites that are linked to the original site. This uses up hours of browse time in exploration, distractions, site-tracking and often, wasted on-line time.

environment. Another participant felt that this would limit the emotion and body language.

Many agreed that unfortunately, the growth in technology would allow space for hate groups and the like to thrive on the Internet, raising new and more challenging issues relating to censorship on the Net. It would allow misuse and abuse of technology due to lack of critical analysis and blind acceptance of information available on the Internet.

By the end of the project, each of the participants felt that he or she had a greater understanding of the topic chosen to research and the medium (Internet) they had used. Participants who were currently teaching noted that the project experience was very useful during classroom discussions. Some commented that they had achieved a wider understanding of a prevalent medium in today's world— "opened their eyes to a wider vision of the future of education." They also had a meaningful learning experience as they found others who were interested in similar things in the exploration process (poetry, social transformation) despite "being half a world away." Some noted that they had achieved a different level in their own research— towards a more positive manner in using the Internet. Participants agreed unanimously that they had gained valuable insights from this experience (especially for those who were novices in the area of technology). One participant was able to access enormous amount of information that otherwise would have remained unavailable or unknown to her. In doing so, this participant felt *"connected"* to the world. (e.g. "I was excited to find a high school reunion web site that allowed ex-students to re-connect").

In planning to *apply their knowledge* and experience gained during this project, participants intended to use the skill and information to enrich their classroom teaching and in the strengthening of their own professional development. One participant commented: "As a first year teacher, I will be in-charge of technology and computers at school. This project has provided me with some background and experience to feel comfortable with the upcoming responsibility." Another noted: "I feel empowered to address inequalities in the classroom, especially after this project. I will be more readily willing to challenge assumptions and stereotyping among students. The access to technology will enhance my resolution to do this." Yet another participant intended to use the technology to complete her thesis work. One participant observed: "I will be able to use information from the Net in a very efficient way; I have already taken a couple of quotes directly off the web sites."

As to whether their *experience on the Internet* had any influence in terms of processes, barriers, resolution strategies, and failures at various levels (personal, interpersonal, professional and societal levels), the participants commented as follows:

At the Personal level: "This project has had a sensitizing experience for me. Made me feel more grown up, because I was learning something new. The technology matured me in a way. A really interesting site was the *Amnesty International*. I travelled in during the summer and saw *Amnesty International*'s activities [in person] and that [with the Internet site] had an extra meaning for me."

At the Interpersonal level: "This experience has made me more empathetic; made more aware of interactions. This experience makes me feel that some barriers have been broken between individuals."

291

At the Professional level: "I have found sites where we could look for jobs. I now have a knowledge and experience about the web and what it can offer me [to enrich my professional development]."

At the Societal level: "I have gained different perspectives of any given problem— allows me to be in other people's shoes; hasn't made a fundamental ideological change but has made any change impressive due to the nature of the medium being so *persuasive* and *pervasive*. One aspect that may result from technology could be tight control and supervision in the classroom."

As to the question relating to their perception following their Internet explorations of current domestic and international events relating to cultural issues the participants preferred not to discuss their own understanding of various international issues but talked about the role of technology rather than the content they had accessed.

In general, the participants felt that their Internet explorations gave them a clearer understanding as to:

- How racism was culturally transmitted through the hate web site cultures.
- How parents could "train" their children through technology [by showing them sites that parents believe in].
- How ignorance could be transmitted through latest technology.
- How the Internet can be very graphic and live.
- How unnerving it was to see and hear on the web instead of just reading about such controversial issues.
- How Euro-centric (Western view) many issues were.

- How the language itself was limiting to non-English users.
- How some pictures could and were manipulative.
- How we had to maintain a critical approach to everything on the Net.

The researcher experiences unfolded during the project. It was possible to interact with people never met before; people who were in communication for a short time in countries far beyond the physical reach or presence. It has definitely provided the added insights to the understanding of differing perspectives and issues. Problems and concerns that are immediate to someone living in Tokyo have become closer and real to someone living in North America. For example, the *CNN Interactive*, is a site most commonly used by Net surfers. The CNN home page remained a major link and source site for this study due to its constant updates, versatility, extensive coverage, speed and accessibility. One of the most important elements of the site is the *CNN Interactive Feedback,* where comments from readers are posted. In one instance, the comments of the primary researcher in this study appeared at this site resulting in an email from a Japanese engineer.

November 19, 1996
Dear sir,
I found your name on CNN comments page. Therefore, please not be surprised to receive this mail from a stranger.

My name is XXX XXXXX, 26 years old, Japanese male, who lives in Tokyo, Japan. I work in a trading company which deals with Non-ferrous metals. Since I want to make friends with many people all over the world, I send you my E-mail this time. (I don't have any other way to get E-mail friend but picking up your mail address on Web site like CNN home page. Please forgive me.)

Please write to me, if you don't mind. I am waiting for your E-mail.

Best regards,
XXXX XXXX

ATTENTION:
I, myself, don't have any connection with CNN Inc., and writing to you this E-mail doesn't have any intention of political and economical purposes.I would apologize to you, if this E-mail gives you any troubles.

This launched a short but informative email interaction with the person about his daily life, his job, and his location. With the business of life that we all have burdened ourselves, communication with the Japanese individual was lost.

A few realities emerged from the experience with people around and with those in communication over the Net. These interactions not only facilitated the understanding of processes and people, but also challenged the perception about our own knowledge and interpretations we create in our minds. A few bright spurts of awakenings occurred in the process of discovery. There appears a clear acknowledgement of how we change in our perception, our thinking, our realization of how we view the *Other*, our evolving identities, our critical understanding of not only our world around us but around others. What kind of identity emerges if one spends time on the Internet? Not unlike other experiences, the experience with the computer and the Internet highlights our own "fluid" and "multiple" identities; it exposes our reactions to relationships that are both positive and negative, forcing us to never remain the same. As our understandings change, our experiences evolve, and our identities unfold, we become cognizant of the fact that it is "the now" that demarcates the reality from unreality for a given situation. What we agree now and how we feel about it presently may be different at a later stage. Technology confirms this transforming nature of human identity, just like the "transformer" concept or the fluid and changing nature of the Cyborg in the movie *Terminator*. We can become better global educators by realizing our own evolution and by recognizing how our relationship with others around us influences our own thinking. It is essential that we keep these perspectives in mind as we raise global issues in our classrooms and stimulate our students to ask challenging questions that may even question our own understanding of reality. Thus, global educators are not merely engaged in influencing their students toward change; they are in the process of defining themselves and their orientation to different perspectives and worldviews.

Chapter 9: Summary and Conclusions

9.1. Summary

The study began with a number of questions relating to the availability and usefulness of cultural issues on the Internet. Within the cultural sphere, three areas were focused, namely, *human rights, anti-racism education,* and *cross-cultural issues*. A number of related questions were raised. The main intent was to explore the role of the Internet in shaping our consciousness to become better global educators.

The content analysis of Web sites offered some insights into the nature of interaction between users engaged in cross-cultural communication. The *Access email Classroom Exchange* had examples of exchange between people across economic/social status, diverse cultures, geographical locations, physical disabilities, and language limitations. The *24 Hours in Cyberspace* provided the opportunity for an international collage to present the various aspects of human lives, while the Web sites like the *KidLink, Kids Online,* and *SchoolNet* offered students and teachers access to classroom resource materials. Sites by the *Worldwatch Institute, German Alert, Institute of Global Education, Institute for Global Communications* with its four sub-sites (*PeaceNet, EcoNet, ConflictNet, LaborNet* and *WomensNet*), and *Human Rights in Iran* were excellent examples of Web sites dealing with democracy, human rights, equality and freedom issues. The Internet can also allow dissemination of legitimate cultural causes, as was seen in case of *Cultural Survival, Centre for Study of Indigenous Peoples,* and *World Conference on Indigenous Peoples*. The *NativeWeb* and *The Village* aboriginal Web sites were two Web sites engaged in efficient networking in a cost-effective manner. The *Amnesty International* is a good example of establishing electronic dissemination for political support, collection of evidential information and maintaining international solidarity; *Amnesty International* and *German Alert* Web sites provided some of the best opportunities for people wanting to disseminate suppressed information. These initiatives were possible without the limitation of local communication systems or the legal or political constraints placed upon by people claiming power.

While users connected with each other exchanged information across borders, there remained no evidence as to whether the interaction involved critical questions pertaining to issues of equity, imbalances, historical incongruities and overall structural violence. During these electronic exchanges, no questions were raised regarding exclusion of the poor who do not have access to technology or the option to be heard. There was no direct recognition among any of the Web sites on the changing aspect of culture or identities. Web sites such as the *American Global Forum*, claimed to address emancipatory education within a democratic structure but did not offer free access to their Web sites without subscription dollars.

Some Web sites such as the *Third World Traveller* and the *Honolulu Community College*, had writers with good intentions who raised issues of undemocratic political structures in the developing world, consequently presenting stereotypes, condescending ideas, uncritical comparisons across countries, perpetuation of the Western myths and misconceptions. The seemingly neutral news Web sites such as the *CNN, BBC, Globe and Mail,* and *New York Times* had filtered the information resulting in their own biases. Yet, they remained the most favored of all sites for current events and relatively open discussions. Some sites like the *Afro-American* have embarked upon "re-presenting" the untold or wronged stories. While the Internet does offer the possibility to do this site's attempt to replace "untold" black histories with "re-written" histories belies the notion of the existence of a single originary identity and/or history. With its information on the diversity among Arab nations the *ArabNet*, reinforces the notion of culture being a human creation that is a product or fruit of people's histories. Despite its vast information, the *ArabNet* link sites remained sanitized by government presentation of culture and the lack of voices of dissent or critique remained obvious.

In most cases, we need to critically question our assumptions about how we define terms that cannot be universalized across cultures, as seen in the case of *The International Child Labour Study*'s definition of "child" and "child labour." Similarly, the neutrality of some Web sites that are seemingly not influenced by their funding departments needs to be questioned. Government sponsored human rights sites belie the reality of being subject to the mandate and expectation of their political masters. In cases where women's issues were presented (*Feminist-Com* and *PACAWom*), the specific concerns were not always necessarily identical in their origin, manifestation and resolution between countries.

The existence of hate sites raises the debate on freedom and censorship. Having experienced the implications of these sites, a reasonable argument can be made for local screening and control by users and Internet Service Providers rather than politically or legally mandated censorship. Sometimes, the vitriolic exchanges between racist and anti-racist sites reinforced the need for a more rational and non-violent approach to dealing with hatred on the Net.

A considerable amount of information, including those considered global education, needed careful screening for accurate information. Stereotyping, inaccuracies, biased opinions, and disinformation about people, places and issues were evident in some cases, as seen in the Honolulu teacher education and the Nepal traveller Web sites. Despite good intentions, assumptions about developing countries—the experiences, the people, the politics, and the histories— distorted facts in some situations.

In essence, it is true that the Internet offers vast resources for global educators but it is imperative that we ensure the authenticity and the legitimacy of any information by confirming the source of such information. According to one source, "Even the most authoritative sources of medical information [including the universities] on the Internet contain errors and should not be taken as gospel" (Knight-Ridder Newspapers, 1998, F5). Despite the source being established, teachers must continue to assess all information critically to raise challenging questions about any available knowledge—whether such information is on the Internet or in any of the traditional sources (print, audio and video). Global educators must also recognize the possibilities and limitations of using the Internet along with implications of technology on our lives. We need to differentiate between traditionally accepted tools and the more impacting nature of the Internet, making it more than an innocuous tool (Postman, 1993; Stoll, 1995, 1995b). Global educators also need to distinguish connections between critical research and liberatory pedagogy (Lather, 1991), i.e., the relationship between language of critique and language of possibility (Giroux, 1993). Global education, being critical education, must attempt to develop empowerment and solidarity among those who attempt to understand the struggles and the ones who live those struggles. Perhaps, the Internet may facilitate this connectivity and enable global educators bring the unheard voices to their students in the classrooms.

All participants expressed the need for becoming more aware of global issues; there was unanimous agreement on the need to become more proactive concerning the health of the planet and nurturing better relationship with people around the world. There was a cautious note on the role of technology in facilitating this relationship. All participants highlighted the positive and negative aspects of the Internet even as they emphasized a critical analysis of the process of using technology and the nature of information available on the Internet. Some participants noted that the development of critical pedagogy and empowerment was dependent upon the global educator rather than the medium. In essence, there was a general consensus that the Internet was useful for furthering the goals and objectives of global education. Some described how their perception of "identity" evolved as they began to establish connections with like-minded people. The notion of "being connected" to the rest of the world made the Internet more powerful and attractive for some participants.

As to whether the Internet contributed to the goals of global education, some participants argued for further appropriation of the communication network system for classroom teaching. While different perspectives and voices could be presented on the Internet, unedited material misrepresenting and stereotyping cultures was a problem for many participants. Hence, there was an agreement to the crucial need for critical and judicious filtering of information available on the Internet.

The Information Superhighway has facilitated emancipatory struggles aimed at releasing political prisoners and more humane treatment of minorities. Even though the Net has allowed the unrestrained proliferation of racists groups, human rights activists have been able to use the very same medium to challenge the haters. Peace activists have been able to use the Net for presenting realities of war and its consequences. As the Internet offers access to innumerable resource materials on the Net, all participants felt that they would definitely use the medium in its various forms in their classroom teaching. The Internet also facilitates a better understanding of global issues, in that, more than one participant felt an increase in sensitivity to global issues. Our browsing the Internet has shown that global educators were able to use the Internet to establish partnerships involving direct correspondence between students in different parts of the world. These experiences have facilitated sharing of stories and local histories between people living in diverse situations. In being able to communicate faster and more efficiently, the global educator would be able to overcome the traditional barriers that have limited exchange of information between individuals and groups. In essence, all participants envisioned the Internet's future in not just communication and connection but also for connectivity between global educators.

Our browsing of the sites provided us with an experience challenging our notion of identity. It also confirmed that the Internet could be used as a powerful tool for classroom teaching, sharing of teacher resources, establishing better connectivity with fellow global educators around the world, joining activists in support of their negotiation for social justice, and accessing enormous amount of information from authentic sources. As explicated earlier, this would suggest peacemakers working toward solidarity and a peaceful world in collaboration and cooperation rather than struggling as individuals in isolation (Toh and Floresca-Cawagas (1990, pp. 11-12). Conversely, there were concerns about the proliferation of hate, crime and pornography on the Net. We went through agreement/ disagreement/ undecided phases on the issue of censorship; in our mind, issues relating to the debate on freedom of speech and the limits of tolerance have not been resolved. The sites of contestation will continue and technology will influence the way we think and act. In spite of the limitations, it was found that the Internet can enhance the global educator's attempt to facilitate the development of a global identity.

9.2. Theoretical Reflections

At the beginning of this study, we started with a few questions relating to the Internet as an effective tool and source for global educators. In pursuing this inquiry, a few sub-sets of questions as to the Internet's role in the development of a global citizen were identified; whether technology had any potential and possible roles in achieving the goals of global education; and if the Internet had an impact upon the development of a "global identity." Another pertinent question offered to be examined was the "quality" of processes that entailed using the Internet for global education. While remaining cautious to the ubiquitous crime of simplistic generalizations, we now come to some basic sense relating to these questions.

The Internet itself does not motivate a person to pursue global education objectives *per se* but may provide a conduit and venue for people who are looking for a tool to access and disseminate information. Just having the information is as good as a horde of books in the best library where the person only has to pick the topic and then look for the appropriate sources. One could also roam through the aisles looking for nothing in particular. Browsing aimlessly may result in serendipitous rewards but incidental discoveries remain quite fragmentary for an organized research in any topic. Similarly, a person surfing the Web aimlessly may access nothing in particular. An individual who does access issues of global relevance will have to be sensitized to the issues and be searching for sites that are specific to the topic. A sensitized person may look for it beyond the conventional sources of information, i.e., the library or the book store and go on to the Internet due to its powerful networking features.

Some of the findings point to the possibility of a technology driven future, which despite some limitations, in most cases, will enhance the learning environment. While it also suggests a cautious belief in the uses of technology and the promise to better access of information, the future of technology in global education is as useful as the user wants it to be. As any tool in the hands of the user, the Internet allows individuals to utilize the available technology for communication and learning. Albeit, the Internet is no ordinary tool— it persuades our thinking, affects our living, influences our culture. Some like Neil Postman even question its effect on our social relations, suggesting that technology is "both friend and enemy" in that they "alter the structure of our interests" (1993, pp. xii, 20). As Sherry Turkle observed, "In our relationship with the computer, we need to ask not just what computers do *for* us but also what they do *to* us... The technology changes us as people, changes our relationships and sense of ourselves (pp. 22, 26, 232). In his inimical but veracious style, Stoll (1995) ponders: "In short, the medium in which we communicate changes how we organize our thoughts. We program computers, but the computers also program us" (p. 46). We struggle to access and then digest all the available information, as if it is the ultimate goal in our lives. As Shenk (1997) notes, "At certain level of input, the law of diminishing returns takes effect; the glut of information no longer adds to our quality of life, but instead begins to cultivate stress, confusion, and even ignorance" (p. 15). Merely having access to voluminous information is not the precursor to enlightenment. Lamy (1990) elaborating this, notes:

> Simply teaching more about the world is not the solution—merely having
> more information may not advance students' understanding. As I have

304

suggested, much of what we notice and the inferences we draw depend upon the lenses through which we filter the raw data. Approaching a study with a jaundiced attitude is likely to confirm, not dispel, prejudices—a racist watching the beating of a person from another racial group may well see justice being done. Developing appropriate conceptual and moral lenses through which to view global interactions may be more crucial than acquiring extensive information (Lamy, 1990, 49).

Does the Internet play a role in the development of a global identity? It is true that the Internet does not cause or shape our ways of thinking about global identity; it only offers an experience that further enhances the development of one's identity. It also gives a newer meaning to the fluidity of identities in real life represented in the virtual life. As some participants emphasized, the Internet not only allowed evolving of multiple identities, but also provided the connectivity increasing their "awareness and knowledge" of themselves in relation to others around the world. Contradictions and ambiguities in the influences of the Internet on the global identity of participants highlight the different experiences, perceptions and understanding of the relationship with technology. Waheed, for example, felt an element of "left-wing propaganda" among sites he identified as being global education in nature and argued that this did not affect his identity while Nalini thought that the global education sites allowed better connectivity and enhanced her identity as a global educator. Ron noted that his life experience complemented his interaction with the Internet to increase his sensitivity to global issues while Gunadasa was less optimistic about technology's role in global education. Over time, Ron did feel that his narrow view of the world broadened through his experiences on and off the Net. Thus, in having transcended the physical boundaries and narrow nationalistic feelings, some participants became what Turkle calls, "the naturalized citizen of the Net" and "not a native" (Greenberg, 1996, p. 161). The "affair" with technology accentuates our own "fluid" and "multiple" identities; it exposes our reactions to relationships that are both

305

positive and negative, forcing us to never remain the same. As our understandings change, our experiences evolve, and our identities unfold.

Thus, the Internet does facilitate the process of accessing and disseminating information; it allows establishing connectivity with other participants who have common interests and it serves as a powerful conduit to linking up with people in different situations. For example, the opportunity to directly link with activists around the world empowers those in isolation. Rob Harrison, co-editor of the UK-based *Ethical Consumer* magazine notes that effective campaigning techniques such as consumer boycotts, direct actions (on-site activism), shareholder actions, letter writing, ethical competitors (manufacturing environmentally friendly, violence-free products), labelling (monitoring companies' adherence to a set of ethical standards, e.g. Rugmark), specialist campaigners (e.g., *Corporate Watch* in the UK), specialist consumers (ethical-shopping guides), and "anti-consumerists" or "downshifters" (less materialistic, anti-consumerism) are all various forms of effective activities. Harrison, addressing the ethical and moral aspect of commercial transactions notes that, "The sheer speed of globalization is such that every purchase we make on the grounds of cheapness and attractiveness alone, without reference to the ethics of its manufacturer, nudges the whole global economy towards ever-lower ethical standards" (Harrison, 1997, p. 27).

On the other hand, it is also possible for "linking" through the Net to be superficial or merely reinforce existing dominant relationships. Thus, the increasingly popular strategy of teachers to encourage their schools and classrooms to link with other schools and classrooms in another country needs to be critically examined in global education terms. Given the inequities in access to computer technology, such linkages or "twinning" may connect primarily students from privileged social backgrounds. If the twinning is across North and South, the information exchanges then may not reflect the diversity of voices, national development realities and problems facing peoples in both contexts. In sum, global education, which needs a critical understanding of alternative development paradigms, may not be currently achieving its goals as we see it being understood and translated.

It is troublesome that these socioeconomic changes along with globalization do not appear to be of any concern to those who may have money and power to influence polity at both local and international levels. Fareed Zakaria, editor of *Foreign Affairs* warns that a new emerging class of "techno-nerds" living in the Silicon Valley's high-tech industries, design and plan computer systems without being interested or aware of societal issues. Zakaria is concerned about this apolitical group of rising entrepreneurial millionaires who do not seem to care about liberty and freedom; politics and foreign affairs; globalization and wars; poverty and crime; and inequities and struggles (Foot, 1998, C13). The wealthy "techno-nerds," according to Zakaria, "do not understand the relevance of international structures like the United Nations, NATO, or even free trade agreements." Zakaria feels that having abdicated their civic responsibilities and "detached themselves from traditional society...these productive, energetic, brilliant people, who will command the heights of the 21st century, are fundamentally apolitical." Their "life without a sense of duty," these techno-wizards' apathy for political institutions is disconcerting to Zakaria: "Missing from this generation of techno-nerds is a conception of how global politics is tied up with their prosperity—that peace most importantly is the product of an enormously difficult political process, that it isn't a normal state of events, and that the global free market is not a naturally occurring phenomenon" (Foot, 1998, C13).

Thus, we may have to deal with three aspects of technology— the effect of technology on our lives, the way we use technology for the betterment of humankind, and the ensuing conflict between "haves and have-nots," perhaps differentiated by the incongruent relationship between financial power and democratic principles.

As to global education *per se*, it is not only exciting to use technology as a tool but issues pertaining to the common good remain much more readily accessible because of the Internet. One may focus on the *issues and concerns* along with *critical reflection* being engaged in a critical analysis to *understand* the issues (cause and effect) to develop a *commitment* to the cause. The *action* at the *personal* level may entail considering non-violent intervention, advocacy, dialogue, and peaceful protest and at the *institutional* level, issues that are systemic and structural including political, economic, and educational changes. By itself, the Internet does not initiate the nurturing of a global identity. Boris Yeltsin's resistance to isolation during the martial law was one good example where the internal censorship was ineffective as Yeltsin's supporters kept the world informed about what was happening in the Soviet Union. This resulted in a democracy movement that facilitated the collapse of the military rulers. The Iranian human rights activists presenting valuable stories of inhuman treatment of Iranian citizens to the world along with the necessary contacts allowed many letter-writing campaigns, resulting in sufficient pressure to help some of the victims. The IGC site on peace offers resource materials and information for global educators allowing them to present information otherwise unavailable to students.

The Internet allows us to not only connect but also share our experiences with different people. According to Darling (1996), listening to stories can be one of the ways of discovering how other people see their world. Recognizing perspectives, understanding personal and cultural narratives interpreting the narratives, enhancing one's appreciation and respect for different cultures and identifying common values and goals that transcend nations, borders and cultures can be revealing experiences that can enrich a global education curriculum (pp. 180-182). Even within a multicultural classroom, the global educator can engage in what Ladson-Billings calls "culturally relevant pedagogy," by drawing upon classroom diversity to link the cultural heritage of a child and by bridging the gap between home and school through real-life connections of narratives (Gibson, 1996, p. 183). Global educators can be more effective teachers by acknowledging the silent voices in their classrooms through such culturally responsive teaching.

In all these, there are ongoing "struggles" between "globalization from above" and "globalization from below," causing a cyberspace of contestation where some transnational corporations and powerful international bodies in the West embark on altruistic endeavors even as activists and grassroots movements vie for disseminating information and gaining spaces for their own voices on the Net. As global educators utilize this new tool, they must also heed the cautionary warnings of Aronowitz & Giroux:

> Some even argue that the computer is the final road to human freedom because it permits each of us to create our own worlds, to escape the straitjacket or linear text, to make of thought a collage of insight. In this new world Marshall McLuhan's most radical fantasy, the global village, is on the brink of realization. Politics exists, but it is viewed as a massive obstacle to the creation of the electronically mediated community in which we are all digitally linked. The struggle for social power, having been rendered obsolete by the now realized dream of total individual autonomy made possible by the machine, may be conceived as an illusion. (Aronowitz & Giroux, 1991, pp. 192-193)

Isobel Hoffmann, director of the Information Technology and Design Centre at the University of Toronto's School of Architecture warns teachers about being dazzled by the new technology or the toys that claim to enhance the learning process. Hoffmann noting that, "teachers should use technology as a tool and not let it play the leading role," adds that "teachers should be in control, should plan the classroom, what's going to be taught and the sequence of how it should be taught" (Marck, 1996, B3). But as explicated earlier, the Internet cannot be considered as a mere tool due to its impact upon our lives and behaviour. In essence, these are warnings that serve as road-markers we need to heed as we use technology without ascribing to it an uncritical and divine position.

9.3. Significance of this Research

In this inter-connected global village, we need to appropriate a clear understanding of the aims and objectives of global education. This is especially true as the interdependent world for each "new generation of youths becomes inexorably more involved in a shrinking world and a more complex international society... It is imperative that our students develop and achieve some sense of their global citizenship. There is simply no other choice if global survival is the decision" (Metzger, 1988, p. 15). The rapid political and economic changes at the international level have an impact on all of us around the world, and hence, global education is a "necessity" for everybody (Kniep, 1985). Apart from the interconnectedness, global education carries with it an emancipatory approach that envisions a reconstructionist world that believes in amelioration and elimination of the *negative* and strengthening of the *positive* in the life situations of humans. According to futurist predictions the arrival of the *third wave* i.e., the communications-based society that has replaced the industrial and the post-

310

industrial societies is crucial as to how we as a society will change and evolve (Olson & Sullivan, 1993). In this changing milieu of electronic society, we may recognize four kinds of people in relation to their responses or reactions to technological developments. They are: (a) the *technophobes* or the traditionalists, who subscribe that technology will do nothing useful but rather only create problems (b) the *sceptics* or the *cynics,* who argue that technology will do something that may not really be useful (c) the *techno-pessimists,* who think that technology is promising but not without its limitations, and (d) the *techno-optimists* or the "technophiles,"[44] who uncritically profess that technology will be the panacea to most of our problems.

9.4. Implications of this Study for Teacher Education

Teacher educators will have to emphasize the need to critically examine the role of technology in global education. They should also encourage student teachers to critically analyze the prevailing understanding of culturally diverse issues. Some Web sites on the Internet can actually serve as good resource materials for serious discussion among teacher educators and their students. The teacher training institutions must re-visit and revise their current curriculums to reflect the existing superficiality and misconceptions about cultural and global issues. A global perspective and cross-cultural/multicultural content can enable the faculty of education to explore issues that are global and local in nature. If possible, student must be encouraged to do their practicum in a cultural setting different from one's own. There must be an ongoing critical analysis of the existing relationship between the one who presents the information and the one who is being represented.

---

[44] Zakaria's "techno-nerds."

311

As to practising teachers, they will have to impress upon their students the uncritical nature of information available on the Internet. They will have to sensitize students to the existence of unedited and unauthentic information amidst the voluminous ocean of questionable material on the Internet. The moderating responsibility of the teacher must not assume the role of censorship but rather evoke challenging questions among learners who browse the Net. Teacher educators may also draw attention to the "double edged" nature of the Internet, in that it remains a powerful source of information but also happens to be the producer of stereotypes and misinformation. Students will also have to recognize the effects of computer addiction along with the way the machine influences the way we think and behave with not only others on the Net but also people in our non-cyberspace life. Teachers could capitalize on the reality that people in power have access to the Internet and that people who are engaged in struggles can reach administrators, politicians, rulers, and other decision-makers. The Internet provides opportunity to disseminate authentic knowledge, maintain electronic solidarity, and establish activism through networking with people engaged in emancipatory struggles. Teachers could explore with their students, the Internet's role in the production of culture, its intervening nature in the reconstruction of identity, and its limiting effect on gullible users. Even as the Internet becomes deterritorialized, culture and identity will also continue to become increasingly deterritorialized. In this study, as culture has been understood as the hybridized state resultant of inter- and intra-relationships, the products of such human encounters are resultant of social and historical construction.

Teachers as global educators can benefit from the enormous capability of the Internet in accessing and utilizing the vast amount of information. Nevertheless, quality, rather than quantity of information, must define the learning transaction, even as teachers act as moderators, rather than surrogate providers of information.

As teachers discuss the relationship between knowledge and power in relation to class dynamics, we need to also go beyond the traditional domination/exploitation debate to include issues of gender, race, and ethnicity. This "multiplicity of relations of power" (Apple) will allow global educators to analyze issues in a more critical way. In doing so, teachers must be wary of becoming the intellectual "experts,"[45] who claim to speak for others (Lather, 1991). It is also imperative that global educators acknowledge that as much as there is no neutral education, there is no neutral research. In our pedagogical practice, we as global educators may have to approach theory as a contextual intervention or practice (Giroux & McLaren, 1994). As global educators, we must recognize the evolving nature of identity, culture and race, in that they are not immutable categories defined by genetic or other fixed markers. If our own identities and the culture we represent evolve as we engage in new experiences, the Internet allows the postmodern fluidities to manifest in the relationship we have with technology (machine) and other humans across cyberspace. Perhaps, our students may want to explore how we interpret reality and define experiences that may be unique to the narrator— meanings that cannot be generalized, universalized, stabilized as permanent markers of absolutes. In making experiences contextual, we can recognize our own cultural limitations in understanding experiences of people from different cultures. Even before learning can become critical, it must be become meaningful to students (Giroux, 1993). Teachers and students may have to bring meaning *to* our experiences before attempting to understand the meaning *of* our experiences.

---

[45] "elitism of intellectuals" (Giroux and McLaren, 1994)

9.5. Implications of this Study for Further Research

This study focused on the experiences of the participants as they browsed in search of sites but did not engage participants in sustained online exchanges such as the chat groups, newsgroups, and electronic mail with different individuals in other countries. It did not include interactions with practicing teachers in schools who deal with students and computers on a daily basis. Perhaps, a study that looks at the actual classroom activities among teachers and students engaged in global education would be quite rewarding. One could also consider ongoing online interaction to further delve into the details of activism and outcomes of using the Internet among individuals, groups, and institutions around the world that are specifically engaged in issues relating to human rights.

9.6. Conclusion

As this personal journey started off with the intent to discover and experience technology's role in influencing our own identities even as realities surrounding other identities around us, an equally important objective was to explore the Internet's role in facilitating the process of pedagogy among global educators. Did this experience result in a transformed thinking? Firstly, the reckoning of identity was challenged. The notion of multiple identities not only was fascinating but also offered some insights into how we would describe ourselves. The primary researcher in this study felt at ease to be a Canadian, born in another country, spoke a set of different languages, and practised a number of unique habits. The greatest discovery in this venture was the realization that we each were a unique person with a set of identities that were in the process of evolution. For the first time, change was not a cause for apprehension; there was

314

no need to fit into boxes and categories defined by others. We all can live our own identities without struggling to accommodate definitions of who we were to be, as decided by others. It was the evidence of experiencing the process of hybridization.

Secondly, it was also realized that the initial excitement of technology somehow tends to blind, the tangible joys of real life not offered by virtual life. In some sense, one might rather spend more time in making sandcastles in the backyard with our families than sit glued to the computer screen for 6 hours downloading the latest Web site dedicated to explaining the significance of a life on the beach. One would agree with the Silicon Valley computer wizard Clifford Stoll, that "the finest computer model is still just a simulation of the physical world [and that] much of what comes across the computer screen is a surrogate for experience" (1995, pp. 148, 149). Perhaps, Sherry Turkle's comments can vividly express the sentiments: "[T]he culture of simulation may help us achieve a vision of multiple but integrated identity whose flexibility, resilience, and capacity for joy comes from having access to our many selves. *But if we have lost reality in the process, we shall have struck a poor bargain*" (emphasis, added) (1995, p. 268).

Finally, earlier in the study, the use of technology in activism looked very attractive. As the project evolved and the hate groups in cyberspace appeared, one was in for a rude awakening. Despite the assumption of being objective and distanced from the subject of inquiry, at one stage, the emotional involvement in contents with which one would naturally disagree and the sheer exposure to verbal violence was quite evident. Having eventually regained composure, one of the researchers launched an initiative, purposefully exposing the hate propaganda on the Internet. A number of opportunities arose where the researcher could

315

present the graphic and contextual materials to the public and beyond the academia stimulating media's interest in a sensational issue. Being able to disseminate this information in a number of venues offered one the satisfaction of having provided more exposure to the racist movement that is gaining power by its presence on the Internet.

Reflection Questions

1. What lessons and implications can be drawn by educators in order to make constructive and appropriate use of technology?

2. Do computer on-line systems enhance the intercultural communication process? Do such interactions result in expected changes in terms of the attitudes of learners toward other cultures and peoples?

3. How does information shared over the electronic communication network have an impact at the personal and social level?

4. What is the role and effect of the new information technology in the overall objectives of global education? How will such communication systems enable our children to develop global consciousness as they enter the 21st century?

5. Amidst current technological advances, how can we prepare ourselves and the next generation to live peacefully and without foregoing sustainable development?

Appendix

**Global Education across Cyberspace: Role of the Internet in
Educating for Global Awareness**

<u>**ORIENTATION**</u>
(Preliminary Questionnaire)

Date:		**Time:**	
Duration:		**Place:**	
Name:		**Telephone:**	
Program:		**Specialty:**	

1. Have you attended any global education course? If YES please elaborate.

2. Have you attended any global education conferences or workshops? If YES please elaborate.

3. Have you travelled abroad on any overseas project? If YES please elaborate.

4. Do you have any experience on the Internet? If so, relating to what?

5. Do you regularly read print materials relevant to global education? If YES please elaborate.

6. Have you participated in any international/intercultural on-campus or off-campus events? If YES please elaborate.

**Global Education across Cyberspace: Role of the Internet in
Educating for Global Awareness**

FOCUS GROUP ONE

Elements covered in the Focus Group session one attempted to address the following questions:

- Why do you want to be a part of this Project?

- Are global issues important to us? Why?

- Do we have to concern ourselves with global issues? Why or why not?

- Do you think we need global education? Why or why not?

- What did you find or expect to find on the Internet that was relevant to cultural issues that are global?

- What are the different cultural issues you have seen or expect to see that would be relevant to this discussion?

- What area/areas of cultural dimension has interested you?

- Did you explore any sites that are relevant to this particular issue/issues?

- How useful was the site in enhancing your understanding of the issue?

- Currently, what is your understanding of this area of concern?

- What do you expect to achieve for yourself by the end of this project?

- Besides this Project, how do you plan to use the information you have accessed?

Item 3

**Global Education across Cyberspace: Role of the Internet in
Educating for Global Awareness**

FOCUS GROUP ONE

Date:_____Wednesday January 24th , 1996
Time:_____4:45 p.m. to 6:30 p.m.
Duration:_____1 hour and 45 minutes_____
Place:__Room N5-106, Education North_____

Name: Code:

4:45 p.m. THE NEED FOR GLOBAL EDUCATION AND MY ROLE IN IT [Sub-Groups]

While it is assumed that we have come together because of our personal interest in this topic, why do we think that global education is important and how do we see ourselves being a part of this thinking and living?

"In my opinion, the two main reasons for the need for global education are:
1._____
_____
_____ "
2._____
_____
_____ "

5:00 p.m. SHARING OUR THOUGHTS [Main Group]

5:20 p.m. CLARIFYING THE CONCEPT OF GLOBAL EDUCATION [Main Group]

While there are a number of definitions of global education, we as a group, will attempt to come to a common understanding (rather than a consensus) as to what *global education* will constitute for this discussion and project.

"According to what I understand, "global education" can be loosely described as:
_____
_____
_____ "

320

5:50 p.m. THE INTERNET AND ITS ROLE IN THE LIVES OF GLOBAL EDUCATORS

The "Information Superhighway" or the Internet has become an important part of our vocabulary and perhaps, a part of some of our lives as educators. What role can the Internet play in achieving the objectives of global education?

"I think that the Internet could be significantly relevant to the objectives of global education because:

_____
_____
_____
_____
                        "

6:15 p.m. A VISION OF THE INTERNET'S FUTURE IN GLOBAL EDUCATION

Envisioning the future is at best, an exercise of hope and expectations. Imagine that you are a global educator in the year 2010. How do you describe the Internet in your life as a classroom teacher? What other aspects of the Internet do you think will influence your living and thoughts? What *possibilities* and *limitations* do you foresee?

"In the year 2010, I envision:

_____
_____
_____
_____
                        "

*"I think, **one major promise/possibility** could be:*

_____
_____
_____
_____
                        "

*and **one major limitation** could be:*

_____
_____
_____
                        "

321

Global Education across Cyberspace: Role of the Internet in Educating for Global Awareness

- **Global education**

    Tye and Kniep (1991) define global education as something that, "involves learning about those problems and issues which cut across national boundaries and about the inter-connectedness of systems—cultural, ecological, economic, political, and technological." (p.47).

- **Global education curriculum**

    A global perspectives curriculum attempts to build an understanding and appreciation of public and private actions which recognize: 1. the linkages between state and non-state actors... 2. the value and importance of cultural commonalities and differences 3. the necessity for foreign and domestic policies which minimize conflict ehavior and reinforce cooperation and accommodation. (Lamy, 1983, p.18)

- **Significance**

    Global education can be dealt within the framework of the troika—*cause, concern and conduct.* Firstly, causes of conflicts, tensions, inequalities, and disturbances; secondly, concern toward our fellow humans in questioning some of the assumptions as to how these causes of disruptions came to be; and finally, defining our own conduct at the personal and interpersonal level and thereby seeking resolutions to issues that are manageable even at a microcosmic level.

- **Concerns and Issues**

    What one may consider as "concerns under the global education umbrella" may include: environment or ecology (concerns such as acid rain, global warming, ozone layer depletion, desert encroachment, water pollution or effluents, deforestation, and toward sustainability); pacifist movement or peace education (nuclear and conventional disarmament, conflict resolution, treaties); political rights (individual rights, freedom and democracy); social justice (human rights- aboriginal rights, anti-racism, anti-prejudice, gender inequality, anti-discrimination, child labour, bonded chattel labour); economic relations (trade sanctions, embargoes, penalties, agreements, treaties, international labour laws, international debt- inflation and recession); development education (functional literacy, dissemination of information, education and self-empowerment); health (basic health needs, population, natality, mortality, migration); basic human needs (nutrition-distribution, access and affordability, poverty and famine, availability of potable water, clothing and decent housing); and cross-cultural awareness (multiculturalism, ethnic diversity, cultural pluralism, and autochthony).

- **Cultural Issues**

    The cultural issues include global culture, "global citizen," indigenous cultures, international conflicts, multiculturalism, racism and gender issues.

- **The Internet**

    Can the Internet provide means and possibilities to allow `critical' global education across the cyberspace?

Item 5

Observation Sheet

What do I look for? <u>Besides</u> other aspects of relevance/ importance to YOU:

Is the site:

1. relevant to global education?

2. within the cultural realm?

3. specific to the area of your interest?

4. easy to access (user-friendly)?

5. descriptive or prescriptive?

6. critical in its approach?

7. a possible teacher resource site?

8. really needed on the Internet? Why or why not?

9. would you use this site again?

Reminder: Please DO NOT FORGET the **SITE #**_____

Item 6

Researcher Observation Sheet   **Date:**_____

_____

_____   Name of Site:_____

Address of Site: http://www._____

Comments:_____

_____

_____

_____

_____

Information Value:_____ **Critical thinking Value:**_____(0 least to 5 most)

Site Emphasis: **File Saved As:**

_____   Name of Site:_____

Address of Site: http://www._____

Comments:_____

_____

_____

_____

_____

Information Value:_____ **Critical thinking Value:**_____(0 least to 5 most)

Site Emphasis: **File Saved As:**

Item 7

Global Education across Cyberspace: Role of the Internet in Educating for Global Awareness

CONVERSATION

Date:_____ Time: _____

Duration:_____ Place:_____

Name:_____

Audiocassette Label_____#_____Code_____

Conversation #:　　　☐ One☐ Two　　　☐ Three

Some sample basic questions:

1. What relevant sites have you discovered? What relevant issues have you explored?

2. How do you feel as to the content and presentation of the issues?

3. Did you interact with other users over the Internet by involving in　Usergroup/ Newsgroup discussions? If so, what is your experience?

4. Do you feel that the available sites contribute to the goals and objectives of global education?

5. How would you use the Internet as a tool for pedagogical process in a successful global education curriculum?

6. Has your experience influenced your current thinking of global concerns?

7. Did this experience have any impact on the way you deal with global issues in your daily life?

8. Has this experience changed your global perspective?

9. Do you feel that the Internet has helped you develop a global identity? (i.e., "a person in a global context")

10. What do you think of the role of the Internet in the year 2010?

11. Do you think the Internet could be better than what it is now?

Item 8

Global Education across Cyberspace: Role of the Internet in Educating for Global Awareness

FOCUS GROUP TWO

Elements covered in the Focus Group session two attempted to address the following questions:

1. Why do we have to concern ourselves with global issues?

2. Do you think we need global education? Why or why not?

3. What area/areas of cultural dimension interested you most?

4. In having been a part of this project, what have you achieved for yourself?

5. Besides this project, how do you plan to use the information you have accessed?

6. [**In terms of** processes; barriers; resolution strategies; and failures] Has your experience on the Internet had any influence on you and the way you interact at the: (a) Personal level (b) Interpersonal level (c) Professional level and (d) Societal level ?

7. How do you perceive the current domestic and international events relating to cultural issues as a result of your Internet explorations?

8. During your experience with the Internet, what specific aspects of technology encouraged/ discouraged you?

Item 9

Global Education across Cyberspace: Role of the Internet in Educating for Global Awareness

FOCUS GROUP TWO

Date:_____Wednesday, November 27th, 1996_____
Time:_____5:00 PM - 7:00 PM_____
Duration:_____1 hour and 30 minutes_____
Place:__7N-114, Education North_____

Name: Code:

- **5:05 p.m. THE NEED FOR GLOBAL EDUCATION AND MY ROLE IN IT.**

Why do we have to concern ourselves with global issues? Why is it important?

In my opinion, the two main reasons we need global education are:

   1._____

   _____

   _____

   2._____

   _____

   _____

- **5:15 p.m. WHAT DID YOU FIND ON THE INTERNET THAT WAS RELEVANT TO CULTURAL ISSUES THAT ARE GLOBAL?**

I found sites that were relevant to cultural issues such as:

   _____

   _____

   _____

   _____

   _____

327

_____

_____

- **5:25 p.m. THE INTERNET AND ITS ROLE IN THE LIVES OF GLOBAL EDUCATORS**

How would you use the Internet as a tool in dealing with issues relevant to global education? Would you allow computers in your classroom during learning activities? Why or why not?

_____

_____

_____

_____

_____

- **5:35 p.m. THE TECHNOLOGY**

How easy was it to gain access to the information you were seeking? Was the time worth spent? Was it fast and easy? Was the information relevant?

Ease: _____

_____

Speed:_____

Relevance:_____

_____

Value:_____

Other Comments: _____

_____

- **5:40 p.m. A VISION OF THE INTERNET'S FUTURE IN GLOBAL EDUCATION**

You had envisioned the future of the Internet at the beginning of this study. How do you now describe the Internet in your life as a classroom teacher? Now that you have used the Internet, what other aspects of the Internet do you think will influence your life and thoughts? What *possibilities* and *limitations* do you foresee?

328

"In the year 2010, I envision:

_____

_____

_____

_____

_____

*"I think, **one major promise/possibility** could be:*

_____

_____

_____ "

*and **one major limitation** could be:*

_____

_____

_____   .

- **5:50 p.m. WHAT DO YOU THINK YOU HAVE ACHIEVED FOR YOURSELF IN HAVING PARTICIPATED IN THIS PROJECT?**

- **5:55-6:30 p.m. GROUP DISCUSSION**

<u>**NOTES:**</u>

6:30-6:45 WRAP-UP

Item 10

List of Web Sites selected for Content Analysis

A Celebration of Black Culture — http://www.msbet.com/bhistory/main.htm
Access email Classroom Exchange — http://www.iglou.com/xchange/ece/index.html
Action for Aboriginal Rights — http://www.cablededucation.ca/cic/nns/berit.html
Africa Online AOL [Nairobi] — http://www.africaonline.co.ke/
AFRO-America@ — http://www.afroam.org/
AIESEC Online — http://www.aiesec.org/
Alberta Human Rights Commission — http://www.gov.ab.ca/~mcd/mcd.htm
Amnesty International — http://www.organic.cm/non.profit/amnesty/
ArabNet — http://www.arab.net/
Censorship, Freedom of Speech, Child Safety on the Internet
   http://omni.voicenet.com/~cranmer/censorship.html
Center for Global Education
   at Augsburg College — http://aug3.augsburg.edu/global/
Children Now — http://www.dnai.com/~children/
Classroom Connect Resource Station — http://www.wentworth.com/
CNN Interactive — http://www.cnn.com
Collaboration in the Classroom — http://gsn.org/gsn/gsn.home.html
Computing Professionals for
   Social Responsibility — http://www.cpsr.org/dox/home.html
Content Blocking — http://ilpf.org/contentblocking.html
Democratic Socialists of America — http://www.dsausa.org/index.html
EdLinks — http://webpages.marshall.edu/~jmullens/ edlinks.html
Encyclopedia of Women's History — http://www.teleport.com/~megaines/women.html
Exploring Ancient World Cultures — http://eawc.evansville.edu
Feminist com Activism — http://www.feminist.com/activ.htm
German Alert — http://www.chantry.com/ga
Global Democracy Network — http://www.gdn.org/
Global SchoolNet/ — http://gsn.org/gsn/gsn.home.html
Honolulu Community College — http://www.hcc.hawaii.edu/hccinfo/
   facdev/main.html
Human Rights in Iran — http://www.tufts.edu/departments/Fletcher/
   multi/humanRights.html
I Have a Dream Foundation — http://www.ihad.org/
I*EARN International — http://www.peg.apc.org/~iearn/intnl.intnl.htm
Institute for Global Communications — http://www.igc.org/igc/
Institute of Global Education
   http://www.pacificrim.net/~nature/univ.html#univ
Intellectual Capital — http://www.intellectualcapital.com/
International Centre — http://www.intlcent.ualberta.ca/IDEP/
   IDEP.Directory.html
International Kids' Space — http://plaza.interport.net/kids_space/
International Schools Cyber Fair 97 — http://www.gsn.org/gsn/cb/index.html
Just for Kids — http://www.ontheinternet.com/kids/kids.htm
Kid's Locker Room — http://www.peg.apc.org/~balson/

330

Kids Online	http://www.slonet.org/global/education/kid.html
KidzPage	http://web.aimnet.com/~veeceet/kids/kidzpage.html
Ku Klux Klan	Link (through Hate Groups on Site)
Links to Right-Extremists on the Net	http://www.cs.uit.no/~paalde/NazismExposed/Scripts/flinks.html
NEWS Electronic Web Service	http://www.thenews.com/
Nizkor Project	http://www.almanac.bc.ca/
Politically Incorrect	http://www.smartnet.net/~fenix/
SchoolNet	http://k12.school.net/
Simon Wiesenthal Center	http://www.wiesenthal.com
Skin Net	http://alpha.ftcnet.com/~skinhds/index2.htm
Slonet Education	http://www.slonet.org/global/education/
Smithsonian	http://www.si.edu/newstart.htm
Stormfront	http://www.stormfront.org/STORMFRONT/
Third World First Group	http://www.ed.ac.uk/~3w1
Third World Traveler	http://pomo.nbn.com/people/stevetwt/
Watchman	http://www2.stormfront.org/watchman/index.html
Webcrawler 100	http://www.webcrawler.com/WebCrawler/WC100.html
Web 66: International School Registry	http://web66.coled.umn.edu/schools.html
White Power Brainwash TV	Link (through Hate Groups on Site)
World Bank	http://www.worldbank.org/
Worldwatch Institute	http://www.worldwatch.org/
Yahooligans!	http://www.yahooligans.com/
Zundelsite	http://www.webcom.com/~ezundel/english/welcome.html

CATEGORY DESCRIPTORS

ERROR: Requested URL Not Found On This Server **404!**

ACTIVISM	**ACT**
ARTICLE	**ARTICLE**
CAREERS & JOBS	**C&J**
CENSORSHIP	**CENSOR**
ENVIRONMENT	**ENV**
FEMINISM	**FEM**
GAME	**GAME**
HUMAN RIGHTS	**HR**
HUMAN RIGHTS ABORIGINAL	**HRABOR.**
HUMAN RIGHTS WOMEN	**HRWOM.**
INFORMATION GENERAL	**INFOGEN** (includes
information on	cultural groups)
INFORMATION DEVELOPMENT	**INFODEVT**
INFORMATION TECHNICAL	**INFOTECH**
INTERNATIONAL	**INTNL** (UN, IMF, WB,
WHO, UNICEF)	
LAW ENFORCEMENT (POLICING)	**LAWE**
NEWS	**NEWS**
NEWSGROUP	**NEWSGROUP**
OTHER	**OTHER**
POLITICS	**POL**
PORNOGRAPHY	**PORNO**
PROMOTIONAL (AD)	**PROMO**
RACISM/ANTI-RACISM	**RAR**
RELIGION	**REL**
RESEARCH	**RES** (Theory, Technical,
Scientific)	
SCHOOL GENERAL	**SCHOOLGEN**
SCHOOL RESOURCES	**SCHOOLRES**
SCHOOL TECHNICAL	**SCHOOLTECH**

Item 12

The Internet Acronyms and Symbols

ACRONYMS (may also be used in small caps):

AFK	Away From Keyboard
BRB	Be Right Back
BBL	Be Back Later
BBFN	Bye Bye For Now
BBIAF	Be Back In A Few Minutes
LOL	Laughing Out Loud
ROTFL	Rolling On the Floor Laughing
FOCL	Falling Of the Chair Laughing
IMO	In My Opinion
IMHO	In My Humble Opinion
MOTOS	Member Of The Opposite Sex
MOTSS	Member Of The Same Sex
OIC	Oh, I See
FAQ	Frequently Asked Question
RTFM	Read the [Expletive] Manual
TTFN	Ta Ta For Now
TTYL	Talk To You Later

EMOTICONS (Most emoticons are read with the head tilted sideways):

:-) =	Smiling	:-D=	Big Smile
.'J =	(Profile) Smiling	.'V =	(Profile) Shouting
(8-) =	Wearing Glasses	:-(=	Sad (or "unsmiley")
:'-(=	Crying	:-0 =	Surprised
:-* =	Oops!	:-@ =	Screaming
;-) =	Winking	:-(=	Frowning
:-D =	Laughing	:-X =	My lips are sealed
:-P =	Sticking tongue out	{:-) =	Wearing a toupee
:-{) =	Smiley with a mustache	:8) =	Pig
:=8) =	Baboon	=:-l =	Cyberpunk
(-o-) =	Imperial Tie Fighter from "Star Wars"		
3:*> =	Rudolph the Red-Nosed Reindeer		

Public domain: Collected from various sources.
Can't find a computer term or meaning of a technical word/acronym? Try the free *On-Line Dictionary of Computing* at http://wfn-shop.princeton.edu/cgi-bin/foldoc/

REFERENCES

Abercrombie, N., Hill, S. & Turner, B. S. (1988). *Dictionary of Sociology* (Second Edition). England: Penguin Books.

Alger, C. F. & Harf, J. E. (1986). Global Education: Why? For Whom? About What? In Freeman, R. E. (Ed.). *Promising Practices in Global Education: A Handbook with Case Studies*. New York: National Council on Foreign Language and International Studies. (ERIC Document Reproduction Service No. ED 265 107).

Alladin, I. & Rymer, J. E. (1996). *Anti-Racist Education: Policy, Implementation and Curriculum*. Ontario: Cambrian College of Applied Arts and Technology.

Anchan, J. P. (1998). "In the Name of Technology: The Holy Shrine." Paper to be presented at the International Child/Youth Conference: "Shaping the Future," Edmonton, Alberta, Canada July 26-August 1, 1998.

Anchan, J. P. (1998). "Towards Non-Threatening Discourses in the Classroom: Action Research Engaging Critical Dialogue to allow Silent Voices of Minorities." Paper to be presented at the International Multicultural Conference: "Preparing Together for the 21st Century," Edmonton, Alberta, Canada July 26-August 1, 1998.

Anchan, J. P. (1998). "Canada: A Nation of Changing Identities " In Richardson, A. (Ed.). *The Canadian Multicultural Experience: Myth and Reality*. Toronto: Prentice Hall (To be published in late fall 1998).

Anchan, J. P. (1998). "Multiculturalism, Race and Stereotypes: School Texts and Student Perceptions." (To be published in late summer 1998). Canadian Heritage, Edmonton, Alberta.

Anchan, J. P. (1998). "Hate Groups and Human Rights on the Internet." Paper presented at the International Week, University of Alberta International Centre on January 28, 1998 in Edmonton, Alberta, Canada.

Anchan, J. P. (1997). "Research that Makes Sense to the Non-Profit Organizations." Panel Session, Metropolis Second National Conference on

Immigration, [Immigration et Métropoles], Montreal, Quebec, November 23-26, 1997.

Anchan, J. P. (1997). "Educating Children to use the Internet Critically: (Hate Groups on the Information Superhighway)." Paper presented at the Canadian Childhood National Conference on November 01, 1997 in Edmonton, Alberta, Canada.

Anchan, J. P. (1997). "Culture Shock and Racism." Paper presented at the Western Canadian Association of Immigrant Serving Agencies (WCAISA) Conference: *Settlement and Integration into the 21st Century* on June 4, 1997 in Edmonton, Alberta, Canada.

Anchan, J. P. (1997). "Cyberspace and Global Education." A paper presentation at the Graduate Student Research Conference: *Educating in Global Times: Race, Class, Gender (and other processes of Normalization)* on March 14, 1997 at the University of Alberta, Canada.

Anchan, J. P. & Holychuk, L. (1996). "Dealing with Racial and Cultural Diversity in the Curriculum." In Alladin, I.(Ed.). *Racism in Canadian Schools*. Toronto: Harcourt Brace & Company, 93-106.

Anchan, J. P. (1995). "Anti-Racism Education and Multiculturalism." Panel Session at the Western Canadian Conference on Chinese Education on August 20, 1995, Edmonton, Alberta, Canada.

Anchan, J. P. (1993). "Global Education: Theory and Practice- A Project Report." A paper presentation at Department of Educational Foundations Seminar, Faculty of Education, University of Alberta, on February 11, 1993 in Edmonton, Alberta, Canada.

Anchan, J. P. (1992). "Implementation of Global Education Programs: A Study of Four Sample Schools in Edmonton." In Alladin, I. (Ed.). *Teaching in a Global Society*. MA: Ginn Press, 63-71.

Anchan, J. P. (1992). Global Education: A Study of Theory and Practice among Sample Schools in Edmonton. Unpublished Master's Thesis, Department of Educational Foundations, University of Alberta, Edmonton, Canada.

Anderson, C.C. (1982). Global Education in the Classroom. **Theory into Practice**, vol.21, # 3, pp.168- 176.

Anderson, L. (1990). A Rationale for Global Education. In Tye, K. A. (Ed.). *Global Education from Thought to Action*. The 1991 ASCD Yearbook. Alexandria, VA: Association for Supervision and Curriculum Development, pp. 13-34.

Anderson, W. T. (Ed.) (1995). *The Truth about the Truth*. New York: G. P. Putnam's Sons.

Andrews, P. (1997, June 5). Internet Users have to Face Threats to Computer Security. *Edmonton Journal* (Edmonton), sec. E9.

Aoki, T.T. (1985). Toward Curriculum Inquiry in a New Key. Curriculum Praxis: Occasional Paper Series No.2, Department of Secondary Education, University of Alberta.

Apple, M. W. (1993). Introduction (Series Editor). In McCarthy, C. & Crichlow, W. (Eds.)(1993). *Race, Identity, and Representation in Education*. New York: Routledge, pp. vii-ix.

Apple, M.W. & Weis, L. (Eds.)(1983) *Ideology and Practice in Schooling*. Philadelphia: Temple University Press.

Arab, P. (1996, August 17). Internet Called New Key to Commercial Success. *Edmonton Journal* (Edmonton), sec. E12.

Armstrong, R. (1997, August 17). It's Official... Internet can be Addictive. *The Edmonton Journal* (Edmonton), sec. A2.

Arnold, G. (1994). *The Third World Handbook*. Second edition. London: Cassell, pp.14-29.

Aronowitz, S., Martinsons, B., Menser, M. & Rich, J. (Eds.) (1996). *Technoscience and Cyberculture*. New York: Routledge.

Aronowitz, S. & Giroux, H.A. (1993). *Education Still Under Siege*. Connecticut: Bergin & Garvey.

Aronowitz, S. & Giroux, H. A. (1991). *Postmodern Education: Politics, Culture, & Social Criticism*. Minneapolis: University of Minnesota Press.

Ashcroft, B., Griffiths, G. & Tiffin, H. (Eds.).(1995). *The Post-Colonial Studies Reader*. New York: Routledge.

Ashford, M. (1996). Peace Education after the Cold War. **Canadian Social Studies**, vol. 30, # 4, pp. 178, 179, 182.

Aull, B., Hacker, B., Postlethwaite, R., Rutstein, N. & Rutstein, T. (1996). Healing Racism: Education's Role. Online article at *Artists Against Racism* site. For more information call Nathan Rutstein at (413)-253-2021 (Massachussetts Institute of Technology).

Babbie, E. (1989). *The Practice of Social Research.* California: Wadsworth Publishing Company.

Bacchus, M. K. (1989). The Concept of Global Education. *The Computer Paper,* May/ June, pp.19-22.

Bacchus, M. K. (1992).[Foreword]. In Alladin, I.(Ed.). *Teaching in a Global Society.* Massachusetts: GINN Press, pp. xi-xv.

Banisky, S. (1997, September 26). What's Fair Is(n't) Fair. *Edmonton Journal* (Edmonton), sec. A18.

Barber, B. R. (1992). Jihad Vs. McWorld. **The Atlantic Monthly**, March, pp. 53-55, 58-63.

Beauchesne, E. (1997, February 13). Ottawa Poised to Build Up Net in our Schools. *Edmonton Journal* (Edmonton), sec. H2.

Becker, G. (1997, November 1). World's Churches to get own Web Sites. *Edmonton Journal* (Edmonton), sec. H5.

Beckley, N. (1997). Another Tibet. *New Internationalist,* May, # 290, p. 4.

Begler, E. (1993). Spinning Wheels and Straw: Balancing Content, Process, and Context in Global Teacher Education Programs. **Theory Into Practice**, vol. 32, # 1, pp. 14-20.

Belluck, P. (1996, December 8). Weaning the Webaholics. *Edmonton Journal* (Edmonton), sec. F4.

Berens, C. (1996, April 28). Spanner in the Works. *Guardian Weekly* (United Kingdom), pp. 28-29.

Berreby, D. "The Numbers Game." *Discover*, April 1990, pp. 42-49.

Bertens, H. (1995). *The Idea of the Postmodern: A History*. London: Routledge.

Bhabha, H. K. (1995). Signs Taken for Wonders. In Ashcroft, B., Griffiths, G. & Tiffin, H. (Eds.). *The Post-Colonial Studies Reader*. New York: Routledge, pp. 29-35.

Bhabha, H. K. (1994). *The Location of Culture*. New York: Routledge.

Binder, S. (1997, June 23). Quebec Language Laws Net Debate: Does the Province have the Right to Order that French be used on Internet Sites?. *Edmonton Journal* (Edmonton), sec. A4.

Bindman, S. (1996, November 23). Rights Body wants to Shut Down Zundel's Site on the Web. *Edmonton Journal* (Edmonton), sec. A3.

Blankert, W. (1992, March 19). "Development Education and the Teacher Colleges in Netherlands." Paper presented at the ATA Alberta Global Education Project Conference, Calgary, p. 2.

Blythe, C. (1996, Month 5). Electronic Cash, Virtual Plastic. *Edmonton Journal* (Edmonton), sec. C1.

Boei, W. (1997, February 19). Internet Trade Still Unpopular. *Edmonton Journal* (Edmonton), sec. D3.

Bogdan, R. (1998). *Qualitative Research for Education: An Introduction to Theory and Methods*. Boston: Allyn and Bacon.

Bogdan, R. & Taylor, S. J. (1975). *Introduction to Qualitative Research Methods: A Phenomenological Approach to the Social Sciences*. Toronto: John Wiley.

Bourdieu, P. (1977). *Reproduction in Education, Society and Culture*. London: Sage.

Bourdieu, P. (1973). "Cultural Reproduction and Social Reproduction." In Brown, R. (Ed.). *Knowledge, Education and Cultural Change*. London: Travistock, pp. 71-112.

Boston, J. A. (1997). Professional Development in Global Education. In Merryfield, M., Jarchow, E. & Pickert, S. (Eds.). *Preparing Teachers to Teach Global Perspectives: A Handbook for Teacher Educators.* California: Corwin Press, Inc., pp. 168-188.

Braun, Jr., J. A. (1992). Caring, Citizenship, and Conscience: The Cornerstones of a Values-Education Curriculum for Elementary Schools. **International Journal of Social Education**, vol. 7, # 2, pp. 47-56).

Bray, J. (1997, February 27). Confounding Tax Code Simplified with Cyberhelp. *Edmonton Journal* (Edmonton), sec. H1.

Brehl, R. (1994, October 14). Information Highway Bypasses 3 Billion. *The Edmonton Journal* (Edmonton), sec. A1.

Britzman, D., Santiago-Valles, K. A., Jimenéz-Muñoz, G. M. & Lamash, L. M. (1991). Dusting off the Erasures: Race, Gender and Pedagogy. **Education and Society**, vol.9, # 2, pp. 89-98.

Broadway, B. (1996, October 5). Churches Reach Out through Cyberspace. *Edmonton Journal* (Edmonton), sec. H5.

Broder, J. M. & Zuckerman, L. (1997, May 11). Millennium Meltdown. *Edmonton Journal* (Edmonton), sec. F3.

Bronskill,J. (1997, July 21). Smugglers Fuel Web of Crime. *The Edmonton Journal* (Edmonton), sec. A1.

Brook, J. & Boal, I. (Eds.). (1995). *Resisting the Virtual Life: The Culture and Politics of Information.* San Francisco: City Lights.

Brown, L. (1995). Nature's Limit. In Brown, L. et al. (Eds.). *State of the World,* New York: W. W. Norton & Company, pp. 3-20.

Brown, S. C. & Kysilka, M. L. (1994). In Search of Multicultural and Global Education in Real Classrooms. **Journal of Curriculum & Supervision**, vol. 9, # 3, pp. 313-316.

Brown, L. R., Flavin, C. & Postel, S. (1991, May-June). The Planet in Jeopardy. *The Futurist*, pp. 10-14.

Cabral, A. (1994). National Liberation and Culture. In Williams, P. & Chrisman, L. (Eds.). *Colonial Disclosure and Post-Colonial Theory: A Reader*. New York: Columbia University Press, pp. 53-65.

Calgary Herald & Journal Staff. (1995, November 16). Internet `Code of Conduct' Drafted. *Edmonton Journal* (Edmonton), sec. A7.

Canadian Heritage (1997a). *1948-1998 Fact Sheet. The Universal Declaration of Human Rights*. Ottawa. Also available at: www.credo98.com

Canadian Heritage (1997b). *A Message from the Minister of Canadian Heritage*. Ottawa.

Canadian Heritage (1997c). *1948-1998 Fact Sheet. Canada: A Record of Respect for Human Rights*. Ottawa. Also available at: www.credo98.com

Canadian Heritage (1997d). *1948-1998 Fact Sheet. Why Canadians Should Care: Canadians and the Universal Declaration of Human Rights*. Ottawa. Also available at: www.credo98.com

Canadian Heritage (1997e). *Multiculturalism: Respect, Equality, Diversity*. Ottawa.

Canadian Human Rights Commission (1995). *Annual Report*. Ottawa: Minister of Supply and Services Canada.

Canadian International Development Agency (1987). *Sharing Our Future*, Minister of Supply and Services Canada.

Carnoy, M. (1974). *Education as Cultural Imperialism*. New York: David McKay.

Carr, W. & Kemmis, S. (1986). *Becoming Critical: Education, Knowledge and Action Research*. Philadelphia: The Falmer Press.

Carroll, J. (1997a). *Surviving the Information Age*. Ontario: Prentice Hall Canada Inc.

Carroll, J. (1997b). The Information Highway is a Bunch of Hooey. Online article at author's home page: jcarroll@jacc.com

Carroll, J. & Broadhead, R. *1997 Canadian Internet Handbook.* Ontario: Prentice Hall Canada Inc.

Carroll, J. & Broadhead, R. *1996 Canadian Internet Handbook.* Ontario: Prentice Hall Canada Inc.

Carson, T. R. (Ed.)(1988). Editor's Introduction. In *Toward Renaissance of Humanity: Rethinking and Reorienting Curriculum and Instruction.* World Council for Curriculum and Instruction. Edmonton: University of Alberta Printing Services, pp. 3-6.

Carson, T. R. (1986). Closing the Gap between Research and Practice: Conversation as a Mode of Doing Research. **Phenomenology+Pedagogy**, vol. 4, # 2, pp. 73-75.

Case, R. & Werner, W. (1997). Building Faculty Commitment for Global Education. In Merryfield, M., Jarchow, E. & Pickert, S. (Eds.). *Preparing Teachers to Teach Global Perspectives: A Handbook for Teacher Educators.* California: Corwin Press, Inc., pp. 189-208.

Case, R. (1996). Promoting "Global Attitudes." **Canadian Social Studies**, vol. 30, # 4, pp. 174-177.

Case, R. (1993). Key Elements of a Global Perspective. **Social Education**, vol. 57, # 6, pp. 318-325.

Cetron, M. & Davies, O. (1991). "50 Trends Shaping the World." In Jackson, R.M. (Ed.). *Global Issues 93/94.* Annual Edition. Connecticut: Dushkin Publishing Group, Inc. pp. 22-29.

CFRN Eyewitness News Executive Summary, January 30, 1998.

CFRN Eyewitness News Executive Summary, December 3, 1997.

CFRN Eyewitness News Executive Summary, December 2, 1997.

CFRN Eyewitness News Executive Summary, November 28, 1997.

CFRN Eyewitness News Executive Summary, October 22, 1997.

CFRN Eyewitness News Executive Summary, October 17, 1997.

CFRN Eyewitness News Executive Summary, October 10, 1997.

CFRN Eyewitness News Executive Summary, April 22, 1997.

Chalmers, R. (1996, May 7). Telus Linking Schools to Net. *Edmonton Journal* (Edmonton), sec. E1.

Chamberlain, S. (1997). Cycles of Violence. *New Internationalist,* June, #291, p. 6.

Charles, G. "Hobson's Choice for Indigenous Peoples." *World Press Review,* September 1992, pp. 26-28.

Chmielewski, D. (1997, August 7). Modern Road Warriors and their Devices. *The Edmonton Journal* (Edmonton), sec. E7.

City of Edmonton (1997). Official Proclamation by Mayor Bill Smith. December 5, 1997.

CNN Online News, February 2, 1998, Web posted at 7 03 p.m. EST (0003 GMT). Clinton proposes increased spending for Internet. http://www.CNN.com.

CNN Online News, December 1, 1997, December 4, 1997, Web posted at 7:25 p.m. EST (0025 GMT). *Wired* activists find strength in cyberspace. http://www.CNN.com.

CNN Online News, Sunday, November 16, 1997, Web posted at 8:03 p.m. EST (0103 GMT). Former Klan Hotbed Elects First Black Mayor. http://www.CNN.com.

CNN Online News, Tuesday, November 11, 1997, Web posted at 9:14 p.m. EST (0214 GMT). U.N. Conference Debates Limits on Internet Speech. http://www.CNN.com.

CNN Online News, Sunday, November 9, 1997, Web posted at 11:26 p.m. EST (0426 GMT). Hate Case raises Internet Free Speech Issues. http://www.CNN.com.

CNN Online News, Wednesday, October 29, 1997, Web posted at 7:33 p.m. EST (0033 GMT). Hardware problems knock out America Online e-mail. http://www.CNN.com.

CNN Online News, Wednesday, October 29b, 1997, Web posted at 12:33 p.m. EST. Sports bookmakers going offshore to flourish online. http://www.CNN.com.

CNN Online News, Tuesday October 21, 1997, Web posted at 5:02 a.m. EDT (0902 GMT). U.S. said Vulnerable to Computer Attack. http://www.CNN.com.

CNN Online News, Friday October 10, 1997, Web posted at 2:35 p.m. GMT. Internet, a $3 Billion Market in 1997 and Growing. http://www.CNN.com.

CNN Online News, Thursday October 9, 1997, Web posted at 3:11 p.m. EDT. Internet successor shows its stuff. http://www.CNN.com.

CNN Online News, Monday, August 22, 1997. http://CNN.com/CNN/Programs/TalkBack/

CNN Online News, Thursday February 27, 1997, Web posted at 1:45 a.m. EST. Cyberspace giving Bigotry a New Lease on Life. http://www.CNN.com.

CNN Online News, Wednesday March 26, 1997, Web posted at 5:45 a.m. EST. Racism at Texaco. http://www.CNN.com.

Coates, J. (1996, November 17). Another Sili-con Job. *Edmonton Journal* (Edmonton), sec. F4.

Cogan, J. J. (1981). Global Education: Opening Children's Eyes to the World. **Principal**, vol. 61, # 2, pp. 8-11.

Cogan, J. J. (1978). Implementing Global Education in the Elementary School: A Case Study. **Social Education**, vol. 42, # 6, pp. 503-505.

Compilation. (1997, March 29). English `Bias' on Web Irks French. *Edmonton Journal* (Edmonton), sec. B4.

Connor, S. (1996). "Cultural Sociology and Cultural Sciences." In Turner, B. S. (Ed.). The Blackwell Companion to Social Theory. Oxford UK : Blackwell. Pp. 340-368.

Cornbleth, C. (1979). Toward Global Perspectives. **Social Studies Journal**, vol. 8, pp. 5-8.

Coombs, P. H. (1985). *The World Crisis in Education: The View from the Eighties*. New York: Oxford.

Cortes, C. E. (1983). Multiethnic and Global Education: Partners for the Eighties? **Phi Delta Kappan**, vol. 64, # 8, pp. 568-571.

Coulter, D. (1995, October 21). At Dawn of the Computer Age, `It was so much fun': How We Stack Up. *Edmonton Journal* (Edmonton) sec. B3.

Crum, M. (1982). Global Education in the United States: A Panoramic View. **International Review of Education**, vol. 28, # 4, pp. 505-509.

Cummins, J. & Sayers, D. (1997). *Brave New Schools: Challenging Cultural Illiteracy through Global Learning Networks*. New York: St. Martin's Press.

Cummins, J. & Sayers, D. (1996). Multicultural Education and Technology: Promise and Pitfalls. **Multicultural Education**, vol. 3, # 3, pp. 4-10.

Darder, A. (1991). *Culture and Power in the Classroom*. New York: Bergin & Garvey.

Darling, L. F. (1996). Deepening our Global Perspective: The Moral Matters in Trickster Tales. **Canadian Social Studies**, vol. 30, # 4, pp. 180-182.

Darling, L. F. (1989). "The Rise of Global Education in North America." Werner, W. & Case, R. (Eds.). Occasional Paper # 21, EDGE Series on Explorations in Development/Global Education, B.C.: Faculty of Education, University of British Columbia & CIDA, p.1.

Dawson, C. (1997, May 25). Schools Enjoy High-Tech Barn-Raising. *Edmonton Journal* (Edmonton), sec. A8.

D'Andrea, M. & Daniels, J. (1996). Promoting Peace in Our Schools: Developmental, Preventive, and Multicultural Considerations. **School Counselor**, vol. 44, #1, pp. 55-64.

Deccan Herald Online, December 9, 1997. Christians to protest against rights violation. http://www.deccanherald.com

CNN Online News, Sunday, November 16, 1997, Web posted at 8:03 p.m. EST (0103 GMT). Former Klan Hotbed Elects First Black Mayor. http://www.CNN.com.

De Groot, P. (1997a, July 3). Welcome to Our Revolution. *The Edmonton Journal* (Edmonton), sec. E8.

De Groot, P. (1997b, June 26). Microsoft Learns a Lesson. *The Edmonton Journal* (Edmonton), sec. E14.

De Groot, P. (1997c, April 3). Engines that Search the Net. *Edmonton Journal* (Edmonton), sec. H1.

De Groot, P. (1995a, January 26). They're only Machines, Right? *Edmonton Journal* (Edmonton), sec. C14.

De Groot, P. (1995b, June 22). Internet: Uncontrollable Global Network. *Edmonton Journal* (Edmonton), sec. E3.

De Groot, P. (1995c, September 14). Fear and Loathing of the Future. *The Edmonton Journal* (Edmonton), sec. E2.

De Groot, P. (1994, February 24). Budget Stresses Role of Technology. *The Edmonton Journal* (Edmonton), sec. D5.

Dei, G. J. (1996). *Anti-Racism Education: Theory and Practice.* Halifax: Fernwood Publishing.

De Kerkhove, D. (1995). *The Skin of Culture: Investigating the New Electronic Reality.* Toronto: Somerville House Publishing.

Denniston, D. (1995). Sustaining Mountain Peoples and Environments. In Brown, L. et al. (Eds.). *State of the World*, New York: W. W. Norton & Company, pp. 38-57.

Dewdney, C. (1995). Introduction. In Kerkhove, D. (1995). *The Skin of Culture: Investigating the New Electronic Reality.* Toronto: Somerville House Publishing.

Diamond, J. (1997, September 25). Good Ideas for Fighting Hate on the Net. *The Edmonton Journal* (Edmonton), sec. E12.

Diamond, J. (1997, July 24). Canadian Join Online Wave. *The Edmonton Journal* (Edmonton), sec. E8.

Dienkelspiel, F. (1997, June 30). Web Smut Dilemma for Librarians. *The Edmonton Journal* (Edmonton), sec. A6.

Doane, C. (1993). Global Issues in 6th Grade? Yes! **Educational Leadership**, Vol. 50, # 7, pp. 19-21.

Donnan, S. (1995, August 11). Kids get Early Lesson in Cyberspace Ethics. *The Edmonton Journal* (Edmonton), sec. E10.

Donovan, P. (1997). Lending a Hand: Big Banks Fund Arms Deals. *New Internationalist,* April, # 289, p. 2.

Dreazen, Y. (2002). American Web Usage Reached 54%, In Autumn, Government Study Says. *Wall Street Journal*, http://online.wsj.com/login?URI=%2Farticle%2F0%2C%2CSB10127897 93162132080%2C00.html%3Fmod%3Dtechnology_main_whats_news

D'Souza, D. (1995). *End of Racism: Principles for a Multiracial Society.* New York: The Free press.

D'Souza, D. (1992). *Illiberal Education: The Politics of Race and Sex on Campus.* New York: Vintage Books.

Duffy, A. (1997, June 25). Chretien's `Save the Forests' Plea: Proposed Convention on Agreement Faces Stiff Opposition — including the U.S. *Edmonton Journal* (Edmonton), sec. F2.

Duvall, M. (1997, February 12). Digital Revolution Seen as Dawn of New Golden Age. *Edmonton Journal* (Edmonton), sec. F1.

Duvall, M. (1996, August 8). Rating Internet Sites Easy with Freeware. *Edmonton Journal* (Edmonton), sec. H3.

Eagleton, T. (1996). *The Illusions of Postmodernism.* Massachusetts: Blackwell Publishers.

Editorial. (1997, June 22). G7 Mandate is Out of Date. *Edmonton Journal* (Edmonton), sec. A8.

Editorial. (1996, December 2). Difficult to Curb Internet Abuses: But the Zundels Must be Corrected. *Edmonton Journal* (Edmonton), sec. A6.

EdTel (1995). Welcome to Our Planet: Public Live Access Network. Promotional Brochure. http://planet.eon.net.

Erickson, R. (1995, August 15). New Software? Who Needs it?. *The Globe and Mail* (Ontario), sec. B8.

Estable, A. & Meyer, M. (1996). *Working Towards Racism-Free Child Care.* Ontario: Margin Publishing.

Evans, J., Schengili-Roberts, K., Bennett, G., Tanaka, D., & Johnston, M. (1997). What's New. *Computer Paper*, vol. 10, # 5, pp.10, 12.

Evans, S. (1992). Decision Making: Developing a Global Perspective. **International Journal of Social Education**, vol. 7, # 2, pp. 10-16.

Evenson, B. (1997, July 10). High Tech Success: Use it or Lose out, says Conference Board. *The Edmonton Journal* (Edmonton), sec. E1.

Fanon, F. (1994). On National Culture. In Williams, P. & Chrisman, L. (Eds.). *Colonial Disclosure and Post-Colonial Theory: A Reader.* New York: Columbia University Press, pp. 36-52.

Farmer, R. (1992-93). International Education as a Worldcentric Perspective: Defining International Education. **New England Journal of History**, vol. 49, # 3, pp. 52-55.

Farrell, J. (1997, May 25). Warning Sounded on Porn Slipping into CDs. *Edmonton Journal* (Edmonton), sec. B3.

Featherstone, M. (1991). *Consumer Culture and Postmodernism.* London: Sage Publications.

Fien, J. (1989). Teaching about Global Issues. **Geographical Education**, vol. 6/1, p.4.

Fife, S. (1996, October 2). Betting on the Net. *Edmonton Journal* (Edmonton), sec. F2.

Floresca-Cawagas, V. (1988). Values Education for Social Transformation. In Carson, T. R. (Ed.). *Toward Renaissance of Humanity: Rethinking and Reorienting Curriculum and Instruction.* World Council for Curriculum and Instruction. Edmonton: University of Alberta Printing Services, pp. 130-138.

Foot, D. K. (1996). Boom, Bust & Echo: How to Perform from the Coming Demographic Shift. Toronto: Macfarlane Walter & Ross.

Foot, R (1998, April 27). `Techno-nerds' are bright, wealthy—and have no sense of duty. *Edmonton Journal* (Edmonton), sec. C13.

Fornäs, J. (1995). *Cultural Theory and Late Modernity.* CA: Sage Publications.

Frankenberg, R. (1993). *White Women, Race Matters: The Social Construction of Whiteness.* Minneapolis, MN: University of Minnesota Press.

French, H. F. (1995). Forging a New Global Partnership. In Brown, L. et al. (Eds.). *State of the World*, New York: W. W. Norton & Company, pp. 170-189.

Freire, P. (1985). *The Politics of Education.* New York: Bergin & Garvey.

Freire, P. (1983). *Pedagogy of the Oppressed.* New York: Continuum Publishing Corporation.

Freire, P. (1978). *Education for Critical Consciousness.* New York: Seabury Press.

Gadd, J. (1996, January 8). Daycares Struggle with Racism. *Edmonton Journal* (Edmonton), sec. C2.

Gal, C. (1996a, November 17). Peerless Lake School Goes Online. *Edmonton Journal* (Edmonton), sec. G5.

Gal, C. (1996b, April 25). Software Protects Net-surfing Kids. *Edmonton Journal* (Edmonton), sec. F5.

Gallagher, N. (1997, February 26). Driving Information Highway can Create Vision Problems. *Edmonton Journal* (Edmonton), sec. C5.

Gardner, D. (1995). When Racial Categories make no Sense. Online version of the original article in the *Globe and Mail*, Canada, October 27, 1995. gardner@helix.net.

Garman, A. (1997). Muslim/Arab Experiences in the Canadian School System. **Multicultural Education Journal**, vol. 15, # 2, pp. 16-27.

Gates, B. (1995). *The Road Ahead*. New York: Viking.

Gibson, S. (1996). Using Culturally Relevant Approaches to Teaching Social Studies. **Canadian Social Studies**, vol. 30, # 4, pp. 183, 184, 185, 191.

Gilliam, E. M. (1990). Quoted in **Synergy**, December, vol. 1, # 1, Newsletter of the Saskatchewan Global Education Project.

Gilliom, M. E. (1993). Mobilizing Teacher Educators to Support Global Education in Pre-service Programs. **Theory Into Practice**, vol. 32, # 1, pp. 40-46.

Gilliom, M. E. (1981). Global Education and the Social Studies. **Theory Into Practice**, vol. 20, # 3, pp. 169-173.

Gillmor, D. (1997, February 27). Net Abuse Risks Freedom. *Edmonton Journal* (Edmonton), sec. H2.

Giroux, H. & McLaren, P. (1994). *Between Borders: Pedagogy and the Politics of Cultural Studies*. New York: Routledge.

Giroux, H. A. (1993). *Border Crossings: Cultural Workers and the Politics of Education*. New York: Routledge.

Giroux, H. A. (1985). *Teachers as Intellectuals*. New York: Bergin & Garvey.

Giroux, H. A. (1983). *Theory and Resistance in Education*. New York: Bergin & Garvey.

Giroux, H. A. (1981). *Ideology, Culture, and the Process of Schooling*. Philadelphia: Temple University Press.

Giroux, H., Penna, A. & Pinar, W. (Eds.). (1981). *Curriculum and Instruction: Alternatives in Education.* California: McCutchan Publishing Corporation.

Globe and Mail (2001, March 22). Canadians Second to Americans as the Most Active Web Surfers in the World. Survey Results. A1.

Gold, M. (1997, May 1). City Man Charged with Spreading Porn on 'Net. *Edmonton Journal* (Edmonton), sec. A1.

Gold, M. (1996, September 28). Unplugging Cyber-Porn. *Edmonton Journal* (Edmonton), sec. H1.

Goldberg, D. T. (Ed.)(1994). Introduction: Multicultural Conditions. In *Multiculturalism: A Critical Reader.* Oxford, UK: Basil Blackwell.

Goodland, J. I. (1979).[Foreword]. In Becker,J.M.(Ed.). *Schooling for a Global Age.* New York: McGraw-Hill Book Company.

Gralla, P. (1996). *How the Internet Works.* California: Ziff-Davis Press.

Greenberg, J. (1996, April). Sex, Lives, and Avatars. **Wired**, vol. 4.04, pp. 106-165.

Greenfield, T. B. (1980). The Man who comes back through the Door in the Wall: Discovering Truth, Discovering Self, Discovering Organization. **Education Administration Quarterly**, vol.16, # 3, pp.118-126.

Gunter, L. (1995, October 28). UN Must Accept its Limitations. *Edmonton Journal* (Edmonton), sec. F3.

Haakenson, P. (1994). Recent Trends in Global/International Education. Bloomington, IN. (ERIC Document Reproduction Service No. ED 373 021).

Hall, G. T. (1992). Justice and Peace Education. **Momentum**, vol. 23, # 1, pp. 80-81.

Hall, S. (1997a). The Local and the Global: Globalization and Ethnicity. In King, A. D. (Ed.). *Culture, Globalization and the World-System: Contemporary Conditions for the Representation of Identity.* Minneapolis: University of Minnesota Press, pp. 19-39.

351

Hall, S. (1997b). Old and New Identities, Old and New Ethnicities. In King, A. D. (Ed.). *Culture, Globalization and the World-System: Contemporary Conditions for the Representation of Identity.* Minneapolis: University of Minnesota Press, pp. 41-68.

Hall, S. (1990). Cultural Identity and Diaspora. In Rutherford, J. (Ed.). *Identity: Community, Culture and Difference.* London: Lawrence & Wishart, pp. 222-237.

Hanvey, R. G. (1983). Global Education—Stage II. **California Journal of Teacher Education**, vol. 10, # 1, pp. 1-10.

Hanvey, R. G. (1976). Cited in Ramler, S.(1991). Global Education for the 21st Century. **Education Leadership**, vol. 48, # 7, April 1991, pp. 44-46.

Hanvey, R. G. (1975). An Attainable Global Perspective. Reprinted in Kniep, W. P. (Ed.).(1987). *Next Steps in Global Education: A Handbook for Curriculum Development.* New York: The American Forum.

Harris, I. (1986). *Peace Education.* Jefferson N. C. and London: McFarland and Co.

Harrison, R. (1997). Bare-Faced Cheek. *New Internationalist,* April, # 289, pp. 26-27.

Haysom, I. (1997a, February 27). Online Magazine only draws Micro-audience. *Edmonton Journal* (Edmonton), sec. H2.

Haysom, I. (1997b, February 18). Crashing into a Computerized Future. *Edmonton Journal* (Edmonton), sec. A1.

Hewes, J., Massing, C. & Singh, L. (1995). *Many Ways to Grow: Responding to Cultural Diversity in Early Childhood Settings.* Edmonton: Alberta Association for Young Children.

Hicks, D. (1990). The World Studies 8-13 Project: A Short History 1980-89. **Westminster Studies in Education**, vol.13, p. 61.

Hicks, D. (Ed.) (1988). "Understanding the Field." In *Education for Peace: Issues, Principles, and Practice in the Classroom.* London: Routledge, pp.3-19.

Highfield, R. (1997, August 24). World Wide Web. *Edmonton Journal* (Edmonton), sec. F7.

Hislop, I. "Looking for Dazzling Satire in Cyberspace." The Guardian Weekly, October 1, 1995, p.12.

Hooper, D. (1997, October 16). Zundel's Web-site Reviles Jews, Professor Says. *Edmonton Journal* (Edmonton), sec. A12.

Human Rights. September 3, 1995 *Human Watch Global Report on Women's Human Rights.*

Humphreys, A. (1997, July 20). Invasion of the Privacy Snatchers. *The Edmonton Journal* (Edmonton), sec. F8.

Husaini, Z.(1990). Peace Education and Global Education: Towards an Integration. In Alladin, M. I. (Ed.), *Perspectives on Global Education.* Edmonton: Centre for International Education and Development, University of Alberta, pp.79-90.

Husted, B. (1997, January 23). Searching for e-mail Addresses. *Edmonton Journal* (Edmonton), sec. H3.

Jantz, R. K. & Weaver, V. P. (1992). Travel Abroad as Culture Study. **International Journal of Social Education**, vol. 7, # 2, pp. 25-36.

Jarchow, E. (1997). The Dean's Role in Infusing Global Perspectives Throughout a College of Education. In Merryfield, M., Jarchow, E. & Pickert, S. (Eds.). *Preparing Teachers to Teach Global Perspectives: A Handbook for Teacher Educators.* California: Corwin Press, Inc., pp. 209-225.

Jary, D. & Jary, J. (Eds.) (1991). *The Harper Collins Dictionary of Sociology.* New York: HarperPerennial.

Jenkins, B. (1997). Combating the Proliferation of Weapons of Mass Destruction. **Update on Law-Related Education**, vol. 21, # 1, pp. 26-28.

Johnston, D; Johnston, D. & Handa, S. (1995). *Getting Canada Online: Understanding the Information Highway.* Toronto: Stoddart.

Johnson, D. (1985). The Contribution of the Humanities to a Global Perspective in Teacher Education. Washington,D.C.: American Association of

Colleges for Teacher Education. (ERIC Document Reproduction Service No. ED 265 114).

Johnsrude, L. (1996, November 25). Candidates Plan Knocking on Plenty of Internet Doors in Pursuit of Votes. *Edmonton Journal* (Edmonton), sec. A5.

Journal News Services. (1995a, October 22) Keeping the Peace, Keeping the Faith. *The Edmonton Journal* (Edmonton), sec. D3,

Journal News Services. (1995b, September 29). Home Computer Users in the Dark but Happy. *The Edmonton Journal* (Edmonton), sec. G4.

Journal Staff. (1996, August 16). Freenet gets Wires Crossed. *Edmonton Journal* (Edmonton), sec. B1.

Kane, H. (1995). Leaving Home. In Brown, L. et al. (Eds.). *State of the World*, New York: W. W. Norton & Company, pp. 132-149.

Katz, G. (1997, December 10). Internet Voice of Serb Protest. *Edmonton Journal* (Edmonton), sec. A5.

Katz, J. (1996, July). Technology. *Wired*, vol. 4.07, pp. 120-123; 166-170.

Kay, H. & Sharlot, M. (1997, September 26). Universities Poorer because of Laws. *Edmonton Journal* (Edmonton), sec. A18.

Keegan, V. (2000, December 14). Divide and Rule. *The Guardian*, http://www.guardianunlimited.co.uk/online/story/0,3605,410922,00.html

Keith, E. (1997, February 18). Government Strings Mean Dollars for Computers are No Gift. *The Edmonton Journal* (Edmonton), sec. A15.

Kelly, K. (1996, September 25). Internet a Good Hunting Ground for Business. *Edmonton Journal* (Edmonton), sec. F3.

Erickson, K. C. (1998). *Doing Team Ethnography: Warnings and Advice*. Thousand Oaks, CA: Sage Publications.

Kidder, R. (1988). The North-South Affluence Gap. **The Christian Science Monitor**, July 25, pp. B6-B8.

King, A. D. (Ed.) (1997a). Prefatory Comments. *Culture, Globalization and the World-System: Contemporary Conditions for the Representation of Identity*. Minneapolis: University of Minnesota Press.

King, A. D. (Ed.) (1997b). Introduction: Spaces of Culture, Spaces of Knowledge. In *Culture, Globalization and the World-System. Contemporary Conditions for the Representation of Identity*. Minneapolis: University of Minnesota Press, pp. 1-18.

Kniep, W. M. (1989). Essentials for a Global Education. *The Computer Paper*, May/June, pp.12-18.

Kniep, W. M. (1986). Defining a Global Education by its Content. **Social Education**, vol. 50, # 6, pp. 437-446.

Kniep, W. M. (1985). Global Education in the Eighties. **Curriculum Review**, vol. 25, # 2, pp.16-18.

Kniep, W.M. (1985a). A Critical Review of the Short History of Global Education. Occasional Paper, Global Perspectives in Education Inc. New York.

Kniep, W. M. (1985b). Global Education in the Eighties. **Curriculum Review**, vol. 25, # 2, pp.16-18.

Knight-Ridder Newspapers. (1998, June 9). Internet Health Sources often contain Errors. *Edmonton Journal* (Edmonton), sec. F5.

Knight-Ridder Newspapers. (1997, March 14). Internet Users Doubled in 18 Months. *Edmonton Journal* (Edmonton), sec. H1.

Knox, P. (1995, October 25). U.S. China talks solve little. *The Globe and Mail* (Toronto), sec. A10.

Kobus, D. K. (1992). Multicultural/Global Education: An Educational Agenda for the Rights of the Child. **Social Education**, vol. 56, # 4, pp. 224-27.

Kobus, D. K. (1983). The Developing Field of Global Education: A Review of the Literature. **Educational Research Quarterly**, vol. 8, # 1, pp. 21-28.

Krueger, R. A. (1988). *Focus Groups: A Practical Guide for Applied Research.* London: Sage Publications.

Kymlicka, W. (1997). Immigrants, Multiculturalism and Canadian Citizenship. Paper presented at the symposium on "Social Cohesion through Social Justice," Canadian Jewish Congress, Ottawa, on November 2. Forthcoming book *Finding our Way: Rethinking Ethnocultural Relations in Canada*, Oxford University Press, 1998.

Lamy, S. L. (1990). Global Education: A Conflict of Images. In Tye, K. A. (Ed.). *Global Education: From Thought to Action.* Alexandira, Va.: Association for Supervision and Curriculum Development.

Lamy, S. L. (1983a). Defining Global Education. **Educational Research Quarterly**, vol. 8, # 1, pp. 9-20.

Lamy, S. L. (1983b). Resources for Global Perspectives Education: A Practitioner's View. **Social Studies Review**, vol. 22, # 2, pp. 43-49.

Lamy, S. L. (1989). The National Interest or Global Interests? *The Computer Paper*, May/June, pp. 40-46.

LaQuey, T. & Ryer, J. (1993). *The Internet Companion: A Beginner's Guide to Global Networking.* Ontario: Addison-Wesley Publishing Company.

Lather, P. (1991). *Getting Smart: Feminist Research and Pedagogy With/in the Postmodern.* New York: Routledge.

Lechte, J. (1994). *Fifty Key Contemporary Thinkers: From Structuralism to Postmodernity.* London: Routledge.

Li, P. (1988). *Ethnic Inequality in a Class Society.* Toronto: Thompson Educational Publishing.

Lickteig, M. J. & Danielson, K. E. (1995). Use Children's Books to Link the Cultures of the World. **Social Studies**, vol. 86, # 2, pp. 69-73.

Linden, E. "Megacities." TIME, January 11, 1993, pp. 28-38.

Livingstone, D. (Ed.) (1987). *Critical Pedagogy & Cultural Power.* New York: Bergin & Garvey Publishers.

Logan, R. K. (1995). *The Fifth Language: Learning a Living in the Computer Age*. Toronto: Stoddart.

MacDonald, J. (1996, November 21). Learning English the CD Way: New Software Teaches English as a Second Language. *Edmonton Journal* (Edmonton), sec. H1.

Mackwood, G. (1991). Hockey Gloves, Chocolate Bars, Asbestos, and Why Trees Fall in the Forest: Teaching Global Economics. **Canadian Social Studies**, vol. 26, # 1, pp. 3-4.

MacLean, M. (1997, April 2). Market Rumors Fly on Free-wheeling Internet. *Edmonton Journal* (Edmonton), sec. F2.

Maloni, K., Greenman, B., Miller, K. & Hearn, J. (1995). *NetGuide*. 2nd Edition. New York: Michael Wolff & Company, Inc.

Marin, V. (1997, May). World Wide Wait (Letter to the Editor). *Computer Paper*, vol. 10, # 5, p.10.

Marck, P. (1997, October 18). Information Technology has Global Audience. *Edmonton Journal* (Edmonton), sec. F4.

Marck, P. (1996, November 16). Don't be Dazzled by Multimedia Toys, Teachers Told. *Edmonton Journal* (Edmonton), sec. B3.

Maroney, T. (1997). The Networked Society: Info Pipelines. TIME, February 3, 1997, pp. 50-51.

Marshall, G. (Ed.) (1994). *The Concise Oxford Dictionary of Sociology*. New York: Oxford University Press.

Marx, K. (1978). "Machinery and Modern Industry." In Tucker, Robert C.(Ed.). *The Marx-Engels Reader*. New York.

MacDonald, M. (1997a, July 7). On-line Banking has Arrived *The Edmonton Journal* (Edmonton), sec. A9.

MacDonald, M. (1997b, June 18). Nimble Cable Ahead in Internet Fight: Giant Telephone Firms have Plenty of Cash, but Infrastructure called Outdated. *Edmonton Journal* (Edmonton), sec. F6.

MacDonald, J. (1996, November 13). Internet Zooms to Town: Videotron Cable Connection Speeds up the Link. *Edmonton Journal* (Edmonton), sec. F2.

MacDonald, J. (1994, February 16). Virtual Reality the `New TV. *The Edmonton Journal* (Edmonton), sec. C10.

Marck, P. (1997, June 25). Clock Ticking on Computer Meltdown. *Edmonton Journal* (Edmonton), sec. F2.

Martin-Kneip, G. O. (1997). Assessing Teachers for Learner-Centered Global Education. In Merryfield, M., Jarchow, E. & Pickert, S. (Eds.). *Preparing Teachers to Teach Global Perspectives: A Handbook for Teacher Educators*. California: Corwin Press, Inc., pp. 99-122.

Mason, M. (1997). *Development and Disorder: A History of the Third World since 1945*. Toronto: Between the Lines.

Matriano, E.C. (1988). WCCI: A Humanizing Force in Global Curriculum Building. In Carson, T. R. (Ed.). *Toward Renaissance of Humanity: Rethinking and Reorienting Curriculum and Instruction*. Presidential Address at the 5th World Conference of the World Council for Curriculum and Instruction, 1986, Japan. Edmonton: University of Alberta Printing Services, pp. 19-27.

Matriano, E. (1987). Global Community Education: A Curriculum Trend for the 80s. WCCI Forum, vol. 1, #1, June, pp. 66-72.

Matriano, E. and Reardon, B. (1976). A Global Community Perspective on Education for Development. A Working Paper for a Global Education Conference. Chulalongkorn University, Bangkok, Thailand.

Mazurek, K. (1987). Multicultural Futures: Education and the Ideology of the Meritocracy. In Wotherspoon, E. (Ed.). *The Political Economy of Canadian Schooling*. Ontario: Methuen, pp. 141-163.

McCarthy, C. & Crichlow, W. (Eds.)(1993). Introduction. In *Race, Identity, and Representation in Education*. New York: Routledge, pp. xiii-xxix.

McConnell, R. (1997, February 20). Computers Ain't So Smart. *Edmonton Journal* (Edmonton), sec. D1.

Mcguire, J. S. & Austin, J. E. (1987). *Beyond Survival:Children's Growth for National Development*, United Nations Children's Fund, New York.

McIntosh, A. (1997, June 25). Espionage in the Corporate World: `Spies' Keep Close Eye on Web Sites, Publications to get Leg Up on Rivals. *Edmonton Journal* (Edmonton), sec. F6.

McLaren, P. L. (1995). Education and Globalization: An Environmental Perspective. An Interview with Edgar Gonzalez-Gaudiano. **International Journal of Educational Reform**, vol. 4, # 1, pp. 72-78.

McLuhan, M. (1995). *Understanding Media: The Extensions of Man*. Cambridge: The MIT Press, Massachusetts.

McLuhan, E. & Zingzrone, F. (Ed.). (1995). *Essential McLuhan.* Ontario: Anansi.

Mehan, H. (1989). Microcomputers in Classrooms: Educational Technology or Social Practice. **Anthropology and Education Quarterly**, vol.20, pp.4-22.

Mendes, E. P. (1997). Human Rights and the New Information Technologies: The Law and Justice of Proportionality and Consensual Alliances. Paper presented at the WebNet World Conference, November 1-5, 1997, Toronto, Canada. Proceedings including this paper available at: http://www/uottawa.ca/~hrrec/

Menzies, H. (1996). *Whose Brave New World? The Information Highway and the New Economy*. Toronto: Between The Lines.

Mercer, J. (1997, May 1). Internet Lists Child Molesters. *Edmonton Journal* (Edmonton), sec. B7.

Merryfield, M. (1997). A Framework for Teacher Education in Global Perspectives. In Merryfield, M., Jarchow, E. & Pickert, S. (Eds.). *Preparing Teachers to Teach Global Perspectives: A Handbook for Teacher Educators*. California: Corwin Press, Inc., pp. 1-24.

Merryfield, M. M. (1995). Making Connections between Multicultural and Global Education: Teacher Educators and Teacher Education Programs. Washington, D.C.: Institution: American Association of Colleges for Teacher Education.

359

Merryfield, M. M. (1995b). Reactions. **Theory & Research in Social Education**, Vol. 23, # 1, pp. 21-33.

Merryfield, M. M. (1995c). Teacher Education in Global and International Education. Washington, D.C.: Office of Educational Research and Improvement. (ERIC Document Reproduction Service No. ED 384 601).

Merryfield, M. M. (1994). Shaping the Curriculum in Global Education: The Influence of Student Characteristics on Teacher Decision-Making. **Journal of Curriculum & Supervision**, vol. 9, # 3, pp. 233-249.

Merryfield, M. M. (1993). Reflective Practice in Global Education Strategies for Teacher Educators. **Theory Into Practice**, vol. 32, # 1, pp. 27-32.

Merryfield, M. M. (1992). Preparing Social Studies Teachers for the Twenty-First Century: Perspectives on Program Effectiveness from a Study of Six Exemplary Teacher Education Programs on Global Education. **Theory & Research in Social Education**, Vol. 20, # 1, pp.17-46.

Metzger, D. J. (1988). The Challenges Facing Global Education. **Louisiana Social Studies Journal**, vol.15, # 1, pp.13-16.

Meyer, M. & Estable, A. (1996). *Awareness, Assessment, and Action...A Tool for Educators Working Towards Anti-Racism in the School System*. Ontario: Margin Publishing.

Meyers, M. (1993). *Teaching to Diversity: Teaching and Learning in the Multi-Ethnic Classroom*. Toronto: Irwin.

Mikkelsen, R. (1997, September 26). Clinton Holds the Door for `Little Rock Nine'. *Edmonton Journal* (Edmonton), sec. A4.

Miller, G. (1997). Introduction: Context and Method in Qualitative Research. In Miller, G. & Dingwall, R. (Eds.). *Context and Method in Qualitative Research*. London: Sage Publications.

Miller, G. & Dingwall, R. (Eds.)(1997). *Context and Method in Qualitative Research*. London: Sage Publications.

Miller, J. (1997a, June 23). Cyber-cheats Browse Net for Credit. *Edmonton Journal* (Edmonton), sec. A2.

Miller, J. (1997b). Between 1984 and 2001 [From the Editor-in-Chief]. *Pc magazine*, March 25, 1997.

Miller, J. (1997c, June 25). Gates Finances Library Charity: Software Billionaire Sets Aside Millions. *Edmonton Journal* (Edmonton), sec. A12.

Milone, Jr., M. N. (1996). Kidz on the Web. **Technology & Learning**, vol. 16, # 8, pp. 34, 40.

Milone, Jr., M. N. (1995). Global Education Begins at Home. **Technology & Learning**, vol. 16, # 3, pp. 44, 48-50, 52.

Mock, K. (1997). Hate and the Internet. **Human Rights Forum**, Summer/Fall, pp. 2-3.

Mohanty, C. T. (1994). On Race and Voice: Challenges for Liberal Education in the 1990s. In Giroux, H. & McLaren, P. *Between Borders: Pedagogy and the Politics of Cultural Studies*. New York: Routledge, pp 145-166.

Moore-Gilbert, B. (1997). *Postcolonial Theory: Contexts, Practices, Politics*. New York: Verso.

Morash, G. (1997, November 30). Internet the `Wave of the Future' for General-Interest Bookstores. *Edmonton Journal* (Edmonton), sec. C4.

Morgan, D. L. (1997). *Focus Groups as Qualitative Research*. Thousand Oaks, CA: Sage Publications.

Moysa, M. & Kent, G. (1995, September 30). Junior High Students Blast Off to School in Cyberspace. *Edmonton Journal* (Edmonton), sec. B3.

Montero-Sieburth, M. & Anderson, G. L. (Eds.)(1998). The Emerging Latin American Paradigm in Qualitative Research. In *Educational Qualitative Research in Latin America: The Struggle for a New Paradigm*. New York: Garland Publishing, Inc.

Muul, I. "Use them or Lose them." *The UNESCO Courier*, January 1989, pp. 29-33.

Naisbitt, J. (1994). *Global Paradox*. New York: Avon Books.

Naisbitt, J. (1982). *Megatrends.* New York: Avon Books.

Nasrin, T. (1997). A Disobedient Woman. *New Internationalist,* April, # 289, pp. 22-23.

NCSA (1993). *An Incomplete Guide to the Internet.* University of Illinois: NCSA Education Group.

Negroponte, N. (1996). *Being Digital.* New York: Vintage Books.

New Internationalist (1981). Today's Press…and Tomorrow's Alternatives. *New Internationalist,* June, #100.

News Clippings (1997, July 18). Anti-Semitism grows on the Internet. *The Edmonton Journal* (Edmonton), sec. A6.

Neilsen Ratings (2001). Online Populations. http://cyberatlas.internet.com.

Ng, R. (1993). Racism, Sexism, and Nation Building in Canada. In McCarthy, C. & Crichlow, W. (Eds.)(1993). *Race, Identity, and Representation in Education.* New York: Routledge, pp. 50-59.

Nnandi, J. E. (1990). Peace Education or Global Education: What's in a Name? In Alladin, M. I. (Ed.), *Perspectives on Global Education.* Edmonton: Centre for International Education and Development, University of Alberta, pp.69-78.

OCLC (1999). OCLC Research Project Measures Scope of the Web. http://www.oclc.org/oclc/research/projects/webstats/

O'Connor, E. (1982). Global Education: A Report on Developments in Western Europe. **Theory into Practice**, vol. 21, # 3, p. 226.

Ogden, F. (1995). *Navigating in Cyberspace: A Guide to the Next Millennium.* [With CD ROM] Toronto: MacFarlane Walter & Ross.

Olson, C. P. & Sullivan, E.V. (1993). "Beyond the Mania: Critical Approaches to Computers in Education." In Stewin, L.L. & McCann, S.J.H. (Eds.). *Contemporary Educational Issues: The Canadian Mosaic.* Toronto: Copp Clark Pitman Ltd., pp. 424-441.

Olson, C. P. (1987). "Who Computes?" In Livingstone,W.D. et al. (Eds.). *Critical Pedagogy & Cultural Power*. New York: Bergin & Garvey, pp.179-204.

Omi, M. & Winant, H. (1993). On the Theoretical Status of the Concept of Race. In McCarthy, C. & Crichlow, W. (Eds.)(1993). *Race, Identity, and Representation in Education*. New York: Routledge, pp. 3-10.

Omi, M. & Winant, H. (1986). *Racial Formation in the United States: From the 1960s to the 1980s*. New York: Routledge and Kegan Paul.

O'Neill, J. (1995). *The Poverty of Postmodernism*. London: Routledge.

Our Global Neighborhood (1995). The Report of Commission on Global Governance. New York: Oxford University Press.

Page, C. (1997, April 7). Internet Extends the Grasp of Cult Leaders. *Edmonton Journal* (Edmonton), sec. A8.

Paquet, C. (1999). CNN Online News, February 12, 1999, Web posted at 9:51 a.m. EST (1451 GMT). Report counts 147 million global Net users. http://www.CNN.com.

Papert, S. (1980). *Mindstorms: Children, Computers, and Powerful Ideas*. New York: Basic Books.

Parry, B. (1995). Problems in Current Theories of Colonial Discourse. In Ashcroft, B., Griffiths, G. & Tiffin, H. (Eds.). *The Post-Colonial Studies Reader*. New York: Routledge, pp. 36-44.

Patton, M. Q. (Ed.)(1985). *Culture and Evaluation*. San Francisco, CA: Jossey-Bass.

Peggy, M. (1990). White Privilege: Unpacking the Invisible Knapsack. **Independent School**, Winter, pp. 31-36.

Pellicano, R. R. (1982). Global Education: A Macro Perspective for Citizenship Education. **Social Studies**, vol. 73, # 3, pp. 125-129.

Pike, G. & Selby, D. (1988). *Global Teacher, Global Learner*. England: Hodder and Stoughton.

Pinar, W. F. (1993). Notes on Understanding Curriculum as a Racial Text. In McCarthy, C. & Crichlow, W. (Eds.)(1993). *Race, Identity, and Representation in Education.* New York: Routledge, pp. 60-70.

Pitts, Jr. L. (1997, September 26). Little Rock: A Sad Tale Never Ended. *Edmonton Journal* (Edmonton), sec. A18.

Poling, J. (1996, November 5). Giant Seizure of Computer Child-porn Worries Police. *Edmonton Journal* (Edmonton), sec. A3.

Port, D. (1997, June 5). Encryption Keeps e-mail Private. *Edmonton Journal* (Edmonton), sec. E9.

Postman, N. (1993). *Technopoly: The Surrender of Culture to Technology.* New York: Vintage Books.

Powell, K. (1996, September 5). Porn Police Hone Skills on the Net. *Edmonton Journal* (Edmonton), sec. B3.

Pradervand, P. (1987). Global Education- Towards a World that Works for All. **Geographical Education**, vol. 5/3, pp.12-18.

Putnam, R. D. (1997). The Decline of Civil Society: How Come? So What? **Optimum- The Journal of Public Sector Management**, vol. 27, #1, pp. 27-36.

Quinlan, T. (1997, August 8). Legendary Computer Geniuses Maintain Creative Tension in Rivalry. *The Edmonton Journal* (Edmonton), sec. H6.

Ramler, S. (1991). **Global Education for the 21st Century. Educational Leadership**, vol. 48, # 7, pp. 44-46.

Ramo, J. C. (1997). Networked Society: Welcome to the *Wired* World. TIME, February 3, 1997, pp. 42-49.

Ramstad, E. (1994a, February 24). Many Left Behind in Computer Revolution. *The Edmonton Journal* (Edmonton), sec. D6.

Ramstad, E. (1994b, June 26). Celebrities Discovering Advantages of Cyberspace. *The Edmonton Journal* (Edmonton), sec. D5.

Reardon, B. A. (Ed.)(1984).Education to Ensure a Future. In *Educating for Global Responsibility: Teacher- Designed Curricula for Peace Education.* New York: Teachers College Press, pp. xix-xxi.

Renner, M. (1995). Budgeting for Disarmament. In Brown, L. et al. (Eds.). *State of the World,* New York: W. W. Norton & Company, pp. 150-169.

Repo, S. (1987). "Consciousness and Popular Media." In Livingstone, W. D. et al. (Eds.). *Critical Pedagogy & Cultural Power.* New York: Bergin & Garvey, pp. 77-97.

Rheingold, H. (1993). *The Virtual Community: Homesteading on the Electronic Frontier.* Reading, MA: Addison-Wesley.

Rifkin, J. (1996). *The End of Work. [Technology, Jobs and Your Future]: The Decline of the Global Labour Force and the Dawn of the Post-Market Era.* New York: Tarcher/ Putnam's Sons.

Robertson, R. (1997). Social Theory, Cultural Relativity and the Problem of Globality. In King, A. D. (Ed.). *Culture, Globalization and the World-System: Contemporary Conditions for the Representation of Identity.* Minneapolis: University of Minnesota Press, pp. 69-90.

Robinette, M. (1997). *Windows 95 for Teachers.* California: IDG Books Worldwide.

Rodriguez, R. (1997, July 21). Cyber Cinema: On the Internet, the World of Movies is a Tangled Web, Indeed. *The Edmonton Journal* (Edmonton), sec. B9.

Rogers, A. (1995) at Global SchoolNet Foundation (http://gsn.org/web/) Created: Monday, November 27, 1995 at 9:56 AM.
Rogers, A. (1994). Global Literacy in a Gutenberg Culture. Online at *Global SchoolNet.* Also an abridged version in, "Living the Global Village", *Electronic Learning Magazine,* May/June, 1994. Pp. 28-29.

Roszak, T. (1986). *The Cult of Information: The Folklore of Computers and the True Art of Thinking.* New York: Pantheon Books.

Roman, L. G. (1993). White is Color! White Defensiveness, Postmodernism, and Anti-racist Pedagogy. In McCarthy, C. & Crichlow, W. (Eds.)(1993).

Race, Identity, and Representation in Education. New York: Routledge, pp. 71-88.

Rowan, G. (1996, April 11). Flat Rate Internet Phoning Proposed: Firm Sidestepping Long-distance Fees. *The Globe and Mail* (Toronto), sec. A1.

Rowan, G. (1995a, November 15). Why the Web will never beat TV. *The Globe and Mail* (Toronto), sec. B11.

Rowan, G. (1995b, November 8). Snippets. *The Global and Mail* (Ottawa), sec. E2.

Rusnell, C. (1996, November 21). Police Urge Parents to Mind the Net. *Edmonton Journal* (Edmonton), sec. B3.

Russo, R. (1997, March 20). Policing Porn on the Internet: Clash of Opinions as U.S. Supreme Court Debates Who will Protect the Children. *Edmonton Journal* (Edmonton), sec.A5.

Salkind, N. J. (1997). *Microsoft Office 97 for Windows for Teachers.* California: IDG Books Worldwide.

Sangari, K. (1995). The Politics of the Possible. In Ashcroft, B., Griffiths, G. & Tiffin, H. (Eds.). *The Post-Colonial Studies Reader.* New York: Routledge, pp. 143-147.

Santoli, M. (1995, November 6). Internet Shakes Up Brokerage Industry. *The Globe and Mail* (Toronto), sec. B14.

Sardar, Z. & Ravetz, J. R. (Eds.). (1996). *Cyberfutures: Culture and Politics on the Information Superhighway.* New York: New York University Press.

Saskatchewan Education (1984). *Beyond Bias: Informational Guidelines for Reducing Negative Bias in Instructional Materials.* Community Education Branch, June 1984.

Schiller, H. I. (1978). Decolonization of Information: Efforts towards a New International Order. **Latin American Perspectives**, vol. 5, #1, pp. 35-48.

SchoolNet (1995). "What New," *The Computer Paper* (Alberta Edition), p. 9.

Schukar, R. (1993). Controversy in Global Education: Lessons for Teacher Educators. **Theory into Practice**, 32, # 1, pp. 52-57.

Seidman, I. (1998). *Interviewing as Qualitative Research: A Guide for Researchers in Education and Social Sciences*. New York: Teachers College Press.

Selby, D. (1993a). Global education in the 1990's, Problem and Opportunities: Visions of 2001. **Global Education - Global Literacy,** vol. 1, # 1, pp. 2-9.

Selby, D. (1993b). Humane Education and Global Education. **Australian Journal of Environmental Education**, vol. 9, pp. 115-133.

Shenk, D. (1997). *Data Smog: Surviving the Information Glut*. New York: HarperEdge.

Shipley, C. & Fish, M. (1996). *How the World Wide Web Works.* California: Ziff-Davis Press.

Simmons, A. "Sixty Million on the Move." *The UNESCO Courier,* January 1992, pp. 30-33.

Silver, S. (1997, June 17). Virtual Sex Makes Money. *Edmonton Journal* (Edmonton), sec. D7.

Silverberg, R. "The Greenhouse Effect: Apocalypse Now or Chicken Little?" *Omni*, July 1991, pp. 50-54.

Skinner, C. "Population Myth and the Third World." *Social Policy*, Summer 1988, pp. 57-62.

Slapin, B. & Seale, D. (1992). *Through Indian Eyes: The Native Experience in Books for Children*. Gabriola Island, BC: New Society Publishers.

Sleeter, C. (Ed.) (1991). *Empowerment through Multicultural Education.* New York: State University of New York Press.

Smart, B. (1996). Postmodern Social Theory. In Turner, B. S. (Ed.). *The Blackwell Companion to Social Theory*. MA: Cambridge USA, pp. 396-428.

Smart, B. (1993). *Postmodernity*. London: Routledge.

Smith, M. (1995, June 22). Linguistic Voodoo can't hide Racism, Anti-Semitism here. *Edmonton Journal* (Edmonton), sec. A15.

Smolan, R. (1996). *24 Hours in Cyberspace.* QUE® Macmillan Publishing Inc. USA.

Snippets. (1994, August 2). Happy Birthday to Internet. *The Global and Mail* (Toronto), sec. E1.

Southam Newspapers, (1997, June 26). Clock Ticking on Computer Meltdown. *Edmonton Journal* (Edmonton), sec. E1.

Southam News. (1996, November 15). CRTC May Regulate Internet, Chair Says. *Edmonton Journal* (Edmonton), sec. C9.

Southam Newspapers. (1996, August 28). Self-policing on Internet Planned. *Edmonton Journal* (Edmonton), sec. B5.

Spencer, (1995). J. R. Under the Gaze: The Experiences of African-Canadian Students in Two Edmonton High Schools. Unpublished master's thesis, Department of Educational Policy Studies, University of Alberta, Edmonton, Alberta.

Spink, V. (1996, July 10). Time for Soul-Searching in East Indian Community [Letter to the Editor]. *Edmonton Journal* (Edmonton), sec. A13.

Stafford, D. ((1997, June 5). Bosses Clamping Down on Net Abuse. *Edmonton Journal* (Edmonton), sec. I14).

Stasiulus, D. (1997). International Migration, Rights, and the Decline of Actually Existing Liberal Democracy. **New Community**, vol. 23, # 2, pp. 192-214.

State of the Internet (2000). U.S. Internet Council, September 1, 2000. United States Internet Council and International Technology and Trade Associates (ITTA) Inc. (www.itta.com)

Steinback, S. & Rathenow, H. (1987). Global Education- Scope and Directions: An Interview with David Selby. **Geographical Education**, vol. 5/3, pp.21-24.

Stepan, C. (1995, June 18). New Computer Program Sends Math Scores Soaring: Pilot Project ran in 14 Schools across Alberta. *Edmonton Journal* (Edmonton), sec. E12.

Stewart, A. (1998). *The Ethnographer's Method. Qualitative Research Methods.* Thousand Oaks, CA: Sage Publications.

Swift, J. (1980). Global Education: What's in it for Us? **English Journal**, vol. 69, # 9, pp. 46-50.

Stewin, L. & McCann, L. (Ed.) (1993). *Contemporary Educational Issues.* Toronto: Copp Clark Pitman Ltd.

Stoll, C. (1995). *Silicon Snake Oil: Second Thoughts on the Information Highway.* New York: Double Day.

Stoll, C. (1995b). CBC Documentary. November 7, 1995.

Stone, B. & Gajilan, A. (1996, Fall/Winter). Top sites from ultimate educational playground. *Newsweek*, (Computers & the Family Special Issue), p. 21.

Sullivan, E.V. (1987). "Critical Pedagogy and Television." In Livingstone, W. D. et al. (Eds.). *Critical Pedagogy & Cultural Power.* New York: Bergin & Garvey, pp. 57-75.

Sultana, R. G. (1995). Ethnography and the Politics of Absence. In McLaren, P. L. & Giarelli, J. M. (Eds.). *Critical Theory and Educational Research.* Albany, NY: State University of New York Press, pp. 113-125.

Surtees, L. (1995, September 28). Competition on Information Highway Urged. *The Globe and Mail* (Toronto), sec. B4.

Synnot, A. & Howes, D. (1996). Canada's Visible Minorities: Identity and Representation." In Amit-Talai & Knowles. C. (Eds.). *Resituating Identities: The Politics of Race, Ethnicity, Culture.* Peterborough: Broadview Press, pp. 137-160.

Sypris, T. (Ed) (1993). Internationalizing the Curriculum. MI: Kalamazoo. Kalamazoo, MI.: Midwest Institute. (ERIC Document Reproduction Service No. ED 393 496).

Tapscott, D. (1998). *Growing Up Digital: The Rise of the Net Generation.* Toronto: McGraw-Hill.

Tapscott, D. (1996). *The Digital Economy: Promise and Peril in the Age of Networked Intelligence.* Toronto: McGraw-Hill.

Tapscott, D. & Caston, A. (1996). *Paradigm Shift: The Promise of Information Technology.* Toronto: McGraw-Hill, Inc.

Taylor, R. (1988a). "Too many Mouths." *Canada and the World*, May.

Taylor, R. (1988b). "Starvation Amidst Plenty." *Canada and the World*, May.

Taylor, R. (1988c). "Unequal Shares", *Canada and The World*, May, p.14.

Taylor, S. J. (1998). *Introduction to Qualitative Research Methods: A Guidebook and Resource.* New York: Wiley.

Tenner, E. (1996). *Why Things Bite Back: Technology and the Revenge of Unintended Consequences.* New York: Alfred A. Knopf, Inc.

The Associated Press. (1997a, August 8). Tired of Computer Crashes, Firm Sues over the Year 2000 Problem. *The Edmonton Journal* (Edmonton), sec. H6.

The Associated Press. (1997b, March 7). NASA Web Site Raided. *Edmonton Journal* (Edmonton), sec. A16.

The Associated Press. (1997c, June 12). Internet Rivals Get Together. *Edmonton Journal* (Edmonton), sec. E9.

The Associated Press. (1996a, August 8). Glitch Zaps Links to America Online. *Edmonton Journal* (Edmonton), sec. G1.

The Associated Press. (1996b, December 17). 40-Hour `Blackout' in Attack on Web. *Edmonton Journal* (Edmonton), sec. A5.

The Associated Press. (1995, September 14). U.S. Homes raided over Computer Porn. *Edmonton Journal* (Edmonton), sec. A5.

The Associate Press. (1995, August 15). When the Clock Strikes 2000, Computers will go Haywire. *Edmonton Journal* (Edmonton), sec. A4.

The Canadian Press. (1997a, August 8). Trade Sanctions Imposed on Burma. *The Vancouver Sun* (Vancouver), sec. D3.

The Canadian Press. (1997b, August 8). New Sanctions against Burma. *The Edmonton Journal* (Edmonton), sec. A7.

The Canadian Press. (1997c, April 9). Web Alert on Hoaxes. *Edmonton Journal* (Edmonton), sec. F6.

The Canadian Press. (1997d, July 4). Police Monitoring Net for Porn. *The Edmonton Journal* (Edmonton), sec. B3.

The Canadian Press. (1997e, September 23). Record Company Associates Charged with Hate Crimes in Ontario. *Edmonton Journal* (Edmonton), sec. B5.

The Canadian Press (1997f, May 18). Rights Watchdog Blasts Government for Ignoring Abuses in China. *Edmonton Journal* (Edmonton), sec. A8.

The Canadian Press. (1997g, June 5). Parents Swap Advice Online. *Edmonton Journal* (Edmonton), sec. F3.

The Canadian Press. (1997h, October 17). Zundel's Genocide View a Fable, Professor tells Tribunal. *Edmonton Journal* (Edmonton), sec. B10.

The Canadian Press. (1996a, October 28). Internet an On-line Lifeline, Futurist Claims. *Edmonton Journal* (Edmonton), sec. B10.

The Canadian Press. (1996b, October 22). Net Users Quick to Warn Police of Kiddie-Porn. *Edmonton Journal* (Edmonton), sec. A16.

The Canadian Press. (1996c, August 8). Students getting Laptops. *The Edmonton Journal* (Edmonton), sec. H4.

The Canadian Press. (1995, October 7). Distance Education Popular. *Edmonton Journal* (Edmonton), sec. B7.

The Canadian Press. (1995, September 19). Firms May get Caught in Net. *Edmonton Journal* (Edmonton), sec. E2.

The Canadian Press. (1994, February 21). Check Roadmap before Riding Data Superhighway, Executive Warns. *The Edmonton Journal* (Edmonton), sec. D8.

The Daily Telegraph. (1997, May 25). Fear Growing of Electronic Terrorism. *Edmonton Journal* (Edmonton), sec. A12.

The Report of the Commission on Global Governance (1994). *Our Global Neighborhood.* New York: Oxford University Press.

The Seattle Times and Journal News Services. (1997, August 7).

The Washington Post. (1996, December 14). Laptop Popularity Takes Off. *The Edmonton Journal* (Edmonton), sec. H6.

The World Guide 1997/98: A View from the South. Oxford: *New Internationalist* Publications Ltd.

Thompson, D. S. (1993). The Integration of Young Children's Literature with Multicultural, Nonsexist, and Global Education Goals and Themes. Iowa State Department of Education. (ERIC Document Reproduction Service No. ED 361 106).

Thorne, B. (Comp. et al) (1992). Model for Infusing a Global Perspective into the Curriculum. Paper presented at the Annual Meeting of Center for Critical Thinking, August 1-4, 1993. (ERIC Document Reproduction Service No. ED 367 575).

Thorne, D. (1996a, November 14). Net Services Paralysed by `Pingers,' Fighting Back. *Edmonton Journal* (Edmonton), sec. B3.

Thorne, D. (1996b, May 9). LearnNet puts Students On-line. *Edmonton Journal* (Edmonton), sec. B3.

Tiffin, H. (1995). Post-colonial Literatures and Counter-discourse. In Ashcroft, B., Griffiths, G. & Tiffin, H. (Eds.). *The Post-Colonial Studies Reader.* New York: Routledge, pp. 95-98.

TIME Comments: "Nabbing the Pirates of Cyberspace." TIME, June 13, 1994, p.44.

Tobin, A. (1997, October 14). Website Anti-Semitic— Linguist. *Edmonton Journal* (Edmonton), sec. B6.

Toffler, A. & Toffler, H. (1991). Economic Time Zones: Fast Versus Slow. **New Perspective Quarterly**, vol. 8, #4, pp. 56-58.

Toh, S. (1993). Bringing the World into the Classroom: Global Literacy and a Question of Paradigms. **Global Education - Global Literacy**, vol. 1, # 1, pp. 9-17.

Toh, S. (1992a, April 23). "Canadian Developments in Global Education." A Report to the CIDA/CWDE Consultation on Global Education, Centre for World Development Education, London.

Toh, S. (1992b, March 19). "Bringing the World into the Classroom: Global Literacy and a Question of Paradigms." Paper presented at the ATA Alberta Global Education Project Conference, Calgary.

Toh, S. & Floresca-Cawagas, V. (1990). *Peaceful Theory and Practice in Values Education*. Quezon City: Phoenix Publishing House, Inc.

Toh, S. (1989). Towards Compassion and Justice: Audiovisual Mass Media and the North-South Divide. **Tijdschrift voor Theaterwetenschap (Audiovisual Mass Media and Education)**, vol. 7, #27+28, August, pp. 71-91.

Toh, S. (1988). Objections to Peace Education. In Toh, S. H. (Ed.). *Issues and Insights on Peace Education*. Armide: IYP. pp. 23-29.

Toh, S. (1988b). The Lotus: A Metaphor for North-South Peace Education. In Carson, T. R. (Ed.). *Toward Renaissance of Humanity: Rethinking and Reorienting Curriculum and Instruction*. World Council for Curriculum and Instruction. Edmonton: University of Alberta Printing Services, pp. 286-300.

Toh, S. and Floresca-Cawagas, V. (1987). *Peace Education: A Framework for the Philippines*. Quezon City: Phoenix Publishing House, Inc.

Toh, S. (1987b). Education for Participation: Third World Perspectives. **WCCI Forum**, vol. 1, #1, June, pp. 20-43.

373

Topouzis, D. (1990). The Feminization of Poverty. *Africa Report*, July-August. The African-American Institute.

Troyna, B. & Williams, J. (1986). *Racism, Education, and the State*. London: Croom Helm.

Tucker, J. L. (1991). Global Education comes to Russia in 1991. Paper presented at the First International Conference on "The Reform of Education in Russia." September 6-14, 1991 at Sochi, Russia. (ERIC Document Reproduction Service No. ED 352 284).

Turkle, S. (1995). *Life on the Screen: Identity in the Age of the Internet*. New York: Simon & Schuster.

Turkle, S. (1984). *The Second Self: Computers and the Human Spirit*. NY: Simon and Schuster.

Turner, B. S. (Ed.) (1996). *The Blackwell Companion to Social Theory*. MA: Cambridge, USA.

Tye, K. & Tye, B. (1993). The Realities of Schooling: Overcoming Teacher Resistance to Global Education. **Theory Into Practice**, vol. 32, # 1, pp. 58-63.

Tye, B. & Tye, K. (1992). *Global Education: A Study of School Change*. Albany: SUNY.

Tye, K.A. & Kniep, W.M. (1991). Global Education around the World. **Education Leadership**, vol. 48, # 7, April 1991, pp. 47-49.

Tyson, C., Benton, P. L., Christenson, B., Gollah, A. & Traore, O. M. (1997). Cross-Cultural Experiences in Teacher Education Courses: Reflections and Advice From American and African Teachers. In Merryfield, M., Jarchow, E. & Pickert, S. (Eds.). *Preparing Teachers to Teach Global Perspectives: A Handbook for Teacher Educators*. California: Corwin Press, Inc., pp. 72-98.

Update. (1997). Borneo to Power Malaysia. *New Internationalist*, May, # 290, p. 4.

Update. (1997). No Reason. *New Internationalist*, April, # 289, p. 6.

Urch, G. E. (1992). Global Education: The Time Is Now. **Educational Horizons**, vol. 71, # 1, pp. 15-17.

Usher, R. and Edwards, R. (1994). *Postmodernism and Education*. New York: Routledge.

Vancouver Sun. (1994, April 23). $22.5M High-tech Network Created. *Edmonton Journal* (Edmonton), sec. E12.

Vatta, D. V. "The United Nations is Out of Control." *The Reader's Digest*, November 1995, pp. 91-96.

Venables, D. (1996). Legal, Political and Social Issues of the Internet. Online version of the Paper presented to the Media Development Association, in Brighton, January 1996. venables@pavilion.co.uk

Wallerstein, I. (1997). The National and the Universal: Can there be such a thing as World Culture? In King, A. D. (Ed.). *Culture, Globalization and the World-System: Contemporary Conditions for the Representation of Identity*. Minneapolis: University of Minnesota Press, pp. 91-105.

Wanless, T. (1996a, October 23). Modem Meiser Joins Revolution in Banking. *Edmonton Journal* (Edmonton), sec. C4.

Wanless, T. (1996b, October 23). World Turns to `Virtual Banking'. *Edmonton Journal* (Edmonton), sec. C4.

Ward, O. (1997). After the War: Letter from Chechnya. *New Internationalist*, April, # 289, p. 3.

Watson, R. & Barry, J. (1995, February 27). Net Wise. *Newsweek*, pp. 36-40.

Wattie, C. (1996, May 27). Zundel's Lawyer says Watchdog Cannot Police Internet Sites. *Edmonton Journal* (Edmonton), sec. A3.

Weaver, V. P. (1988). Education that is Multicultural and Global. **The Social Studies**, vol. 79, pp. 107-109.

Weber, P. (1995). Protecting Oceanic Fisheries and Jobs. In Brown, L. et al. (Eds.). *State of the World*, New York: W. W. Norton & Company, pp. 21-37.

Werner, W. (1996). Starting Points for Global Education. **Canadian Social Studies,** Vol. 30, # 4, pp.171-173.

Werner, W. (1993). Whither Global Education? What's Worth Reading. **Canadian Social Studies**, vol. 27, # 3, pp. 121-122.

West, C. (1993). The New Cultural Politics of Difference. In McCarthy, C. & Crichlow, W. (Eds.)(1993). *Race, Identity, and Representation in Education.* New York: Routledge, pp. 11-23.

Wheeler, D. (1992). "KidLink in War and Peace." A Paper presented at the Annual Conference of the American Educational Research Association, San Fransisco, April 21, 1992.

Wheelwright, G. (1994). But What, Really, is a Modem? *The Computer Paper,* October, vol. 7, # 10, p.47.

Whisnietsky, D. H. (1993). Using Computer Technology to Create a Global Classroom. Fastback 356. Bloomington, IN. (ERIC Document Reproduction Service No. ED 371 742).

White, P. (1988). "Countering the Critics." In *Education for Peace: Issues, Principles, and Practice in the Classroom.* London: Routledge, pp.36-50.

Whitefield, M. (1996, September 26). Those High-Tech Gadgets of the Future are Showing Up Now. *Edmonton Journal* (Edmonton), sec. G1.

Williams, I. (1997, March 1). Instructions for Pipe Bomb Found on the Net, say Police. *Edmonton Journal* (Edmonton), sec. B2.

Williams, P. & Chrisman, L. (Eds.). (1994). *Colonial Disclosure and Post-Colonial Theory: A Reader.* New York: Columbia University Press.

Wilson, A. H. (1997). Infusing Global Perspectives Throughout a Secondary Social Studies Program. In Merryfield, M., Jarchow, E. & Pickert, S. (Eds.). *Preparing Teachers to Teach Global Perspectives: A Handbook for Teacher Educators.* California: Corwin Press, Inc., pp. 143-167.

Wood, R. J. (1991). Toward Cultural Empathy: A Framework for Global Education. **Educational Record**, vol. 72, # 4, pp. 10-13.

Wooster, J. S. (1993) Authentic Assessment: A Strategy for Preparing Teachers to Respond to Curricular Mandates in Global Education. **Theory Into Practice**, vol. 32, # 1, pp. 47-51.

Wresch, W. (1996). *Disconnected: Haves and Have-Nots in the Information Age.* New Brunswick: Rutgers University Press.

Wright, L. (1993, August 10). Learning has Low Priority, Conference told. *The Edmonton Journal* (Edmonton), sec. A2.

Wright, E. H. & Harrell, P. (1985). *Teaching about Developing Nations: The Role of Food and Hunger.* Atlanta: Development Education Project, The International Service Association for Health, Inc. P.O. Box 15086, GA 30333.

Wronski, S. P. (1988). Global Education: Charges and Counter-Charges. **Michigan Social Studies Journal**, vol. 2, # 2, pp.147-150.

Yellin, S. (1994, January 31). High Tech Highway an Equal-access Road. *Edmonton Journal* (Edmonton), sec. A4.

Yin, R. K. (1984). *Case Study Research: Design and Methods.* Newbury Park, CA: Sage.

Young, J. E. & Sachs, A. (1995). Creating a Sustainable Materials Economy. In Brown, L. et al. (Eds.). *State of the World*, New York: W. W. Norton & Company, pp. 76-94.

INDEX

MELLEN STUDIES IN EDUCATION